Hiking Hot Springs in the Southwest

Hiking Hot Springs in the Southwest

A Guide to the Area's Best Backcountry Hot Springs

Chris Andrews

FALCONGUIDES

ESSEX, CONNECTICUT

FALCONGUIDES®

An imprint of Globe Pequot, the trade division of
The Rowman & Littlefield Publishing Group, Inc.
4501 Forbes Blvd., Ste. 200
Lanham, MD 20706
www.rowman.com

Falcon and FalconGuides are registered trademarks and Make Adventure Your Story is a trademark
of The Rowman & Littlefield Publishing Group, Inc.

Distributed by NATIONAL BOOK NETWORK

Photos by Chris Andrews unless otherwise noted
Maps by Melissa Baker, The Rowman & Littlefield Publishing Group, Inc.

British Library Cataloguing in Publication Information available

Library of Congress Cataloging-in-Publication Data

Names: Andrews, Chris, author.
Title: Hiking hot springs in the Southwest : a guide to the area's best backcountry hot springs /
   Chris Andrews.
Description: Guilford, Connecticut : FalconGuides, [2022] | Includes index. | Summary: "Author
   Chris Andrews reveals his favorite 'hot spots,' from primitive pools in the backcountry to
handcrafted
   pools close to civilization"— Provided by publisher.
Identifiers: LCCN 2021054699 (print) | LCCN 2021054700 (ebook) | ISBN 9781493036561
(paperback) | ISBN 9781493036578 (epub)
Subjects: LCSH: Hiking—Southwest, New—Guidebooks. | Hot springs—Southwest,
New—Guidebooks.
Classification: LCC GV199.42.S68 A64 2022 (print) | LCC GV199.42.S68 (ebook) |
   DDC 796.510979—dc23
LC record available at https://lccn.loc.gov/2021054699
LC ebook record available at https://lccn.loc.gov/2021054700

CONTENTS

Nevada

Arizona

Utah

Colorado

New Mexico

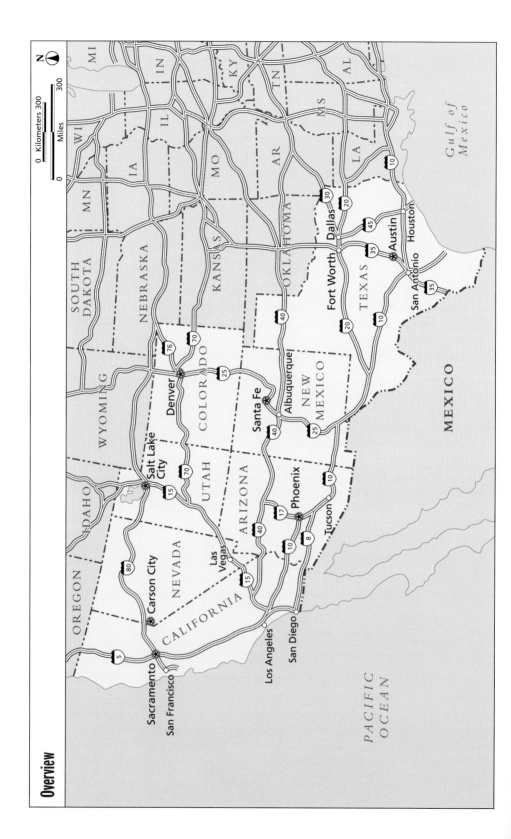

Overview

ACKNOWLEDGMENTS

I would like to thank my many friends and family members who have helped with the research and writing, especially my dear proofreader, Jane West, and hot springs authors Sally Jackson, Evie Litton, Karin Burroughs, and Skip Hill (sadly deceased). Others are Michi Catanese, Steve Benoit, Beth McCowan, Lexi Miller, Jennette Jurado, Cathryn Hoyt, Annie Gilliland, Sonya Popelka, Geoff and Patsy Matthews, Jillian Aragon, Michael Lukens, Keith Brown, John Blackwell, Shaun Astor, Jenny Kotlyar—Founder of Limitless Hiker, Rebecca Sowards-Emmerd, Dan Foye, Andrew Madsen, Lyndon Scott, Anna and Dugan Bates, Kelly DeLange, Glen Wadsworth, and Julie and John Baker. Also, a heartfelt thank you to all the Forest Service, Bureau of Land Management, and National Park Service rangers and personnel who patiently answered my many questions and gave me guidance regarding the safest ways to access these springs.

MEET YOUR GUIDES

Chris Andrews is an industrial hygienist who was born in San Diego and spent most of his life in Idaho where he currently resides. About thirty years ago, he stumbled on the *Thermal Springs List for the United States*, published in 1980 by the National Oceanic and Atmospheric Administration.

As the title implies, this document gives information about nearly all the hot springs in the United States, but most important to him were the approximate GPS coordinates. Armed with his GPS and a truckload of maps, he hit the road on his long weekends searching for them all.

Thirty years, six Chevy pickups, and a million miles later, he has soaked in some amazing places with great friends he met along the way. With his mountain-high spirit and desert-dry humor, he has contributed accurate information, updates, and photos to numerous hot springs magazines and guidebooks. He enjoys sharing his knowledge so that others can experience some of the most breathtaking views and soaks out there.

Blue Meek-Field is originally from eastern Washington, and her love for adventure, hot water, and photography has led her to numerous hot springs in the Northwest, Southwest, and Canada. With many miles under her feet, she is an expert at locating signs, mile markers, forks in the road, trails, tracks, routes, and steam. Blue is always eager to explore and soak in new hot springs, and deserves much of the credit for this guide. I cannot thank her enough for her efforts; she was right by my side on most of the hikes. In addition, Blue wrote most of the captions.

INTRODUCTION

This book is a companion guide to the FalconGuide *Hiking Hot Springs in the Pacific Northwest* by hot springs author Evie Litton. That guide was first published in 1990, and the fifth edition was most recently revised in 2014 by Evie and New Zealand hot springs author Sally Jackson. It has been extremely successful, and the idea came up for a companion guide for hiking hot springs in the Southwest. Due to the logistical challenges of living overseas, Sally invited me to get involved with this book. Sally has been a friend, mentor, and an integral part of the creation of the information provided in this book.

There are several Southwest Touring Hot Springs guides also published by FalconGuides:

> *Touring California and Nevada Hot Springs* by Matt C. Bischoff
> *Touring New Mexico Hot Springs* by Matt C. Bischoff
> *Touring Arizona Hot Springs* by Matt C. Bischoff
> *Touring Colorado Hot Springs* by Susan Joy Paul

These touring guides include the roadside and commercial soaks, as well as information about some of the Southwest hot springs at the end of hikes. This book is not meant to replace those guides, but instead be used as a supplement providing more detailed information and directions for the hikes.

How to Use This Guide

Hiking Hot Springs in the Southwest is a guide to hot soaks at the end of hikes in California, Nevada, Arizona, Utah, Colorado, New Mexico, and Texas. The springs marked on the locator maps are listed numerically. Hot springs are listed by state, and generally in descending latitude (from north to south) except when springs are grouped by region.

I have listed a few hot springs that can be driven to because they are either a trailhead, close to a trailhead, or just too good not to share.

Heading Descriptions

General description: A short synopsis of what to expect and if swimwear is required.

Difficulty: A relative, subjective estimate of the hike. This is not based on any official rating system, just my humble assessment and the collective opinions of others who have hiked there before me.

Distance: Based on GPS tracks, or collective information for the few hikes that I could not personally get to prior to the publication date.

General location: In most cases, the approximate distance and direction of the trailhead from the nearest town.

Elevation gain: In hiking and mountaineering circles, elevation gain refers to the sum of every gain in elevation in a round-trip. In simple terms, it is the total number of feet of elevation that you must climb. Elevation gain (and distance) will give you an idea of how strenuous a hike might be. Due to the multiple ups and downs along a hike, a GPS is required to accurately quantify elevation gain. You can often get a general idea of how strenuous a hike may be from the differences in elevation between the trailhead and the hot springs. I will report elevation gain unless the elevation gain per mile is insignificant, or in simpler terms, a pretty easy hike.

Trailhead elevation: An approximate measure of seasonal access, and information regarding the elevation change on the hike.

Hot springs elevation: Another approximate measure of seasonal access and piece of information regarding the elevation changes on a hike. The difference between trailhead elevation and hot springs elevation gives you information about how strenuous a hike might be. If a hike has significant ups and downs along the hike, I also report elevation gain.

GPS: A handheld GPS unit, or a phone application, with topographical maps is an especially worthwhile investment if you plan on spending a lot of time in the backcountry. There are a few hot springs where I have noted that a GPS is essential because of a critical junction or something similar. The coordinates are all listed in degrees format (dd.ddddd). To be consistent with other guides, I am reporting coordinates to five decimal places. This may help you if you are using Google Earth; however, a coordinate reported to four decimal places is more than enough to locate a destination on a handheld unit. The fifth decimal place represents about 3.6 feet in latitude (north) and less than 2 feet in longitude (west).

The accuracy of waypoints recorded on a handheld GPS is proportional to the number of satellites in view at the time. Whenever possible, I have verified coordinates using Google Earth to ensure accurate information. Due to dense foliage or slot canyons, some verification was not possible; however, I have confidence in my Garmin GPS.

You can enter these coordinates directly into Google Maps for directions, or Google Earth for a satellite perspective.

Map: The applicable USGS 7.5-minute or 15-minute topographical map is generally listed for each hike.

Restrictions: Any required passes, day-use only, dangerous river fords, or seasonal closures.

Best time of year: Though the Southwest's moderate climate allows year-round access to most hot springs, there are road closures to work around and some high-elevation hot springs that are not safely accessed. This heading gives some guidance for the better times to access the springs.

Camping: Generally, the closest US Forest Service or BLM campgrounds and some primitive camping opportunities. The lists are not all-inclusive.

Contact: Who to talk to for more information, including weather, up-to-date road information, closures, permits, passes, and so on.

Finding the trailhead: Due to the improvements of GPS navigation software available on phones and other devices, you can enter a trailhead name (or something similar) and often find it easily. Popular trailheads are well-known and easily found on your device. Alternatively, you can also enter the GPS coordinates directly into Google Maps and get driving directions. Generally, Google Maps directions work well, though not always. It can sometimes lead you astray on long dirt-road trips, as it may try to send you on the most direct route. East Walker Hot Springs in Nevada is an example. The shortest dirt-road route may be impassable for many vehicles. I try to note this in the individual directions.

The hike: The description of the route, including distances between points, campsites, river fords, along with some points of interest. This information should be used in conjunction with topographic maps for all hikes, especially the longer ones.

The hot springs: The description of the soaking pools, source temperatures and any means of controlling them, the general setting and scenery, an idea of how much company you might expect, and a description of the pools.

Things to Know Before You Hit the Trail

Private Property

Please always respect private land. Some hot springs in this book are on private land, and the owners have allowed access as long as the springs are not abused; that sounds fair. Many rivers, creeks, and public roads cross private land but are still considered legal routes of access and open to the public. Oftentimes, landowners install signs to imply that the roads (or creeks) are private when they are not. Do your research and ensure your intended route is indeed public access. The public is expected to respect private property, and landowners need to respect public access to the same extent.

Hot Pools

If you see a pool, or the remains of a pool, at a location, it is because someone found a way to make the water a comfortable temperature. Though prohibited, it is common to see built rock and cement pools. A good pool builder will always install a drain for cleaning. I have witnessed the work of some highly clever, even ingenious, people who devised ways of making a pool a comfortable temperature. In desert pools, it might be as simple as diverting the hot water and allowing a pool to cool to the ambient temperature. Then hot water is added until the desired temperature is reached. If pools like these are drained and then refilled, it might take a day or two for it to cool, so be cautious about draining pools. It is customary to leave these pools full for the next person. It is much easier to heat up a pool than to wait for it to cool. Pool size is an important consideration too. Too often pools are built too big to maintain a comfortable soaking temperature. Radium Hot Springs in Colorado is a good example. I have seen the pool built so large that the hot water source cannot keep the pool warm enough. At my last visit the pool was about 15 feet in diameter, which kept it at about 97°F (36°C). Had it been any larger, it would have been considerably cooler.

Social Media and Hot Springs

Many hot springs show up on social media and are visited by people who aren't prepared for the trip or know the etiquette. This is an ongoing problem and makes it harder for us enthusiasts to keep pools accessible. Too often access is restricted or removed due to misuse or because someone is injured because they were not prepared for the visit. In the time it has taken me to write this, two formerly accessible hiking hot springs were closed to the public because of misuse. Northern California's West Valley Reservoir and Colorado's Rico Hot Springs were both removed prior to publication.

I often carry extra water bottles to give away in the desert canyons below Hoover Dam. I have met many Las Vegas tourists who had an area hot spring pop up on their phone that they wanted to check out but were unprepared. In addition, I pack trash bags to pick up empty water bottles on my way out.

Theft at Trailheads

This is an ongoing problem. Don't leave anything in your vehicle you cannot afford to lose. Take it with you, or hide it.

Glass

Broken glass at hot springs is horrible. This ranks pretty high on my pet-peeve list. To help remedy this, I always pack extra socks for the people who bring glass bottles. In addition to the friendly, but lengthy, education I provide, I give them socks to enclose their bottles. In return, I (usually) get a promise that it will never happen again. I understand that many people enjoy wine as they watch a sunset, so buy boxed wine. Recycle the box, and carry the wine in the plastic bag. Simple.

Dogs

Conundrum Hot Springs has a great solution to manage dogs at hot springs. No dogs are allowed in the Conundrum Hot Springs Permit Zone. Dogs must be leashed out of consideration for other people and wildlife. There is an area outside of the permit zone where dogs must be tied waiting for their owners to retrieve them for the hike down. This may sound harsh, but dogs and hot springs don't mix well for many reasons. Scalding water is one of them; to dogs, it just looks like water.

Etiquette

If you've been hot springing for a while, you probably know all of this, but it is good to repeat. It is most polite to ask before joining people in a pool. I always ask, "Is there room for one more?" I have never been declined. If there are people waiting, please limit your time. California's Miracle Hot Springs has a sign asking people to limit their soak to 30 minutes if people are waiting. That sounds reasonable. You may encounter nudity at some hot springs, especially the more remote ones. Many hot springs have signs that require swimwear. Should you wish to soak without swimwear, ensure the local laws allow it, and be respectful of others.

Leave No Trace

The Forest Service says it well: "The principles of Leave No Trace might seem unimportant until you consider the combined effects of millions of outdoor visitors. One poorly located campsite or campfire may have little significance, but thousands of such instances seriously degrade the outdoor experience for all. Leaving no trace is everyone's responsibility."

A great reminder for us all to minimize our impacts and leave everything better than when we found it. BLUE MEEK-FIELD

Walk and camp on durable surfaces. Pack out everything you brought in, plus any other garbage left behind by others. Use permitted stoves instead of fires. Don't collect souvenirs. Be considerate of wildlife and other people. Plan and be prepared for contingencies.

Make It a Safe Trip

Safety: Let someone know where you're going and check in when agreed. Consider using a personal locator beacon or a satellite GPS. Do not expect cell phone service. When you are out of cell phone coverage, put your phone in airplane mode to conserve the battery. Don't expect your phone battery to last; take spare external batteries. Ensure that you have plenty of food, water, gasoline, and spare tires (yes, that is plural). Always have first-aid supplies. Download maps on your GPS or phone while you still have cell service, and remember that paper maps still work well. Take layers of clothing. Take extra socks (lots of them). Take a good headlamp (or two), with extra batteries. Invest in a good pair of water sandals (they are expensive, but worth it). Always mark the trailhead on your GPS. Don't hike alone. Be very careful fording rivers and creeks. Always take care of your feet. Always practice bear safety principles. Know what to do if you encounter a mountain lion. Use common sense and be aware of your surroundings.

These contents never leave my pack: waterproof rain jacket, sweatshirt, Leuko tape, headlamp, batteries, hiking poles, first-aid/survival kit, water filter, plastic bags, multiple pairs of socks, Swiss Army Knife, GPS, energy gel packets, medications, multiple large garbage bags (they're not just for garbage), good water shoes, parachute cord, multiple bandanas, a hat, and a card with my name and address.

Naegleria fowleri: No hot springs book would be complete without a warning about this. Signs warning of this are a common occurrence at hot springs and trailheads. *Naegleria fowleri* (*N. fowleri*) is commonly referred to as the "brain-eating amoeba" and is found in warm and hot surface water, including freshwater ponds, lakes, rivers, and hot springs. The defense against the amoeba is to not allow water to enter your nose.

Other Resources

- *Thermal Springs List for the United States*, published in 1980 by the National Oceanic and Atmospheric Administration (NOAA). This document gives the GPS coordinates for all the springs NOAA has documented. I have found about twenty that are not included in the book, but otherwise it is pretty complete.
- State Geothermal Maps, published for each state by the US Department of Energy. The maps show the locations of hot springs and provide data (temperature, flow, some mineral content). These maps are very large, but also useful. They are hard to find; get them when you can.

- *Thermal Springs of the United States and Other Countries of the World*, Geological Survey Professional Paper 492. This is the hot springer's bible. The directions are vague, but it's good information to have in conjunction with the other documents.
- The US Department of Energy National Renewable Energy Laboratory's Interactive Geothermal Prospector provides a huge amount of information about geothermal energy in the United States and is available online.

The Ones That Got Away . . .

Some of the springs in this section are mentioned in another guidebook as if they are accessible. These springs were not overlooked, but instead are not included because the current property status does not allow inclusion. There are still hot springs out there that appear closed but can still be legally accessed via public waterways. Many western states own the land to the high-water mark. California is an exception and owns the land to the normal low-water mark. These technicalities make many areas accessible.

San Juan Capistrano Hot Springs was considered for inclusion but was removed due to access issues. The hot springs are close to a road, and there are 12-foot-tall fences along the road that are posted against trespassing. The signs also warn of video surveillance. However, if you take a 5-mile hike through the Casper Wilderness Park, you arrive at the hot springs from the back side. Upon arrival you are greeted by a sign that states that no swimming or wading is allowed. The pools are in good shape and appear like they have been used recently—interesting.

West Valley Reservoir Hot Springs, Rico Hot Springs, and Chattanooga Hot Springs were considered and excluded from this book because they are all on private property.

Map Legend

15	Interstate Highway	⌣	Bridge
50	US Highway	⚠	Campground
41	State Highway	⌒	Hot Spring
001	County/Forest Road	▬	Lodging
	Local Road	🅿	Parking
-------	Unpaved Road	▲	Peak/Summit
⊢─┼─┼─⊣	Railroad	■	Point of Interest
•─•─•─•	Powerline	🚻	Restrooms
- - - - -	Featured Trail	○	Town
- - - -	Trail	①	Trailhead
～～	Small River or Creek	≋	Waterfall
～ ～	Intermittent Stream	▢	National Forest/Park
⬭	Body of Water	⬚	National Wilderness Area
≈	Marsh	▢	State/County Park
		▢	Conservation Area

California

C alifornia has more hot springs at the ends of hikes than any other southwestern state. Nevada has the most documented hot springs (332) in the United States, according to the NOAA's *Thermal Springs List for the United States*. California comes in a close second place at 304. Although many of the 304 are used for geothermal energy production, there are still plenty available for recreation. Many of the recreational springs are commercial spas, pools, and retreats but there are still plenty of wild hot springs available to be used by the public. As the title of this book implies, I am writing about hot springs at the end of hikes, though I might throw in a few roadside hot springs that are simply too great to miss. Unless there are several hot springs in a small geographical area, I will list these hiking hot springs by their descending latitude, or from north to south.

Season

California is well known for its moderate climate so the hiking season virtually never ends. This climate draws millions to the Golden State every year. The hikes in California can mostly be done year-round; however, you might need to travel farther than usual to get to certain trailheads. I love winter in California as it seems to be the best time to get a little solitude while hiking to hot springs. The cooler weather can also bring more people out because it's not so blasted hot; but all in all, you'll find fewer people trying to jam their way into campgrounds and trailheads.

Two of the pools at Hunt Hot Springs viewed from above PHOTO BY BLUE MEEK-FIELD

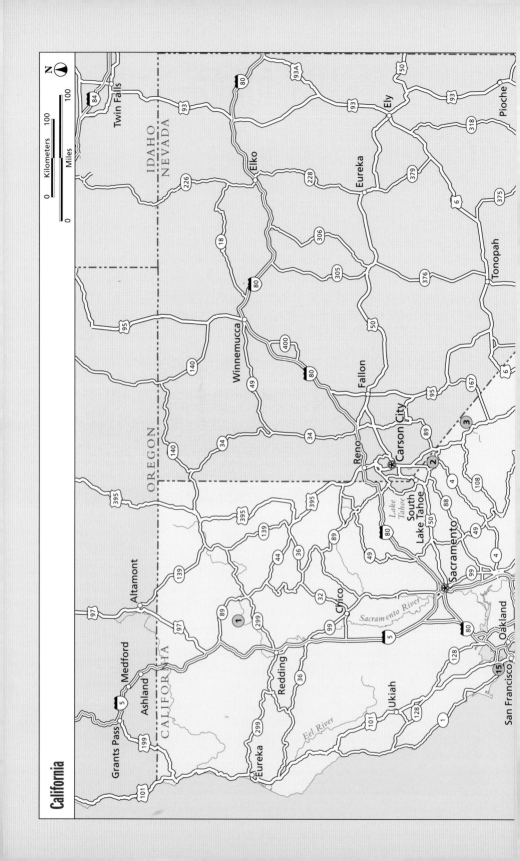

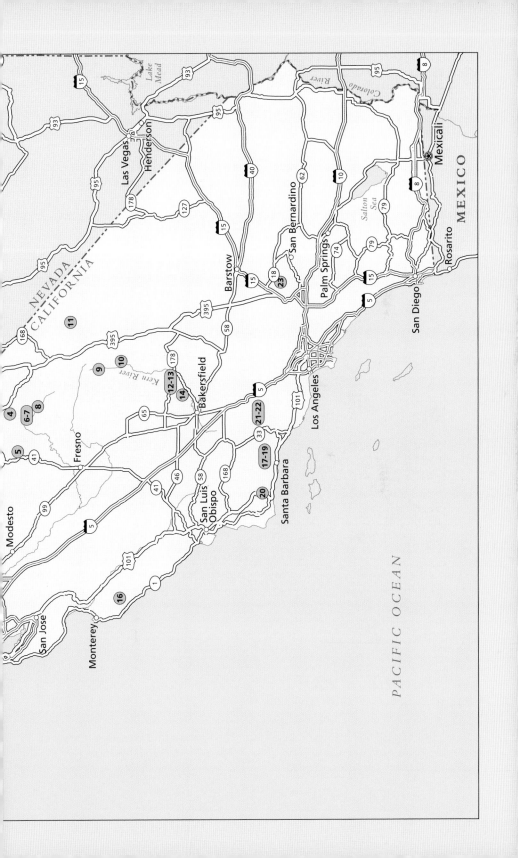

1 Hunt and Kosk Hot Springs

General description: Two separate hot springs a few hundred yards apart on Kosk Creek in the gorgeous Shasta Cascades region. These springs are combined here because you can't get to Kosk without going to Hunt Hot Springs. Swimwear seems customary.

Difficulty: Easy to Hunt, then a short, moderate hike over the hill to Kosk

Distance: 1.5 miles round-trip

General location: About 57 miles northeast of Redding

Elevation gain: 145 feet

Trailhead elevation: 1,650 feet

Hot springs elevation: 1,640 feet

Map: USGS Big Bend 15-minute (springs are shown)

Restrictions: The area is on private property and is open to the public as long as they behave. If you're reading this, you are the segment of the crowd who clean up after others and help landowners continue to allow access to these beautiful places.

Best time of year: Year-round

Camping: The Forest Service's Deadlun Campground is about 10 miles from the trailhead.

Contact: None

Finding the trailhead: Due to the improvements of GPS navigation software available on phones and other devices, you can simply enter Hunt Hot Springs trailhead (or something similar) and find it easily. Otherwise, from Redding, take CA 299 East for 39 miles to Big Bend Road. Turn left (north) and travel about 15.7 miles, through the town of Big Bend, then Big Bend Road crosses the Big Bend River and becomes Summit Lake Road. Continue on Summit Lake Road for 0.9 mile, then continue straight on a dirt road as Summit Lake Road curves around to the right. Continue north for 0.9 mile. The parking area is on the left (west) side of the road, just before a left turn to a bridge crossing Kosk Creek. GPS: 41.03993, -121.92919

The Hike

At the trailhead there is a sign that reads, "Private Property, Permission to pass revocable at any time." Underneath this are two more signs, which say, "No Camping" and "No Dogs." Stay on the trail closest to the creek on this easy half-mile walk to the first tub at Hunt (GPS: 41.03376, -121.93171). After the first tub, keep walking along the creek to the others. To get to Kosk, walk up the well-worn trail heading up the hill, then down to the tub at Kosk (GPS: 41.03231, -121.93207).

The Hot Springs

Despite being fairly remote in northern California, these two springs seem to draw large crowds on weekends. The very short hike to Hunt Hot Springs can be done by nearly anyone. The short hike up and down the hill from Hunt to Kosk Hot Springs might weed a few people out. That is good, because Hunt can handle many more people than Kosk, though you still might have to wait for other groups to finish. The pools have changed over the years, as they get deconstructed and reconstructed by people who have new and sometimes better ideas. It's possible that you won't see the

Hunt and Kosk Hot Springs

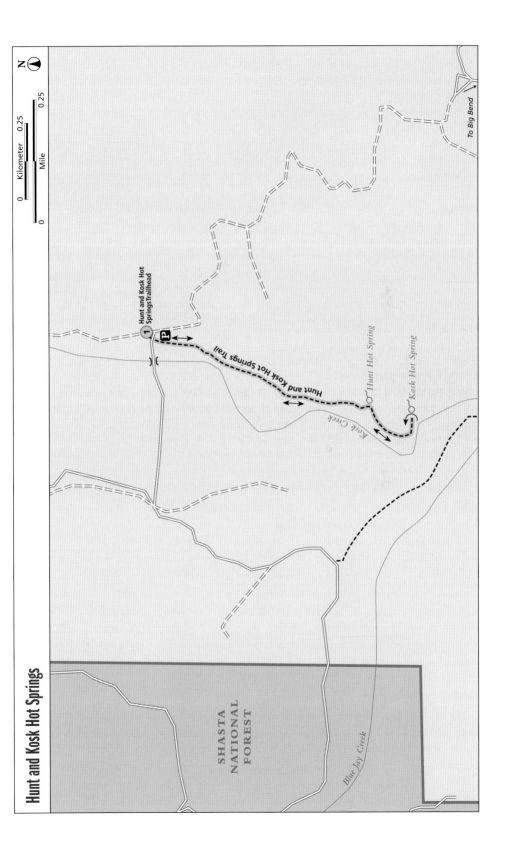

N

0   0.25   Kilometer   0.25
0   Mile

SHASTA
NATIONAL
FOREST

Blue Jay Creek

Hunt and Kosk Hot Springs Trailhead

P

Hunt and Kosk Hot Springs Trail

Kosk Creek

Hunt Hot Spring

Kosk Hot Spring

To Big Bend

These riverside pools are high enough to be washed out, and get a lot of use. If it gets crowded, you can hike over the hill to Kosk. PHOTOS BY BLUE MEEK-FIELD

pools I show here in the photos, but perhaps will see better ideas. The pools built in Kosk Creek often get washed away seasonally.

Hunt Hot Springs: Hot water comes out of the ground at about 135°F (57°C) and into the first pool you see. The flow is diverted to maintain the temperature in the large rock and cement pool. That pool was recently built and can get too hot for soaking if the hot water is not diverted to allow the pool to cool to a comfortable temperature. About 150 feet past that pool and down along the creek are three well-built rock and cement pools perched on boulders above the creek. More hot water comes out of the ground at about 135°F and flows into these pools. The water cools as it flows into the successive pools. There is another smaller cement pool and additional rock and sand pools down in the creek. Despite plenty of soaking room, it can still get crowded.

Kosk Hot Springs: From Hunt, walk up the hill on a well-worn trail and back down the other side to get to a favorite pool for many. This 4-by-12-foot pool is wrapped around a rock shelf about 8 vertical feet above the creek. It's an excellent tub with a great view and fewer people, which make it easy to see why it's a favorite.

Above: The newest pool built at Hunt Hot Springs is the first pool you see when you arrive. Additional pools are just downstream a bit by the creek.

Below left: Just over the hill from Hunt Hot Springs are these additional soaks at Kosk Hot Springs. With all these pools, it's easy to spend a day or few. Check out the number of camping options in the Big Bend area.

Below right: The view across Kosk Creek while sitting in a pool at Kosk Hot Springs

Sierra Nevada Area

One of the extra pools at Carson River Hot Springs. This tucked-away pool can be accessed from the Nevada trailhead without fording the river.

2 Carson River Hot Springs

General description: Three hot springs with well-crafted rock and cement pools on the East Fork of the Carson River in the Humboldt-Toiyabe National Forest. Accessible from both California and Nevada. Swimwear is a local decision.

Difficulty: Easy to moderate from either trailhead

Distance: 10.4 miles (California) or 15.8 miles (Nevada) round-trip to the main Carson Hot Springs pool

General location: About 6 miles northeast of Markleeville, as the crow flies

Elevation gain: California: 2,340 feet; Nevada: 1,790 feet

Trailhead elevation: California: 5,820 feet; Nevada: 5,920 feet

Hot springs elevation: 5,220 feet

Map: Humboldt-Toiyabe National Forest Carson-Iceberg Wilderness (springs are not shown)

Restrictions: The springs are on both sides of the river, which is often not crossable early in the year. The hike from the Nevada trailhead crosses private land, sometimes near previously cultivated fields. Though it is a Forest Service road across private land, there have been reports that the landowner has tried blocking access in the past.

Best time of year: Spring through late fall as roads are impassable in the winter. Crossing the river can be very dangerous during spring runoff.

Camping: There are many primitive camping opportunities in the Humboldt-Toiyabe National Forest. People often camp in the ponderosa pine grove at the Markleeville trailhead. As always, camp far enough away from the springs so that others may enjoy them as well.

Contact: Humboldt-Toiyabe National Forest, Carson Ranger District: (775) 882-2766

History: Carson River Hot Springs is on the Barney Riley Off-Highway Vehicle (OHV) Trail and gets a fair amount of use by off-road vehicles.

Finding the trailheads: California trailhead: From Markleeville, head north on CA 89 for about 5.5 miles and turn right on Diamond Valley Road for about 2.8 miles, then turn right on Airport Road. Continue 1.1 miles and turn left on Scossa Canyon Road. At 0.7 mile, bear left and continue for 0.1 mile to the trailhead at a grove of ponderosa pines. GPS: 38.75901, -119.75794

Nevada trailhead: From Gardnerville, head southeast on US 395 for about 12 miles and turn right on Leviathan Mine Road. Continue 1.7 miles to a large parking area on your left. GPS: 38.79814, -119.63791

The Hike

California trailhead: This 5.2-mile hike follows a two-track road the entire way. In about 0.3 mile from the trailhead, bear left at a fork and go north. Continue on the main trail as it undulates and winds north and northeast until you reach the ridgeline. From there the trail continues to rise and fall over several hilltops. The ridgeline winds along, giving you several opportunities to stop and take photos of the river below. From this spot the road leading down the hill from the Nevada access is also visible on the opposite side of the canyon, giving you an idea of your destination. The main Carson River pools are located where the road meets the river. The springs

Left: A peaceful soak on the Carson River accessible from the California side unless the river is low enough to ford. This highly scenic hike from either trailhead is best visited later in the year when the river is low enough to ford.

Right: Built on a rock ledge just above the Carson River is this peaceful soaking pool away from the potential weekend crowds at the main pool. Accessible from the California trailhead without a river ford.

are visible just prior to starting your descent. Continue down to the pools to enjoy a well-deserved soak. Enjoy the beautiful flora and fauna on this long but moderate hike. I like to have my GPS handy to keep track of my destination.

Nevada trailhead: When I was there last, the Forest Service road passed through signposted private property a few times. There were signs marking the forest boundaries. This is a stunning area with lots to see along the way, including spectacular views of the High Sierra.

From the parking area the trail is an old two-track road that departs from the north side of Leviathan Mine Road, heading west and slightly downhill. This road is no longer shown on some Forest Service maps, but Google Maps calls it Leviathan Mine Road. This is slightly confusing because you just left Leviathan Mine Road. Though lower in elevation, this road roughly parallels Leviathan Mine Road for about 0.6 mile. At 0.7 mile there is a meadow where you bear right to stay on the main road, then in 0.2 more mile, bear left to continue on the main road down the valley. After 2.2 miles the road meets up with Bryant Creek and gets more scenic and fully shaded as you follow Bryant Creek downstream. The road crosses Bryant Creek in another half-mile, then approximately 2.9 miles from the trailhead, the road leaves Bryant Creek and heads gently uphill for about a half-mile.

Carson River Hot Springs

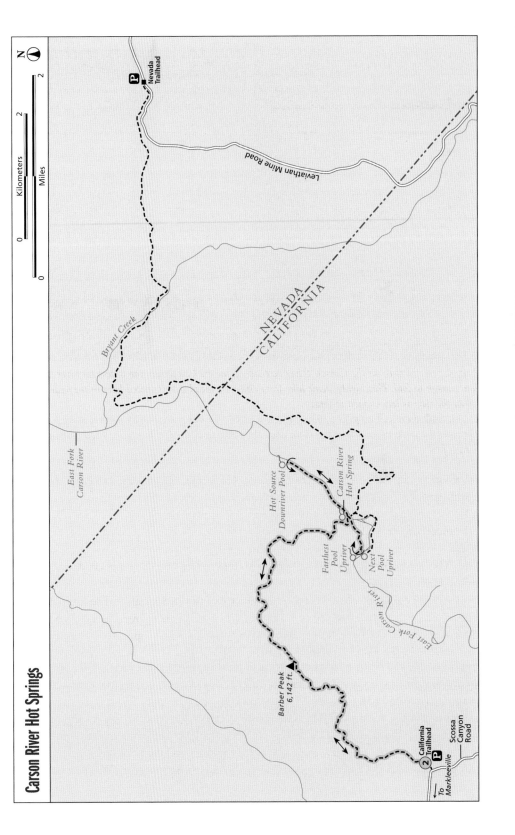

N

Kilometers
0   2

Miles
0   2

Nevada Trailhead

P

Leviathan Mine Road

Bryant Creek

East Fork Carson River

NEVADA
CALIFORNIA

Hot Source
Downriver Pool

Carson River
Hot Spring

Farthest Pool
Upriver

Next Pool
Upriver

East Fork Carson River

Barber Peak
6,142 ft.

California
Trailhead

P

Scossa
Canyon
Road

To
Markleeville

Stay on the road as it starts descending, then leaves the trees and makes a big curve around to the left. The road is fully exposed until it joins Horseshoe Bend Road at about 3.8 miles from the trailhead. Stay left and continue south with partial shade for a little way, then it opens up with pines on your left and the East Fork of the Carson River on your right. The road continues in partial shade for about 0.6 mile, then passes through open ground until it comes to an old house at about 4.9 miles into the hike. The main road continues past the house, passes through some trees, then heads southwest. It crosses into California (though you may not notice), then at about 5.8 miles from the trailhead, you turn right (west), as Horseshoe Bend Road becomes Little Cottonwood Canyon.

The road goes downhill gently then skirts the left side of the fields on its way to the river, mostly exposed for the next 2 miles, though there are occasional shady spots. At about 7.1 miles, turn right on Barney Riley Off-Highway Vehicle (OHV) Road and continue the last 0.7 mile to the river. You can see the main pools directly across the river. If the river level allows, ford it to get to the main pools. The pool on the east side of the river (called the "next pool upriver") is about 0.4 mile west of your position, but about a 0.6-mile walk upstream, if you follow the trail along the river.

The Hot Springs

Each of these three hot springs easily deserves its own entry in this book, but they are all at the end of the same hike, so it wouldn't really make sense to split them up. You can hike from either California or Nevada; both are beautiful hikes, and whether or not you can cross the river is the factor to consider when deciding which trailhead to use. Two of the springs are on the west side of the river, and the third is on the east. Crossing the river early in the year is often very dangerous, so you might consider using the California trailhead to access the main, and most popular, pool.

These three hot springs are not listed in the NOAA's *Thermal Springs List for the United States*, and they do not have official names. The springs referred to here as Carson River Hot Springs is the largest and the most popular. Volunteers have built robust rock and cement pools at all three of these springs on both sides of the river. The springs are generally accessed by rafts, kayaks, and OHVs, and are often overnight stops for rafting guides. On weekends there's likely to be big trucks and kids with loud music at the main Carson Hot Springs pools. You might want to plan accordingly or camp upstream at one of the other pools.

Carson River Hot Springs (GPS: 38.76959, –119.71471): Water comes out of the hill above and flows into a pool measuring about 8 by 11 feet. The 110°F (43°C) source feeds the pool via a PVC pipe that can be moved to control temperature. There is another source and a nice 6-by-10-foot rock and cement pool 130 feet away from the river and the main pool. The 110°F source can be diverted to control the pool temperature at this pool as well. There are other soaking opportunities in the outflows, from this and the main pool. Carson River Hot Springs and the pool farthest upriver can be visited via the California trailhead without crossing the river. The next pool upriver from the main Carson River pool can be visited from the Nevada trailhead without crossing the river.

Next pool upriver (Nevada access; GPS: 38.76755, -119.72144): Located about 0.6 mile upriver from the main Carson River pool is a smaller cement and rock pool. This 6-by-8-foot, rock-bottomed pool has enough flow to keep the temperature in the mid-90s (35°C). There are often seasonal pools made down by the river in the outflow.

Farthest pool upriver (California access; GPS: 38.76873, -119.72191): Located upriver even farther from the main Carson River pools is a 5-by-12-foot cement and rock pool that sits above the river, with enough flow to maintain a comfortable 104°F (40°C), depending on the ambient temperature. This long, narrow pool is worth the trip upriver to see. Like the others, there are often pools made down by the river in the outflow. You can follow the river's edge, or there is a 0.5-mile dirt road that gets pretty close to the pool.

Hot source downriver pool (California access; GPS: 38.77902, -119.70490): In addition to all the soaking opportunities described above, there is another hot springs downstream about a mile. In previous years, hot water came out of the rocks, flowed over an edge, and dropped into a pool. At my last visit, water was still flowing but not quite like before. There was no pool there; maybe you'll find one now.

Top: A relaxing view in a peaceful pool accessible from the Nevada trailhead without a river ford

Middle: Though the pool is gone and the water is not flowing as it did in the past, this is a hot source to keep your eye on. This former waterfall pool was hard to beat.

Bottom: A second nice rock and cement pool near the main Carson River pool

3 Travertine Hot Springs

General description: Located on Bureau of Land Management land, the pools are built on large mineral terraces with views of the High Sierra mountains. There is plenty of hiking around the immediate area, exploring the springs and various pools. Swimwear seems to be the norm at the main pools.

Difficulty: Easy

Distance: 0.5-mile round-trip

General location: About 2 miles southeast of Bridgeport

Elevation gain: Negligible

Trailhead elevation: 6,760 feet

Hot springs elevation: 6,745 feet

Map: USGS Bodie 15-minute (springs are shown)

Restrictions: No camping at the springs

Best time of year: Year-round

Camping: Not near the springs, but there are a few suitable pullouts on the road leading to it.

Contact: Bureau of Land Management, Bridgeport Ranger District Office: (760) 932-7070

History: In the late nineteenth century, travertine was mined from the site and used as stone and surfacing material for buildings. For hundreds of years the hot mineral springs have been used by local indigenous people for warmth, healing mineral water, and cleansing. Not much has changed, as we are still doing this today.

Finding the hot springs: From Bridgeport, drive south on US 395 for 0.8 mile to Jack Sawyer Road. Turn left (east) for 0.2 mile, then bear left on a dirt road for 1.1 miles to the parking area. GPS: 38.24572, -119.20412

The Hot Springs

No really long hikes are involved with this one, but you can certainly get a mile or two on your boots finding the various pools listed here and exploring for more. Travertine Hot Springs is too good to leave out of this guide, especially because it is so close to the Carson River Hot Springs trailhead, and one of the access routes to Saline Valley Hot Springs.

There are multiple rock and cement pools around the edges of a spectacular travertine formation, as well as several more pools within the area. Hot water comes out of the ground at temperatures up to 180°F (82°C), then is diverted into pools to maintain comfortable soaking temperatures. Near the parking area there is also a large cement pool (GPS: 38.24613,

The upper pool by the parking lot is accessible for all. If you are able, continue to the rest of the pools. PHOTOS BY BLUE MEEK-FIELD

Pools built around a beautiful travertine mineral tufa dome. The tufa dome and surrounding areas are very delicate, so please remain on trails and off the tufa dome. Lots of volunteer work goes into maintaining this fragile area.

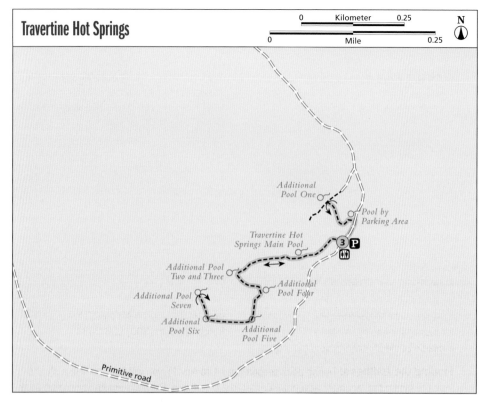

0   Kilometer   0.25

0   Mile   0.25

N

Additional Pool One

Pool by Parking Area

Travertine Hot Springs Main Pool

Additional Pool Two and Three

Additional Pool Seven

Additional Pool Four

Additional Pool Six

Additional Pool Five

Primitive road

One of many steaming sources of hot water on its way to a soaking pool

-119.20395), complete with a foot bath, capable of holding six close friends. This pool maintains a temperature of about 100°F (38°C).

The pools built around the travertine formation (GPS: 38.24539, -119.20526) are wonderful, and the area is too great not to explore. Pools are also built in the outflows. Spend some time hiking around to see it all. New pools get built occasionally, as there is no shortage of hot water here.

The GPS coordinates for the additional pools have not been printed in guidebooks before and include pool one (GPS: 38.24655, -119.20459), pools two and three (GPS: 38.24495, -119.20715), pool four (GPS: 38.24467, -119.20627), and pool five (GPS: 38.24420, -119.20663). You may enjoy the cooler pool six (GPS: 38.24430, -119.20728) or pool seven (GPS: 38.24462, -119.20744).

Though there is no shade, these hot springs are often considered the Taj Mahal of hot springs, as it is hard to take a bad photo of them.

4 Iva Bell (Fish Creek) Hot Springs

General description: At least four beautiful pools, maybe more, in pristine surroundings in the eastern Sierra in the Inyo National Forest, at the end of a long hike. Despite the long hike, swimwear is a mix.

Difficulty: Moderate but long

Distance: 24.4 miles round-trip

General location: About 8 miles southwest of Mammoth Lakes, as the crow flies, but at least 26 miles to get to the trailhead

Elevation gain: 3,880 feet

Trailhead elevation: 7,650 feet

Hot springs elevation: 7,280 feet

Map: USGS Devil's Postpile 15-minute and Crystal Crag 7.5-minute (springs are shown)

Restrictions: A wilderness permit is required for overnight camping. Wilderness permits are available at the Mammoth Mountain Adven-

ture Center. Reserve early, as the permits are subject to a quota during the peak season (May 1-Nov 1). These hot springs are not often visited in the winter months due to snow and the road being closed in the winter, adding an additional 13 miles to an already long hike.

Best time of year: Spring through fall

Camping: Multiple backcountry campsites near the springs and along the way. People often camp just before, or after, crossing Fish Creek, prior to the 4-mile hike up the hill to the hot springs. Near the trailhead, Red's Meadow Hot Springs Resort and Campground is a popular stop for people hiking the Pacific Crest Trail and the John Muir Trail.

Contact: Inyo National Forest, Mammoth Ranger Station: (800) 626-6684

Finding the trailhead: During peak season (May 1 to Nov 1), you will need to take a shuttle from the Mammoth Mountain Adventure Center to the trailhead. From Mammoth Lakes, turn north on Minaret Road (CA 203) and drive 4.1 miles to the Mammoth Mountain Adventure Center (10001 Minaret Rd.). Buy a shuttle ticket from the center and take the shuttle to the Rainbow Falls/Fish Creek trailhead.

During the off-season, continue on Minaret Road past the Mammoth Mountain Adventure Center for approximately 9.3 miles to the trailhead. Follow the signs as Minaret Road becomes Postpile Road, then Minaret Summit Road. Parking GPS: 37.61423, -119.07656; trailhead GPS: 37.61349, -119.07662

The Hike

This scenic hike is on the Fish Creek Trail. This 12.2-mile (one-way) hike has nearly 2,000 feet of elevation gain. The trail starts out following an old wagon route, then meets up with Crater Creek and follows it downstream. The first mile of the trail gets a lot of use as it is the route to Rainbow Falls, a very popular day-hike destination. It's worth the effort to take a look at the 101-foot falls, if you have the time. The first couple of miles of this hike go through an area severely scarred by the 1992 Rainbow Fire that burned most of the Devils Postpile National Monument. The effects are still seen. Though a devastating event, it now provides scenic views from the trail. About 0.1 mile from the trailhead, the Fish Creek Trail intersects with the Pacific Crest Trail (PCT) and the John Muir Trail (JMT); hikers on those trails will often take a 25-mile round-trip detour to visit these springs.

Quiet pools in the peaceful meadows of the Sierra Nevada. Lay your head on a granite boulder and forget all about the hike out.

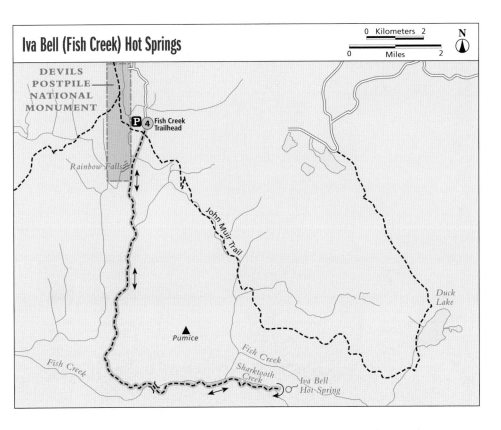

Iva Bell (Fish Creek) Hot Springs

0 Kilometers 2

0 Miles 2

N

DEVILS
POSTPILE
NATIONAL
MONUMENT

P 4 Fish Creek
Trailhead

Rainbow Falls

John Muir Trail

Duck
Lake

▲ Pumice

Fish Creek

Fish Creek

Sharktooth
Creek

Iva Bell
Hot Spring

From the trailhead, follow the wide, sandy trail for about 400 feet to the intersection with the PCT and JMT. Continue straight through this intersection and then head gently downhill for 0.9 mile. Here the trail splits and leads most day hikers to Rainbow Falls. Stay left on the Fish Creek Trail and hike south down the scenic valley dotted with big chunks of granite. The wide-open fire-created views are magnificent, and you can see the forest regeneration in progress. However, there are not many shady spots in the burn scar, so enjoy them when you can. Once through the burn scar, there's plenty of shade as you walk through groves of fir and pine interspersed with stands of quaking aspen and all kinds of ferns.

Continue along the forested valley walled by the huge granite slabs for which the Sierras are known. About 2.7 miles from the trailhead, the trail meets up with Crater Creek and follows its west side for about 0.9 mile, before crossing to the east side and into the John Muir Wilderness.

The trail continues descending mostly southwest on bare granite for about 0.7 mile, to where Crater Creek heads west and the trail heads south. The trail descends for another half-mile or so, then starts heading up. It climbs a couple sets of switchbacks and continues on a 0.9-mile climb. The trail descends for 0.5 mile, then climbs through pines and aspens in preparation for the often-spoken-of "7-mile descent" (meaning 7 miles from the trailhead). The trail descends via switchbacks for 1.4 miles

A cold waterfall up the hill

into the Fish Creek Valley. You will pass several campsites prior to the bridge. You might consider leaving most of your pack here, before continuing up the trail about 4 miles to the springs.

Cross over Fish Creek on an impressively sturdy bridge (GPS: 37.53409, -119.07316) and turn left. Follow the trail east along Fish Creek through heavy forest up to the hot springs. There are now cedars, more ferns, and multiple varieties of berries mixed in with the conifers. About 10.6 miles from the trailhead, the trail leaves Fish Creek and continues east up Sharktooth Creek (GPS: 37.53642, -119.04406) for about 1.3 miles more to a bridge over the creek. Continue approximately 0.3 mile to the first of the hot pools.

The Hot Springs

This Inyo National Forest hike should be on the list of every serious hot-springer. You'll be rewarded with at least four beautiful pools in pristine surroundings of the Eastern Sierras. Several rock and sand pools are on a rocky hillside overlooking the scenic valley below. Water flows out of the ground at 110°F directly into the pools which are dug large enough to maintain comfortable soaking temperatures. One pool is at (GPS 37.53289, -119.02405) and another at (GPS 37.53280, -119.02358). The pools are not easy to spot, so follow the trails around until you do. When I got home and looked at my GPS tracks, I was amazed at all of the places I explored, and still wonder what I missed. I kept thinking there might be some a little higher. I explored up another 500 vertical feet to over 7700 feet, but only found cold water. Keep looking, there still might be some new pools to be found.

5 Lewis Creek Warm Springs

General description: A cozy rock and sand pool surrounded by trees, at the end of a short hike, just off the Lewis Creek National Recreation Trail. Swimwear is optional, but you may want to have it with you due to the springs' popularity.

Difficulty: Easy

Distance: 0.5 mile round-trip

General location: About 7 miles north of Oakhurst

Elevation gain: Negligible

Trailhead elevation: 3,915 feet

Warm springs elevation: 3,815 feet

Map: USGS White Chief Mountain 7.5-minute (springs are not shown)

Restrictions: No glass

Best time of year: Spring through fall

Camping: Many Forest Service campgrounds in the area; Greys Mountain, Soquel, Nelder Grove, Kelty Meadow, Fresno Dome, and Big Sandy Campgrounds are the closest. All are within about 10 miles of the trailhead.

Contact: Sierra National Forest, Bass Lake Ranger District: (559) 877-2218

Finding the trailhead: Begin from the intersection of CA 41 and CA 49 in Oakhurst. Drive north on CA 41 for about 7.4 miles to a large parking area on the right signed "Lewis Creek." GPS: 37.41661, -119.62640

Warm two-person pool in a nicely wooded area. You can smell the sulfur but it doesn't stick to your skin. Lewis Fork is right there to rinse off if you wish. Add a few extra minutes to your hike and check out Corlieu Falls. PHOTOS BY BLUE MEEK-FIELD

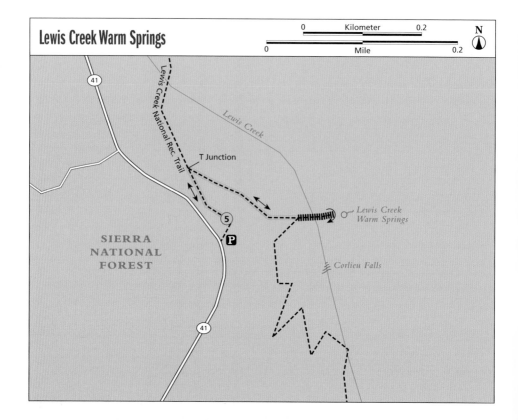

The Hike

From the north end of the parking area, follow the trail approximately 350 feet to a T junction with Lewis Creek Trail. Take the right fork and continue until the trail widens out and there is a series of steps going down to the creek. At the bottom of the steps, cross the creek and pick your way downstream until you find the pool (GPS: 37.41680, -119.62453), just above Corlieu Falls. It's a short hike at about 0.25 mile, but it can be a little rough for some. This pleasant trail is shaded by dogwoods and evergreens. Most of the people on the trail are hiking to the waterfalls and are not aware of the warm springs. If you turn left at the T junction and continue 1.6 miles, you will reach Red Rock Falls. The waterfalls are best in the springtime.

The Warm Springs

Also known as Corlieu Falls Hot Springs, this beautiful rock and sand pool nestles among the boulders, under a canopy of trees. Warm water comes out of cracks in the rocks and flows into the rock-bottomed, two-person pool, which holds a temperature of about 85°F (29°C). The mineralized water smells of sulfur and feels very silky. This peaceful soak is pleasant despite the mosquitoes.

6 Mono Hot Springs

General description: Multiple hot pools on a hillside overlooking the South Fork of the San Joaquin River in the Sierra National Forest, across from the Mono Hot Springs Resort. Swimwear is common during the daytime.

Difficulty: Easy

Distance: 0.75-mile loop

General location: About 18 miles northeast of Lakeshore, accessed via a long, winding dirt road

Elevation gain: Negligible

Trailhead elevation: 6,590 feet

Hot springs elevation: 6,560–6,600 feet

Map: USGS Kaiser Peak 15-minute (some springs are shown). Another map is available from Mono Hot Springs Resort (at no cost) that will help you on this hot-water scavenger hunt. The owners of the resort are top-quality folk; please support them if the season allows.

Restrictions: The road is closed in winter. Please respect the private property of the Mono Hot Springs Resort. The campground and resort are closed Nov through May, the dates varying

year to year. The entire south side of the river is Forest Service land, so nudity can be prohibited if not done with discretion.

Best time of year: Spring through late fall, as roads are closed in winter.

Camping: Cabins and soaks are available at the Mono Hot Springs Resort. In addition, Mono Hot Springs Campground is a Forest Service campground adjacent to the resort on the north side of the San Joaquin River. Another one, Mono Creek Campground, is a few miles farther north on Edison Lake Road.

Contact: Sierra National Forest, High Sierra Ranger District: (559) 855-5355

History: In 1934 the Civilian Conservation Corps constructed a bathhouse and several buildings on the south side of the San Joaquin River. Some foundations are still visible, and some of the original concrete pools are still used today. If it wasn't for the Big Creek (hydroelectric) Project, the road to Mono Hot Springs would never have been built.

Finding the trailhead: From Fresno, travel northeast on CA 168 for nearly 70 miles toward the town of Lakeshore. Drive by Huntington Lake and, as soon as you cross Rancheria Creek, turn right on Kaiser Pass Road, heading northeast. This is one of the highest roads in California, and listed as one of America's most dangerous roads. This one-lane engineering marvel is paved to the pass and has several wide pullouts so cars can get around each other.

At 15.7 miles you come to the Bosillo Campground; the High Sierra Ranger Station is just past that. Continue on Kaiser Pass Road for 1 more mile and turn left on Edison Lake Road, signed for Mono Hot Springs Resort. In about 1.1 miles cross a steel bridge; remember this bridge, because it's where you park for the Rose Garden and Little Eden Warm Springs hike. Continue on Edison Lake Road for another 0.5 mile and cross the bridge over the South Fork of the San Joaquin River. Park in the pullouts on either side of this bridge (GPS: 37.32614, -119.01338). From the pullout on the south side of the bridge, follow the wide trail west and start the hunt.

The alternate trailhead is in the Mono Hot Springs Resort parking area, outside the campground. Park and walk down to the log bridge across the San Joaquin River. GPS: 37.32658, -119.01715

The Hike

The first pool, The Rock, is about 300 feet from the trailhead. It is about a 0.75-mile loop if you want to find all the pools, but you may (and should) get sidetracked.

From the alternate trailhead, make your way down to the South Fork San Joaquin River and cross it on the log bridge to the south side (GPS: 37.32545, -119.01705). Stay on the well-worn trail for 150 feet and you will find the Old Pedro pools. From there, follow the trails until you have found them all, or a pool that suits you.

It is a pretty short hike to the next entry in this book, Little Eden and Rose Garden Warm Springs. There is a trail that leads to Little Eden Warm Springs, then it's a short walk across the road to Rose Garden Warm Springs.

The Hot Springs

Most of the source temperatures are 109°F (43°C), but the pool temperatures are affected by water flow and ambient temperature. Some of the hot pools have names as shown in the GPS table. The Mono Hot Springs Resort has a free map that will help guide you through the maze of hot springs. You could easily find more springs if you have the time and energy. These are described in the approximate order of appearance if hiking from the trailhead by the road. If you choose to start at the alternate trailhead from the Forest Service campground and Mono Hot Springs Resort, then reverse the order.

The Rock (GPS: 37.32604, -119.01437): A nice three- to four-person soaking pool that stays close to 92°F (33°C).

Mud Bath (GPS: 37.32582, -119.01446): For those who like to coat themselves in mud for health and beauty reasons, this tepid pool may be tempting. For the rest of us, this pool is just worth a look. It was around 70°F (21°C) on my visit.

Left: The Rock is the first pool you get to from the main trailhead. It's a good one.
Right: Clusters of rock and sand pools along the San Joaquin River. These pools are usually underwater in the spring. PHOTOS BY BLUE MEEK-FIELD

Mono Hot Springs

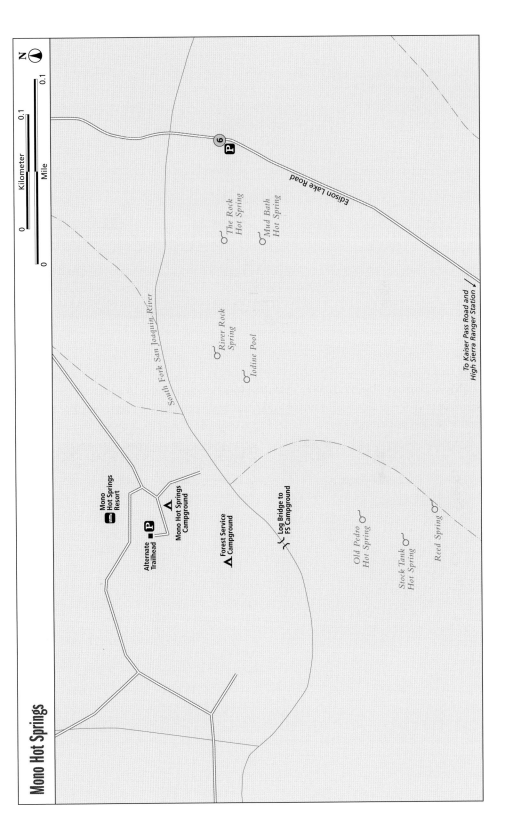

N

Kilometer
0   0.1   0.1

Mile
0   0.1

Mono Hot Springs Resort

Alternate Trailhead

Mono Hot Springs Campground

Forest Service Campground

Log Bridge to FS Campground

South Fork San Joaquin River

River Rock Spring

Iodine Pool

The Rock Hot Spring

Mud Bath Hot Spring

Edison Lake Road

Old Pedro Hot Spring

Stock Tank Hot Spring

Reed Spring

To Kaiser Pass Road and High Sierra Ranger Station

6
P

More concrete pools surrounded by reeds. When the sun hits them just right, the reflection off the water provides a peaceful ambience.

Find these concrete, neck-deep soaking pools not far from the Mono Hot Springs Campground

River Rock Springs (GPS: 37.32611, -119.01551): Large rock and sand pools down by the river. The upper pool stays around 95°F (35°C). These pools are excellent places to soak before hopping into the river for a cool down.

Iodine Pool GPS: 37.32595, -119.01561): A 7-by-8-foot concrete pool that stays around 90°F (32°C). This is a remnant of the first soaking pools from the original 1930s infrastructure.

Hidden Spring (GPS coordinates not listed): A cozy two-person soaker hidden in the grass next to a huge boulder, which stays around 90°F (32°C).

Reed Spring (GPS: 37.32453, -119.01691): A 7-by-8-foot concrete pool that is much cooler. This too is a remnant of the first soaking pools from the original 1930s infrastructure.

Stock tank next to water storage tank (GPS: 37.32473, -119.01718): A one-person stock tank next to a large concrete water storage tank, fed by hot water dripping down a pipe from the tank. Temperature can be controlled by diverting the water source.

A slightly warm, sulfuric, mud-bottomed pool. Be careful though, with this mud. As much fun as it can be to slather yourself in it, it has been known to stain clothing (if you're wearing any).

The warmest of the soaks, Old Pedro is one of the area favorites.

Old Pedro (GPS: 37.32505, –119.01695): A 6-by-7-foot concrete tub just across the river from the resort. This 105°F (40.5°C) tub is the most popular, and the first one you come to if you start from the alternate trailhead by the campground and cross the log bridge. This is also a remnant of the first soaking pools from the original 1930s infrastructure.

7 Little Eden and Rose Garden Warm Springs

General description: Two secluded pools, one on each side of the road, each with a short hike. Not necessarily hiking hot springs, but you drive right past them on the way to the trailheads for Mono Hot Springs and Blayney Meadows Hot Springs. Swimwear is a local decision.

Difficulty: Easy

Distance: 0.25-mile round-trip to visit both warm springs

General location: About 17 miles northeast of Lakeshore

Elevation gain: Negligible

Trailhead elevation: 6,850 feet

Warm springs elevation: Little Eden: 6,780 feet; Rose Garden: 6,880 feet

Map: USGS Kaiser Peak 15-minute (springs are not shown)

Restrictions: The road is closed in winter.

Best time of year: Spring through fall

Camping: The Forest Service's Mono Hot Springs Campground is about a mile away adjacent to the Mono Hot Springs Resort. Another one, Mono Creek Campground, is a few miles farther up Edison Lake Road.

Contact: Sierra National Forest, High Sierra Ranger District: (559) 855-5355

Finding the trailhead: From Fresno, travel northeast on CA 168 for nearly 70 miles toward the town of Lakeshore. Drive by Huntington Lake and, as soon as you cross Rancheria Creek, turn right on Kaiser Pass Road, heading northeast. This is one of the highest roads in California, and listed as one of America's most dangerous roads. This one-lane engineering marvel is paved to the pass and has several wide pullouts so cars can get around each other.

At 15.7 miles you come to the Bosillo Campground; the High Sierra Ranger Station is just past that. Continue on Kaiser Pass Road for 1 more mile and turn left on Edison Lake Road, signed for Mono Hot Springs Resort. In about 1.1 miles cross a steel bridge and park near it. (You can also walk to these warm springs from the hot springs at Mono.) If you choose to park near the steel bridge, walk 150 feet west, back down the Edison Lake Road, to where you see the trail heading down the hill to Little Eden. GPS: 37.32181, -119.01840

The Hike

Little Eden: From the trailhead, find the steep trail heading north down the hill. You have to scramble down some boulders, and this can be tricky for some. It is about 280 feet to the pool. GPS: 37.32243, -119.01850

Rose Garden: From the same trailhead, walk back down the road (west) for about 50 feet and find a trail heading southwest up the hill. It is less than 100 feet from the road. GPS: 37.32160, -119.01860

The Warm Springs

Little Eden: A large pine tree and a few smaller ones provide partial shade at this rock and sand pool, which stays about 90°F (32°C). It is about 4 feet deep and has a lovely view overlooking the Mono Valley. There was a floating wooden table on my visit.

Above and below left: A peaceful, pond-temperature pool worth finding
Below right: Although right off the road, this bubbly pool is surrounded by vegetation, which lends it some privacy. PHOTOS BY BLUE MEEK–FIELD

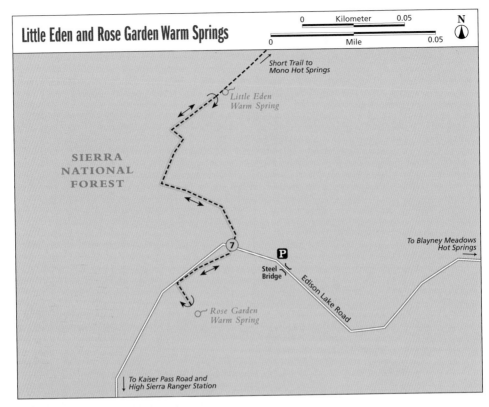

0   Kilometer   0.05

N

0   Mile   0.05

Short Trail to
Mono Hot Springs

Little Eden
Warm Spring

SIERRA
NATIONAL
FOREST

To Blayney Meadows
Hot Springs

7

P

Steel
Bridge

Edison Lake Road

Rose Garden
Warm Spring

To Kaiser Pass Road and
High Sierra Ranger Station

A seemingly local custom of making mud faces along the pool's bank

Rose Garden: A 6-by-10-foot oval rock and sand pool with a mud bottom. Gas bubbles come up from the bottom, making this a different soaking experience. The temperature is generally around the low to mid-90s (33–35°C), though it can vary with the ambient temperature. The pool is partially shrouded by pines and brush, just up off the road, and hidden from view.

8 Blayney Meadows Hot Springs

General description: A few soaking opportunities in a grassy meadow on the side of the South Fork of the San Joaquin River. The hot springs is at the end of a fairly easy 8.5-mile hike in the John Muir Wilderness in the Sierra National Forest. Swimwear is a local decision.
Difficulty: Easy, but with a potentially serious river ford
Distance: About 17.2 miles round-trip
General location: About 25 miles northeast of Lakeshore
Elevation gain: 2,360 feet
Trailhead elevation: 7,360 feet
Hot springs elevation: 7,670 feet
Map: USGS Blackcap Mountain 15-minute (springs are shown)
Restrictions: The Kaiser Pass Road is closed in the winter. A wilderness pass is required for overnight hiking, available from Forest Service offices. Fording the river can be dangerous in high-water times. No camping near the springs.
Best time of year: Summer through fall
Camping: Florence Lake Campground is at the trailhead, and there are multiple camping opportunities along the trail. Two primitive Forest Service campgrounds, Boulder Creek and Lower Blayney, are along the trail.
Contact: Sierra National Forest, High Sierra Ranger District: (559) 855-5355
History: Listed as Blaney Meadows in the NOAA's *Thermal Springs List for the United States*, this hot springs area is near the John Muir Trail and also the Muir Trail Ranch, which has cabins and lots of soaking opportunities.

Finding the trailhead: From Fresno, travel northeast on CA 168 for nearly 70 miles toward the town of Lakeshore. Drive by Huntington Lake and, as soon as you cross Rancheria Creek, turn right on Kaiser Pass Road, heading northeast. This is one of the highest roads in California, and listed as one of America's most dangerous roads. This one-lane engineering marvel is paved to the pass and has several wide pullouts so cars can get around each other.

At 15.7 miles you come to the Bosillo Campground; the High Sierra Ranger Station is just past that. Continue on Kaiser Pass Road for 1 more mile and turn left on Edison Lake Road, signed for Mono Hot Springs Resort. In about 1.1 miles cross a steel bridge; in another 0.5 mile cross the bridge over the South Fork of the San Joaquin River. Continue on Edison Lake Road for another 6.5 miles to the parking area near Florence Lake Campground and the boat ramps. GPS: 37.27735, -118.97503

The Hike

Beginning at the parking area/trailhead, follow the road downhill out of the parking lot and past the campground. Turn right (west) for about 300 feet and then turn left, following the road down along the west edge of the lake. After 0.4 mile from the parking lot, a dirt trail (signed for Blayney Meadows and Muir Trail Ranch) leaves the right side of the road (GPS: 37.27344, -118.97435). Turn right and head south on this well-defined trail for about 3.3 scenic, sometimes shady miles to the south end of the lake. The trail is flat as it winds through and across granite slabs. Pass Boulder Creek Campground at 3.7 miles and cross the footbridge over the South Fork of the San Joaquin River at 3.9 miles from the trailhead (GPS: 37.24249, -118.94334).

Located in the meadow across the river from Muir Trail Ranch is this mud-bottomed pool; just beyond is a warm pond that feels great on a hot day.

After crossing the bridge, the trail heads east and follows an old road for several miles until you get to the sign and the turn to the hot springs. It's often shady and mostly flat as it winds east across meadows, through dense forested areas, and across granite slabs until you come to a gate at about 7 miles. Go through the gate and hike through the trees on the north side of a large meadow. Continue on the shady trail as it skirts around the north side of the ranch property. After about 1.4 miles past the gate, you'll come to a sign (GPS: 37.23700, -118.87997) directing you to turn right for the 700 feet to the river. The hot pools are in the meadow immediately across the river, and the warm pond is just beyond that. When I last visited, there was a rope across the river to help with the ford over to the meadow. GPS: 37.23518, -118.88145

The Hot Springs

It's unfortunate that one of the better pools, located up against the rock mound, belongs to the Muir Trail Ranch. According to Fresno County assessor's maps, the ranch installed their boundary fence 135 feet too far to the south. In doing so, they encroached on Forest Service land and at least one hot pool. The most obvious pool (GPS: 37.23437, -118.88202) is quite shallow, so not as appealing as the ranch's pool to the northwest. Thankfully there's a third hot pool (GPS: 37.23407, -118.88254) that's deeper (and not on contested ground!). It's round and about 14 feet across, with

Blayney Meadows Hot Springs

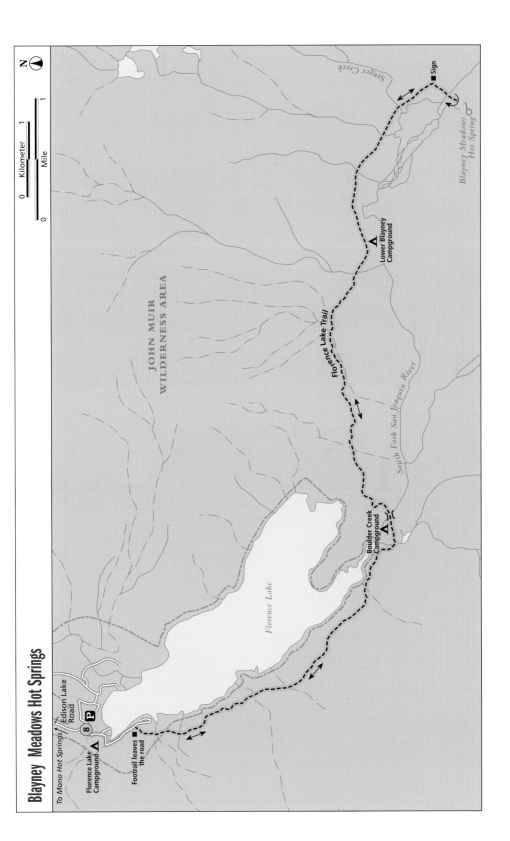

There are a few pools across the river from Muir Trail Ranch. Recently they have built a fence, which may block access to pools like these.

Above left and right: Before you cross the river, you can find some warm seeps that may be nice on a hot day. PHOTOS BY BLUE MEEK-FIELD

a mud bottom. It sometimes runs too hot for comfort in the warmer months. Nearby is a nice swimming pond (GPS: 37.23369, -118.88323) that's warmed by the geothermal outflow. Though considerably cooler, it is refreshing on a hot day. The two meadow pools receive no shade, while the ranch's pool is under a few trees.

There are also hot-water seeps on both sides of the South Fork of the San Joaquin River where you might find some places to soak.

Notes: The John Muir Trail (JMT) and Pacific Crest Trail (PCT) pass within a mile of this trail beyond the hot springs. The Muir Trail Ranch is a popular resupply point for hikers on those trails.

A ferry operates on Florence Lake during the peak season, ferrying JMT and PCT hikers, campers, and guests of the Muir Trail Ranch. No reservations are required, and it runs three times a day. Tickets are available at the Florence Lake store.

9 Kern Hot Springs

General description: A modest source that flows into a small concrete soaking box at the end of a very long hike in Sequoia National Park. Swimwear is a local decision.
Difficulty: Difficult
Distance (the short way): About 22.0 miles each way
General location: About 57 miles east of Visalia
Elevation gain (the short way): 8,700 feet
Trailhead elevation: 7,860 feet
Hot springs elevation: 6,900 feet

Map: USGS Mineral King 7.5-minute (hike), USGS Chagoopa Falls 7.5-minute and Kern Peak 15-minute (springs are shown)
Restrictions: Snow is likely to be problematic on the roads and the hike; plan accordingly.
Best time of year: Summer through fall
Camping: Camping near Kern Hot Springs must be in designated spaces. Primitive camping is available virtually everywhere else.
Contact: National Park Service, Mineral King Ranger Station: (559) 565-3768

Finding the trailhead: The long way: The beginning point for the High Sierra Trail (HST) is Crescent Meadow in Sequoia National Park (GPS: 36.55480, -118.74897). This can be found on your phone or GPS; otherwise, from Visalia drive east on CA 198 for about 50.6 miles. Turn right on Crescent Meadow Road and drive 2.6 miles to the trailhead.

The short way: You can enter "Mineral King Ranger Station" on your phone or GPS and get there easily. Otherwise, from Visalia, drive east on CA 198 for about 32 miles to Three Rivers, then turn right (east) on Mineral King Road. Follow Mineral King Road for 23.4 miles to the Mineral King Ranger Station on the left. Continue a little over a mile to a fork with a locked service gate to the left and the White Chief Trailhead parking area to the right. The locked service gate at this fork is the trailhead GPS: 36.45060, -118.59507.

You cannot park at this trailhead; you must park at either the White Chief Trailhead parking area (GPS: 36.44894, -118.59546) (continue 750 feet down the right fork from the service gate intersection) or at the Sawtooth Trailhead parking area (GPS: 36.45289, -118.59666).

The Hike

The long way (elevation gain: about 15,000 feet): Kern Hot Springs is about 37 miles from Crescent Meadow on the popular 72-mile High Sierra Trail, which crosses the Sierra Nevada from west to east. The National Park Service has provided the details of the High Sierra Trail, which are included in the appendix.

The short way: From the signed trailhead at the locked service gate, follow the trail for Franklin Lakes and Farewell Gap as it heads south along the east side of the East Fork of the Kaweah River. Just short of a mile from the trailhead, Crystal Creek makes its cascading trip down the hillside and enters the East Fork of the Kaweah River. This is the first of many picture-worthy scenes along this hike, which also include the rainbow-colored rocks, the namesake for Rainbow Mountain. Approximately 1.8 miles from the trailhead, the trail crosses Franklin Creek and begins a 1.0-mile climb via switchbacks to a fork in the trail, about 3.25 miles into the hike. Turn

It was a long hike, but you made it to the most remote hot springs in this book. Enjoy the soak along the river, you earned it! PHOTO BY LYNDON SCOTT

left toward the Franklin Lakes and continue around the side of Tulare Peak. At about 4.4 miles, cross Franklin Creek and arrive at the eastern point of the lower Franklin Lake. The views of the valleys with the alpine lakes in the foreground are stunning. There are no bad photos taken here.

Hike along the northern shore of the lake (elevation 10,300 feet) then up several switchbacks on the steep climb toward Franklin Pass (11,600 feet). Shortly after the switchbacks above the lakes, cross the boundary for the Sequoia & Kings Canyon Wilderness and walk along the side of Rainbow Mountain to Franklin Pass, approximately 8.3 miles from the trailhead. The view is spectacular, with peaks in every direction and the Kern River Canyon to the east (4,700 feet of elevation below).

Continue straight past the intersection with the infrequently used trail to Shotgun Pass, and arrive at the next intersection about 2.0 miles after crossing Franklin

Kern Hot Springs

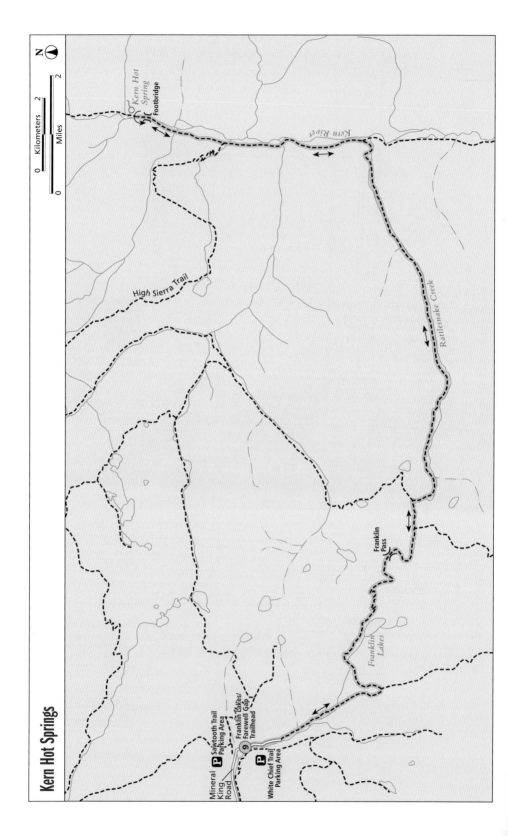

N

0   Kilometers   2
0   Miles   2

Kern Hot Spring

Footbridge

High Sierra Trail

Kern River

Rattlesnake Creek

Franklin Pass

Franklin Lakes

Mineral King Road

Sawtooth Trail Parking Area

Franklin Lakes/ Farewell Gap Trailhead

White Chief Trail Parking Area

Pass. This intersection is well-signed for Rattlesnake Canyon and the Kern River to the right, and the more frequently used trail to Forester Lake and Little Claire Lake to the left. Turn right toward Rattlesnake Canyon and follow this long, continuous descent along the north side of Rattlesnake Creek for approximately 7.5 miles until the trail intersects with the Kern River Trail. Turn left and hike up the west side of the Kern River for approximately 2.7 miles until the trail is joined by the High Sierra Trail. Continue north about 1.3 miles on the Kern River/High Sierra Trail to the footbridge over the Kern River (GPS: 36.47349, -118.40703). Cross the bridge to the east side and continue north for about 0.4 mile to the hot springs on the left (GPS: 36.47813, -118.40624).

The Hot Springs

Hot water at 115°F (46°C) flows into a small concrete soaking box near the edge of the Kern River, then into another small pool, and continues out into another small rock and sand pool at the river's edge. The tub has a short fence partially around it for privacy from the trail. The wildflowers, the rumbling river, and the peaks high above make the long hike worthwhile.

10 Jordan Hot Springs

General description: Several soaking options at the end of the long, downhill Casa Vieja Trail in the Golden Trout Wilderness. Swimwear is a local decision.
Difficulty: Easy
Distance: 10.8 miles round-trip
General location: Southwest of Lone Pine and about 52 miles by road from Little Lake
Elevation gain: 3,010 feet
Trailhead elevation: 8,950 feet
Hot springs elevation: 6,510 feet
Map: USGS Hockett Peak 15-minute (springs are shown)

Restrictions: Roads often closed in the winter months
Best time of year: Spring through fall
Camping: There is camping at the trailhead, but no water.
Contact: Sequoia National Forest, Kern River Ranger District: (760) 376-3781; Inyo National Forest, Eastern Sierra Visitor Center: (760) 876-6200
History: This is now a National Historic Landmark, as the hot springs used to be a resort with stock animals bringing in people and supplies. The resort was left to return to nature when it became a wilderness area.

Finding the trailhead: The Casa Vieja Trail begins at the Blackrock Trailhead, and you can find it on your phone or GPS. Otherwise, drive 7 miles south of Little Lake on US 395 and turn west on 9 Mile Canyon Road/CR 141. Continue 23.9 miles and bear left on Sherman Pass Road/FR 22S05. After another 12.8 miles, turn right on Fish Creek/FR 21S03. Proceed 3.5 miles and keep left to stay on FR 21S03, then continue 4.7 miles to the Blackrock Trailhead. GPS: 36.17584, -118.26912

The Hike

This hike is not overly steep; it's just a very long, continuous, downhill walk. The trailhead is at the far north side of the pack station/parking area. Once on the wide trail, hike gently downhill through the trees for about 1.5 miles and you should start to see the Casa Viejo Meadows ahead. Continue on the shaded trail through the trees, skirting the west side of the pristine meadow. About 2.1 miles from the trailhead, the trail steps down into the meadow for about 70 feet to cross Ninemile Creek (GPS: 36.20191, -118.27328); turn left, following the creek. Get ready, as you are about to lose nearly 1,900 feet of elevation in the next 3 miles. The trail crosses the creek several times as you hike down the canyon, but they are not difficult crossings. Stay on the trail as it winds down the canyon for another 1.5 miles to where the trail leaves the shade and follows around the north side of the meadow. The trail starts down another shaded canyon for 1.5 more miles to a clearing at the bottom. Off to the right, you'll find a large camping spot and an old cabin in the tall grass and brush. The trail was not very clear here at my last visit, but the hot springs are about 450 feet to the northwest on the other side of all the trees and brush.

I tried both ways and found it best to cross Ninemile Creek, head north for about 200 feet, then turn left for about 300 more feet to the springs (GPS: 36.22957,

Hidden away in a remote meadow, sunrises and sunsets don't get much better than from here.

The "coffin pool" is built for one, just like its namesake.

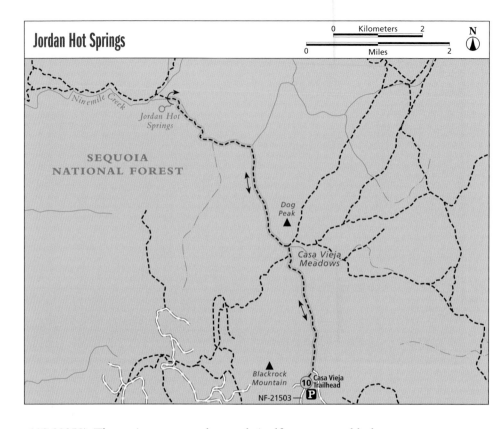

0   Kilometers   2

0   Miles   2

N

Ninemile Creek

Jordan Hot Springs

SEQUOIA
NATIONAL FOREST

Dog Peak

Casa Vieja Meadows

Blackrock Mountain

Casa Vieja Trailhead

NF-21503

-118.30258). The springs are on the creek itself, so you could also try to stay on the creek and pick your way through the brush. Perhaps there will be a better path trampled down by the time you get there.

Note: There is also a Jordan Hot Springs in New Mexico.

The Hot Springs

The pools are along Ninemile Creek at the end of a grassy meadow. It's an amazing setting far away from civilization. Hot water comes out of the ground at over 110°F (43°C) and flows down into a shallow 10-by-20-foot pool created by rocks and sandbags. The flow is enough to keep the pool about 104°F (40°C). The water cools a little as it flows over the dam into a coffin-sized pool. Additional 110°F water, from a small source, is also piped into the coffin pool, which maintains a temperature of about 100°F (38°C). From here the water flows into another rock and sand pool by the creek that is close to body temperature. About 25 feet away, another hot water source flows out of the ground and down a beautifully colored mineral-deposit slide into a small rock and sand pool by the creek. On my last visit, there was not enough flow to keep it above body temperature, but the yellow to green color spectrum of the slide made it worth the little scrambling required to get down to it.

Above left: Jordan's main pool, surrounded by green foliage and surrounding hills
Above right: An additional pool sits beneath this waterfall over a dazzling yellow- to green-colored display of mineral deposits.

One of the many old structures to be explored in this new wilderness area. They have been left to nature.

Also in the Sierra Nevada

Buckeye Hot Springs (GPS: 38.23901 -119.32549): A natural soak you can drive to that is definitely worth the stop.

Hot Creek Geological Site

Just east of Mammoth Lakes is the Hot Creek Geological Site of the Long Valley Caldera. There you will find several pools in which to soak. I don't consider them hiking hot springs, but you will do plenty of walking to get to them all. They are close to trailheads, and definitely worth the time to see. Some are better than others, and most are known by at least one other name. I'll list them how I know them.

Name	North	West
Little Hot Creek	37.68996	-118.84245
Alkali Pool	37.66940	-118.78252
Shepherd	37.66693	-118.80334
Hilltop	37.66397	-118.78940
Crab Cooker	37.66276	-118.80015
Wild Willy's	37.66104	-118.76777
Hot Creek Geological Site	37.66084	-118.82782
The Rock Tub	37.64758	-118.80806

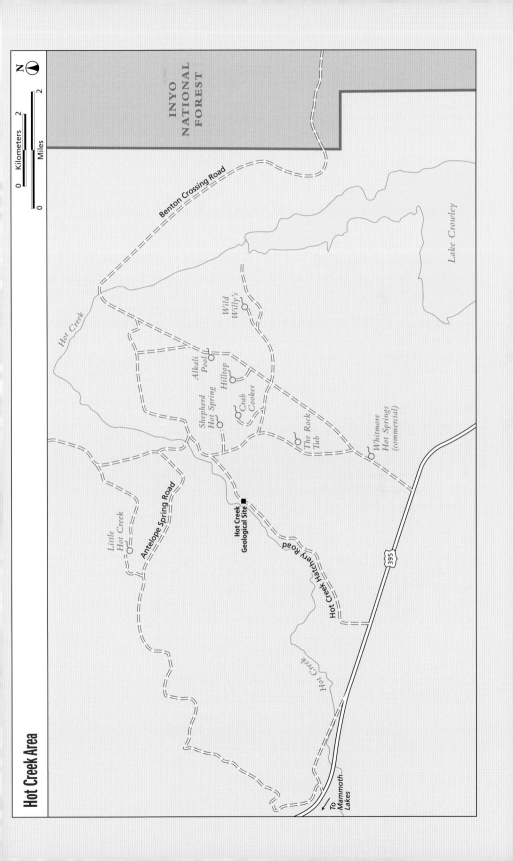

Hot Creek Area

N

0 Kilometers 2
0 Miles 2

INYO NATIONAL FOREST

Benton Crossing Road

Hot Creek

Lake Crowley

Wild Willy's

Alkali Pool

Shepherd Hot Spring

Hilltop

Crab Cooker

The Rock Tub

Whitmore Hot Springs (commercial)

Little Hot Creek

Antelope Spring Road

Hot Creek Geological Site

Hot Creek Hatchery Road

Hot Creek

395

To Mammoth Lakes

11 Upper Saline Valley Hot Springs

General description: An exceptional collection of hot springs in Death Valley National Monument that you have to see to believe. Swimwear is not required at this time.

Difficulty: Easy

Distance: 4.4 miles round-trip

General location: About 67 miles southeast of Bishop

Elevation gain: Negligible

Trailhead elevation: 1,480 feet

Hot springs elevation: 1,840 feet

Map: USGS Dry Mountain 15-minute (springs are shown)

Restrictions: Roads may be impassable in winter. The final road up the valley is extremely rough, so a high-clearance vehicle is essential. Two spare tires are a great idea. This area is blisteringly hot, so be sure to take all the supplies you need and plenty of water.

Best time of year: Winter through spring

Camping: There are multiple places to camp near the two lower pool areas, and places to camp at the upper pools. Take plenty of extra days' worth of food and water; you may not want to leave. There are primitive showers and kitchens at both of the lower areas.

Contact: National Park Service: (760) 786-3200

History: Saline Valley has a caretaker who has been there for several decades. This miraculous man has kept the pools in order, provided first aid, performed countless acts of service, and been an ambassador of goodwill for as long as I have known him. The National Park Service recognizes his immense value and has made some arrangements to let him be part of a team to keep the area safe and clean.

Finding the trailhead: Surprisingly, your phone or GPS will find these directions for you, though you might want to double-check them to ensure they look correct compared to the written ones. Depending on the weather, you can drive to Saline Valley Hot Springs from the north, south, or east—if you're super adventurous and have the right vehicle. The route from the east involves crossing Steele Pass from Nevada. I won't discuss that route here, but you can find details on the internet.

Northern route: From Big Pine, head north on US 395 for 0.6 mile and turn right on CA 168 East for 2.3 miles. Turn right onto Death Valley Road/Waucoba Road and drive 3.4 miles. Continue straight for 9.6 more miles as Waucoba Road gets a name change to Waucoba Springs Road. Continue straight again, this time for 14.3 more miles as Waucoba Springs Road gets a name change to Waucoba Saline Road. Turn left on Saline Valley Road for 4.6 miles to an unmarked intersection where you turn left. (There are multiple washes that look like roads; make sure you find the one with multiple tire tracks.) After turning left, slowly proceed about 4.9 miles, then continue straight on South Warm Springs Road for 2.5 miles to the lower Saline Valley Pools.

About 0.6 mile up South Warm Springs Road past the lower Saline Valley Pools, you come to the second set of pools, the Saline Valley Palm Pools. GPS: 36.81328, -117.76555

Southern route: From US 395 near Olancha, drive east on CA 190 for 31.5 miles and turn left onto Saline Valley Alt Route. Go 4.7 miles, then continue straight as Saline Valley Alt Route gets a name change to Saline Valley Road. Continue 40.7 miles to an unmarked intersection where you turn right. (There are multiple washes that look like roads; make sure you find the one with multiple tire tracks.) After turning right, slowly proceed about 4.9 miles, then continue straight on South Warm Springs Road for 2.5 miles to the lower Saline Valley Pools. About 0.6 mile up South Warm Springs Road past the lower Saline Valley Pools, you come to the second set of pools, the Saline Valley Palm Pools.

Note: The northern route (from Big Pine) is often in better condition than the southern route; however, it is higher in elevation and can get closed due to snow. You should check road conditions before you start. The common advice is to plan 3 hours for this trip. At the risk of sounding uncommon, if you are an experienced backcountry driver with the right vehicle, the trip can be done in half that.

The squishy-bottomed upper pools are shaded by a few lone palms and some foliage—peaceful solitude a couple of miles away from the more popular pools.

Also in the Area

There are ancient campsites with rocks where corn was ground. There are mine sites, Cold Spring Canyon, and all kinds of geological and archaeological wonders. Saline Valley has several "regulars" who, if you ask around, may be happy to offer information about some informal day hikes.

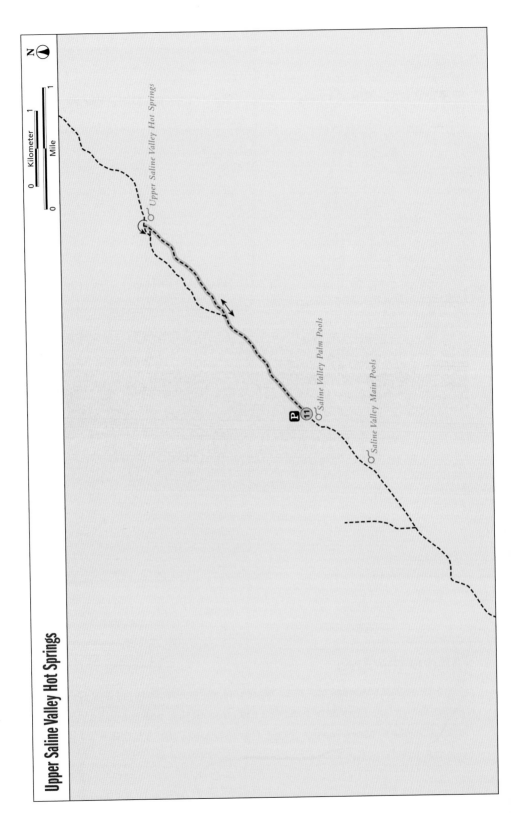

Upper Saline Valley Hot Springs

N

Kilometer
0   1

0   1
Mile

Upper Saline Valley Hot Springs

Saline Valley Palm Pools

Saline Valley Main Pools

P

Top: Blue taking a break from photography and enjoying the spectacular view
Bottom: The shaded Crystal Pool and a book is a great afternoon. PHOTO BY BLUE MEEK-FIELD

The Hike

The trailhead for the hike to the upper pools is accessible from the Saline Valley Palm Pools (GPS: 36.81288, -117.76612), another spectacular set of pools 0.6 mile northeast of the lower (main) Saline Valley Pools (GPS: 36.80575, -117.77308). These hot springs are described in detail in the FalconGuide *Touring California and Nevada Hot Springs* by Matt C. Bischoff. I doubt you will ever find a better trailhead from which to depart, and return to.

Left: Wonderful hot springs, and the locals are friendly.
Right: Crystal-clear pools are more than inviting to any soaker. This pool is waiting for you back at the trailhead. PHOTOS BY BLUE MEEK-FIELD

From the trailhead at the Palm Pools, park at the farthest northeast end and start walking up the old road. It's generally considered too rough and rutted for driving on, though some have done it. The trail follows the road up a wide valley with multicolored hills on both sides. The wind and water have shaped the desert floor as the road winds through a maze of creosote shrub–dotted washes. You are gaining elevation; however, it's so gradual over this 2.1 miles, it's hard to notice. Before long you see the palm trees taking shape and you realize it's not a mirage. Walk to the palms and the fenced area. Pass through the gate and wander through the maze of grass and brush until you discover the pools. GPS: 36.83236, -117.73780

The Hot Springs

The upper hot springs consists of two very secluded natural pools under the shade of some palm trees. Water flows out of the ground at 100°F (38°C) into a small pool with a rock bottom, big enough for three or four people. There is a smaller, cooler pool right next to it.

What's Your Favorite Hot Spring?

This is a question I have been asked a couple of hundred times over the years. If I am sitting in a hot springs when asked the question, my standard answer is, "The one I'm in right now," but that doesn't really answer the question. It's always been hard to pick a single favorite, but I can usually list my top five. Saline Valley is always one of those five. When I visit, I often take supplies for an extra week in case I don't want to leave just yet.

Kern River Area

The Kern River area has two hot springs very close together and a third down the road a little. The Forest Service is doing a nice job managing the springs, which have been closed off and on over the years. They are still working on a long-term management plan to ensure the springs can be enjoyed for years to come.

There are two hot springs on the Kern River within a few miles of each other, and Pyramid Hot Springs is back down the road a little. PHOTO BY MICHI CATANESE

12 Remington Hot Springs

General description: An extremely popular set of rock, sand, and cement pools on the Kern River in the Sequoia National Forest. Swimwear is required, and often adhered to.

Difficulty: Easy, with some tough spots

Distance: 0.4 mile round-trip

General location: About 40 miles northeast of Bakersfield

Elevation gain: 170 feet

Trailhead elevation: 2,460 feet

Hot springs elevation: 2,240 feet

Map: USGS Miracle Hot Springs 7.5-minute (springs are not shown)

Restrictions: Day-use only; no glass, no fires

Best time of year: Spring through fall

Camping: Hobo Campground is about 2 miles away; Sandy Flat Campground is 3.2 miles away.

Contact: Sequoia National Forest, Kern River Ranger District: (760) 376-3781

Finding the trailhead: From Bakersfield, head east on CA 178 for approximately 37 miles and turn right on Borel Road. In 0.3 mile, at the T intersection, turn right on Kern Canyon Road and drive 3.4 miles (passing the Miracle Hot Springs parking at 1.9 miles) to the unsigned parking area on the right (east). GPS: 35.57641, -118.55264

The Hike

The 0.2-mile trail begins from the northeast corner of the parking area. There is a Forest Service sign at the trailhead and a sign saying the area is maintained by the

Three beautifully constructed pools on the edge of the Kern River PHOTO BY MICHI CATANESE

Intricate stonework adorns this upper one-person pool. Photo by Michi Catanese

Kern River Hot Springs Angels. There are several trails in the area, but take the path farthest to the right. Hike down the hill on this well-worn trail, passing periodic wooden handrails, small switchbacks, and a two-person rock and cement pool surrounded by tall grass and trees. From there, continue down the stone steps toward the river.

Remington and Miracle Hot Springs

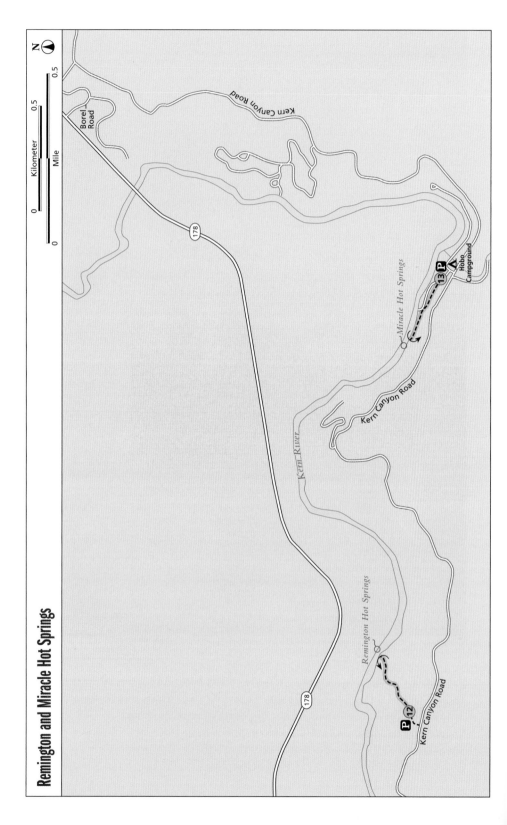

The Hot Springs

Three main pools of varying temperatures sit alongside the Kern River (GPS: 35.57763, -118.54983). The pools are renowned for their crystal-clear water and elaborate stone masonry work. Hot water comes out of the rocks at 106°F (41°C) into a rectangular 3-by-7-foot tub that maintains a temperature of about 103°F (39°C). The outflow cools as it flows into two interconnected pools that stay about 100°F (38°C). One is about an 8-by-12-foot teardrop-shaped pool, and the other is about a 6-by-8-foot oval. These last two pools have stone benches offering places to sit. The main pools have cement and stone bottoms and drains, which are handy for cleaning.

On the trail down to the springs, you passed a two-person rock and cement pool built up against a boulder. Warm water bubbles up from the bottom to keep this pool in the mid- to high 80s (30–32°C). The rock and cement pools are high enough above the river that they don't get flooded often, though it happens occasionally.

An additional pool on the river, for a total of five PHOTO BY MICHI CATANESE

13 Miracle Hot Springs

See map on page 62.
General description: Another very popular set of rock, sand, and cement pools on the Kern River in the Sequoia National Forest at the end of short hike. Swimwear is a requirement that most people adhere to.
Difficulty: Easy
Distance: 0.2 mile round-trip
General location: About 38 miles northeast of Bakersfield
Elevation gain: Negligible
Trailhead elevation: 2,285 feet
Hot springs elevation: 2,270 feet
Map: USGS Miracle Hot Springs 7.5-minute (springs are shown)

Restrictions: Day-use only; no glass, no fires
Best time of year: Spring through fall
Camping: Hobo Campground is at the trailhead; Sandy Flat Campground is 1.2 miles away.
Contact: Sequoia National Forest, Kern River Ranger District: (760) 376-3781
History: Once known as Compressor Hot Springs, then later called Hobo Hot Springs, reportedly named after workers who lived there while building the Borel Power plant. A hotel with a bathhouse was constructed. The pools are reported to be what remained after the hotel burned.

Finding the trailhead: From Bakersfield, head east on CA 178 for approximately 37 miles and turn right on Borel Road. In 0.3 mile, at the T intersection, turn right on Kern Canyon Road and drive 1.9 miles to the unsigned parking area on your right. The trailhead is at the far west end of the parking area. GPS: 35.57497, -118.53081

Pools made from nearby rocks help these various soaks fit perfectly into their natural surroundings.
PHOTOS BY MICHI CATANESE

The Hike

From the parking area, head west on the dirt road for about 500 feet to where the foot trail begins. Continue on this well-used path 0.1 mile to the riverside pools (GPS: 35.57631, -118.53378). The boulder-lined trail is mostly shady and flat, with a few rocks to scramble down at the end.

The Hot Springs

Multiple rock and cement pools line the edge of the Kern River. Hot water comes out of the rocks at 105°F (40.5°C) and cools slightly as it flows through interconnected pools. Most of the pools are fully in the sun, though some pools have a little shade. In July 2021, there were seven pools, one with a nice rock and cement mural in the bottom.

The pools have changed dramatically over the years, and more changes are in store, as the Forest Service would prefer that the pools not contain cement. The

◄ *The largest pool at Miracle Hot Springs with enough room and seating for a third-grade class, though I'd probably soak elsewhere on that day.* PHOTO BY MICHI CATANESE

Intricate rockwork adorns this pool with the hot spring's namesake. PHOTO BY MICHI CATANESE

Forest Service is working on a long-term plan for management of this place, which has opened and closed many times in the last decade. Litter is a big problem at Miracle Hot Springs, though the Kern River Hot Springs Angels, a dedicated group of volunteers, do a great job of trying to keep it clean. It is still a struggle for them to stay ahead of the crowds who apparently forget their manners. The Kern River Hot Springs Angels have a Facebook page if you are interested in supporting them or joining their cause.

The pool is under this cube-shaped rock ▶
on the wrong side of the Kern River.

14 Pyramid Hot Springs

General description: A small two-person pool on the wrong side of the Kern River and only available during low water. Swimwear is a local decision.

Difficulty: Easy to hard, depending on river crossing

Distance: 0.2 mile round-trip if the river is low enough

General location: About 15 miles northeast of Bakersfield

Elevation gain: Negligible

Trailhead elevation: 1,330 feet

Hot springs elevation: 1,330 feet

Map: USGS Rio Bravo Ranch 7.5-minute (springs are not shown)

Restrictions: The pool is on the opposite side of the Kern River, which can be very dangerous. In addition, the pool is also underwater much of the time.

Best time of year: Summer through fall. The river can be impossible to cross at times.

Camping: Hobo Campground and Sandy Flat Campground are two Forest Service campgrounds located about 25 miles northeast up the canyon.

Contact: Sequoia National Forest, Kern River Ranger District: (760) 376-3781

Finding the trailhead: From Bakersfield, drive northeast on CA 178 into the Kern River Canyon. About 2 miles after entering the canyon, pass a dam and hydroelectric power plant on the left side, then continue another 2.3 miles to the pullout on the left. The namesake pyramid-shaped rock is at the north end of the parking area. GPS: 35.47740, -118.75201

When the water is low enough, you can access and enjoy this cozy pool. A big thanks to Shaun Astor for sharing this amazing photo. Photo by Shaun Astor

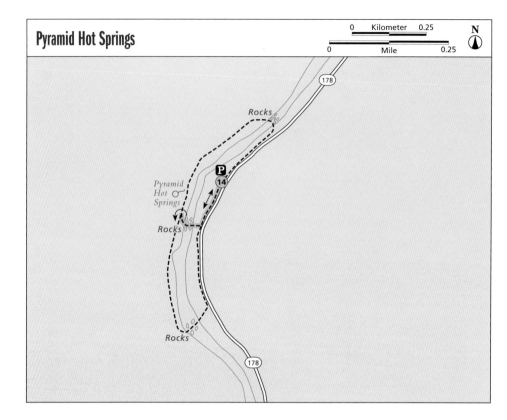

Pyramid Hot Springs

The Hike

The goal is to cross the Kern River safely. One way is to go downstream about 450 feet from the south end of the pullout where there are large boulders that may help if the water is low enough. There are some faint trails close to the river on both sides. Alternatively, there are three rocky spots upstream that may allow you to get across, but getting back downstream to the springs is pretty tough.

The Hot Springs

The small two-person pool sits at the base of a large cube-shaped boulder on the west side of the river (GPS: 35.47706, -118.75313). The hot water comes out of the ground at about 110°F (43°C), and the flow is enough to maintain the pool temperature at 102°F (39°C), when the river is low enough.

After the concrete pool was removed, this small pool is all that remains at the "legendary" Sykes Hot Springs. The area needs to recover after decades of overuse. Though long and brutal, the hike is beautiful.

15 Steep Ravine Hot Springs

General description: An extremely popular pool at the end of a quarter-mile scramble down to the Pacific Ocean. This pool, in Mount Tamalpais State Park, is about 15 miles north of the Golden Gate Bridge. Swimwear is rare.

Difficulty: Moderate

Distance: 0.5 mile round-trip, though it seems like more

General location: About 15 miles north of San Francisco

Elevation gain: 320 feet

Trailhead elevation: 350 feet

Hot springs elevation: 0 feet (or so)

Map: USGS Bolinas 7.5-minute (springs are not shown)

Restrictions: The spring is really close to mean sea level and only accessible during a minus tide. Check the tide charts for Stinson Beach to find the few days that this pool is exposed. If it is not a minus tide, there is no need to go there. Tide predictions can be found at https://tidesandcurrents.noaa.gov/tide_predictions.html.

Best time of year: Year-round

Camping: There are many camping opportunities nearby in Mount Tamalpais State Park.

Pantoll Campground, Bootjack Campground, and Steep Ravine Campground and Cabins are 3 choices.

Contact: Mount Tamalpais State Park: (415) 388-2070

History: The online reviews are mostly negative due to the cooler water temperature and the crowds. It is reported that some of the locals are not so pleased about Steep Ravine's growing popularity, as it was fairly secret for a long time. It isn't all negative, though; there is a local group that is keeping the pool usable by digging, sandbagging, and even siphoning out cold water. The NOAA documented a hot spring in the *Thermal Springs List for the United States* about half a mile south of this one and named it Rocky Point (GPS: 37.880, -122.627). I spoke with some locals who said there was a spring at that location, but noted the hot water moved north a little after a fairly recent seismic event. I can't vouch for the accuracy of the water moving north, but I can say with certainty that after exploring every inch around the USGS coordinates, I found many things, but no hot water. I even dug deep holes in the beach looking for hot water, with no success.

Finding the trailhead: From Mill Valley, proceed north on CA 1 for 10.4 miles to a small parking area on the left side of CA 1 at mile marker 11.20. It's difficult to find a place to park during extremely low tides. You might be able get a spot either north or south of the trailhead and walk the highway back to the trailhead. It is hard enough to find a spot to turn a vehicle around on the busy CA 1, so be careful walking along it if you cannot park at the trailhead. GPS: 37.88714, -122.62859

The Hike

From the trailhead, proceed down the obvious trail as it switches back and forth a few times on the way to the beach. The trail has more switches than were being used; it appears people have skipped some in their desire to get to the beach. Near the end, there are a few spots that are really more of a scramble than a hike. Enjoy the beautiful coastal flora, while avoiding the poison oak. It goes without saying, the view over the Pacific Ocean is spectacular.

Hiding in the rocks (look closely at the bottom of the photo), you will find the large pool, which is usually packed like a can of sardines. Don't expect to have this one to yourself. Squeeze in, make friends, and try to enjoy a very different soaking experience.

The Hot Springs

The pool is nestled underneath some boulders (GPS: 37.88649, -122.63084), and the 90°F (32°C) water seeps up through the sand near the back. The closer you can get back into the enclosed space under the boulders, the warmer your soak will be. The pool is quite noisy because of all the people, and it makes you question the sanitary aspects. The pool could fit a dozen people comfortably, though on my visit, there were many more. It really is neat knowing you're soaking below sea level, and the view is amazing, but the crowds are not for everyone. The local custom is naked, and swimwear can sometimes invite scorn.

It is known by a few names: Steep Ravine seems most popular, with Rocky Point Hot Springs and Marin Tidal Pool coming in second and third in the naming game. You may also hear it called "1120 hot springs," due to the 11.20 mile-marker sign at the trailhead.

Steep Ravine Hot Springs

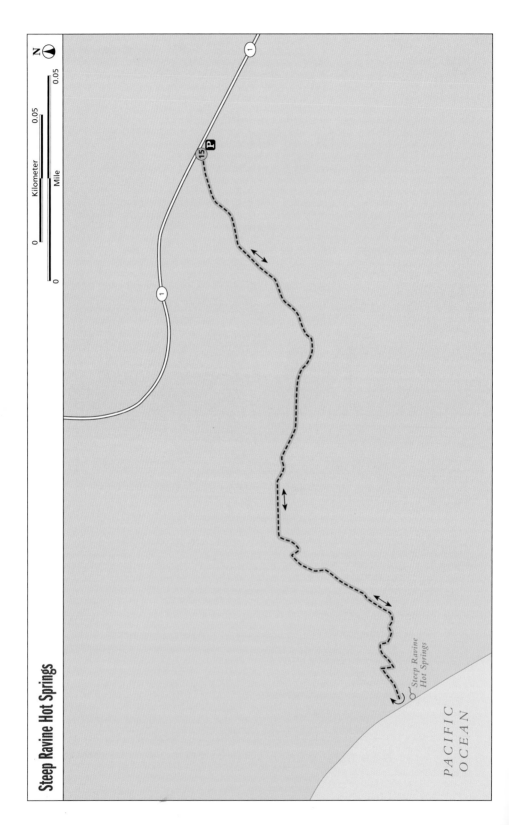

A look down the trail with the Pacific sunset in the background

Fish in a Can

After a couple of days searching for hot water at the USGS-listed coordinates half a mile down the beach, I was pretty excited about finding the actual location, and was determined to soak. When I got down to the pool and saw people jammed in so tight, it reminded me of fish stranded in a pool after the water receded. Not deterred yet, I stripped down to the local customary outfit and sat there like a respectable soaker waiting for someone to leave. Several people came down the trail, took a look, and retreated. After most of an hour, no one had left, but I kept waiting. I tried discreetly counting the soakers and lost track around nineteen. It was difficult because some were stacked two high, maybe more. Then a couple came down the trail, dropped their clothes, and wiggled into the pool in front of me. I doubt they knew I was waiting; they evidently knew more about the local situation than I did. Discouraged, I got dressed and walked down the beach where I might get a photo while still respecting their privacy. After that, I hiked back up the trail and drove away. Quite honestly, I know better places to soak.

16 Sykes Hot Springs

General description: A small pool above the Big Sur River at the end of a grueling hike in the Big Sur Wild and Scenic River and Ventana Wilderness in the Los Padres National Forest. This is a heavily trafficked trail, and you will probably have to wait in line to soak. Swimwear required.

Difficulty: Difficult

Distance: 19.6 miles round-trip

General location: About 7 miles south of Big Sur

Elevation gain: 5,240 feet

Trailhead elevation: 310 feet

Hot springs elevation: 1,070 feet

Map: USGS Partington Ridge 7.5-minute (springs are not shown)

Restrictions: There is a fee for parking. Campfires and smoking are prohibited during fire season. A California campfire permit is required for all flames, including camp stoves. Permits are available at the Big Sur Station. This area is subject to forest fires and washouts that frequently damage the trails. Nudity can be cited on Forest Service land, and rangers visit the site regularly.

Best time of year: Spring through fall

Camping: Several very nice camping spots partway in. Pfeiffer Big Sur State Park is near the trailhead.

Contact: Los Padres National Forest, Big Sur Station: (831) 667-2315

History: For years, Sykes Hot Springs was a legendary hangout for people getting away from civilization. People camped there in numbers beyond what was legal and ethical, and far beyond what the land could accommodate. Today the pools are not what they once were. The Forest Service has partnered with the Ventana Wilderness Alliance, who do a fantastic job managing this out-of-the-way place. The Forest Service wants to manage this hot springs in a manner that prevents overuse. Expect the introduction of a permitting system to limit the impact on this place, which still seems to attract far more hikers than the ecosystem allows. It is ironic that it attracts so many visitors, because the hike is long and brutal and the single pool is really not worth the effort. It is a beautiful place, but there are much better places to soak, without waiting in a line.

Finding the trailhead: From Big Sur, travel 6.7 miles south on CA 1 to Big Sur Station, managed by the Los Padres Forest Association. GPS: 36.24638, -121.78013

The Hike

The Pine Ridge Trail to Sykes Hot Springs begins at the south end of the Big Sur Station. There is over 5,200 feet of elevation gain on this hike. Though only a 760-foot elevation difference between the trailhead and hot springs, you hike that elevation difference nearly seven times by the time you finish this 19.6-mile round-trip. Redwood groves, steep rocky sections, and cliffs form the terrain.

The trail begins easily enough for the first mile, I believe only to lure you into feeling that you can do it. The next 1.7 miles of hiking uphill, gaining nearly a thousand feet of elevation, will make you question that initial feeling. The next 0.3 mile is downhill, so you start to feel positive again, not noticing that you just lost about 200 of the 1,000 feet of elevation you just gained. Don't worry, you will gain it all back, plus some more over the next mile. After that, you undulate for the next 2.5 miles,

After a fire scorched the surrounding area, followed by historic rains, much of the trail and pool area were washed out. The Forest Service is helping this overused hot springs get back to a more natural feel. Though this is a spectacular hike, if it is a soak you're looking for, there are better places. Remember to leave no trace and help this gem recover.

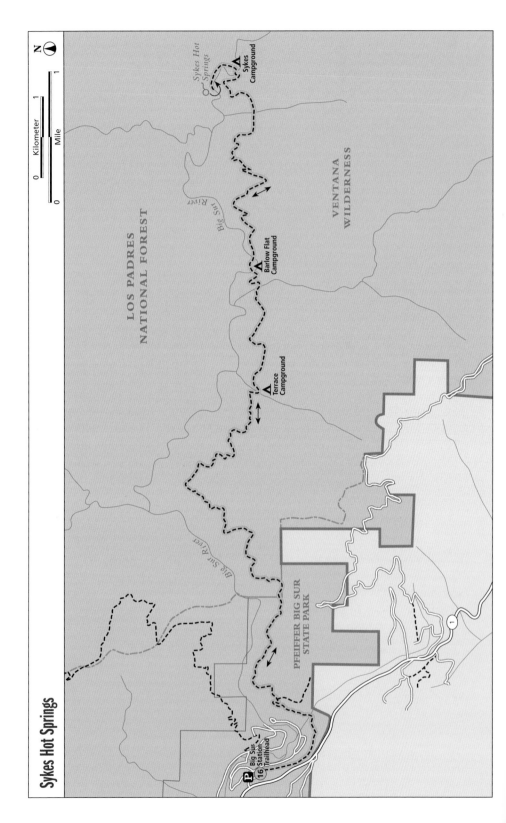

Sykes Hot Springs

This small pool is all that is left, and the building of new pools is prohibited. Expect to wait in a line for a turn to soak.

gaining elevation and losing it, but overall losing more than you are gaining, to the 6.5-mile mark at an elevation of about 950 feet. The next 1.3 miles are the big push as you gain about 750 feet of elevation to arrive at the high point of the hike at close to 1,700 feet. Continue on the trail downhill for another 1.3 miles before fording the Big Sur River. Turn left and proceed 0.4 mile to the hot springs. GPS: 36.25170, –121.68990

The Hot Springs

A small three-person rock and sand pool sits high above the river so as not to be affected by washouts. Water comes out of the rocks at about 102°F (39°C) at enough flow to keep the pool temperature in the mid-90s (35°C) depending on the ambient temperature. A second source comes out of the rocks a short distance away. There once was a pool built near the source, but now the water flows down into the creek.

The Los Padres National Forest issued this statement regarding Sykes Hot Springs: "The hot springs at Sykes Camp lay within the federally protected Big Sur Wild and Scenic River and Ventana Wilderness Areas where human-made improvements are not permitted. In the past, illegal tubs were constructed to capture water from the springs. Sykes Camp was seriously damaged in the 2016 Soberanes Fire and these tubs and other unauthorized infrastructure were removed as part of the extensive restoration of the area carried out over the last five years. Visitors who attempt to rebuild these tubs will be subject to citation and prosecution under federal law."

Southern California Area

This therapeutic hot waterfall at Sespe Hot Springs is a welcome, and well-deserved, sight after nearly 15 miles in your boots.

17 Big Caliente Hot Springs

General description: Two unexpected rock and cement creations at the end of a short hike in the Los Padres National Forest. Swimwear is required, but could be optional with discretion.

Difficulty: Easy to moderate depending on trailhead

Distance: 0.2 mile round-trip from the lower concrete pool, but can be way more

General location: About 28 miles northeast of Santa Barbara

Elevation gain: Negligible (if you can drive to the trailhead)

Trailhead elevation: 1,900 feet

Hot springs elevation: 1,890 feet

Map: USGS Hildreth Peak 7.5-minute (springs are shown)

Restrictions: Day-use only

Best time of year: Spring through fall, though summer might be too hot

Camping: Overnight camping must be in designated Forest Service campgrounds: Mid Santa Ynez, Rock Camp, P-Bar Flats, and Mono Campgrounds.

Contact: Los Padres National Forest, Santa Barbara Ranger District: (805) 448-6487

History: Big Caliente is also known as Agua Caliente by the NOAA, and in many other circles. For many years, Big and Little Caliente Hot Springs have been accessible by vehicles. Due to wildfires and their effects on erosion control in recent years, the roads to the springs have been closed more often than open. I spoke with the Forest Service in 2021, and their plan is to perform the necessary road work to keep the springs accessible by vehicles; however, the public should expect that some roads will close often.

Finding the trailhead: From the intersection of CA 192 and Mountain Drive (just north of Santa Barbara), drive northeast on Mountain Drive for 0.2 mile, then take a slight left on Gibraltar Road. Continue for 6.6 miles, turn right onto East Camino Cielo, and drive 6.7 miles. Continue straight as East Camino Cielo becomes Romero Canyon Road for 330 feet, then Romero Canyon Road turns left and becomes Romero Camuesa Road for 1.3 miles. Take a slight right to stay on Romero Camuesa Road for 4.2 miles. Turn right onto FR 5N16 and continue 2.6 miles to the lower tub on the right (GPS: 34.53909, -119.56458). The trailhead for the upper pools is approximately 280 feet farther, at the northeast end of the day-use area. GPS: 34.53938, -119.56369

The Hike

From the trailhead, hike north on the trail for about 180 feet, then turn right and drop down to, and across, the wash, heading east for about 150 feet to the upper pools. GPS: 34.53997, -119.56342

The Hot Springs

At the lower tub, hot water up to 120°F (49°C) is piped directly into a concrete pool big enough to fit a dozen people, though it has been known to fit many more. The temperature can be controlled by adjusting the inflow. There is a little shade from some oak and palm trees.

Above: Two beautiful gems tucked away along the hillside.
Below: Rock and concrete pool beautifully adorned with seashells. One larger shell acts as the spout of the drain. PHOTOS BY BLUE MEEK-FIELD

Big and Little Caliente Hot Springs

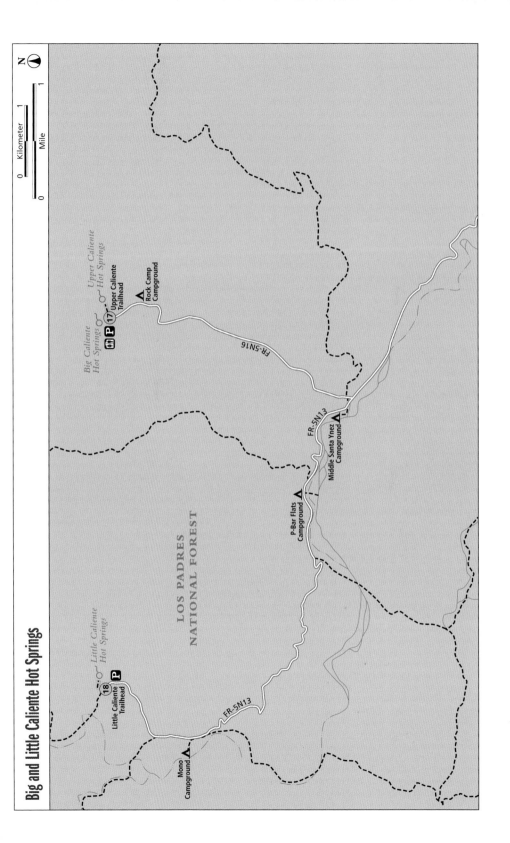

This large concrete pool with a nearby dressing area can get crowded when the roads are open.

The upper hot pools at the end of the short hike are about 8-foot-diameter, well-created rock and cement pools. Seashells have been artfully incorporated into the pools for function and aesthetics. Temperature is controlled by diverting the hot water hoses. The canyon is full of grasses, bamboo, cacti, palms, and other desert flora.

Note: Road closures often prevent access to these trailheads. In those cases, hikers can still walk to the springs by following the driving directions. On my last visit, erosion had closed roads, making it necessary to hike from the Divide Peak gate, a 31.4-mile round-trip. All for the sake of research!

18 Little Caliente Hot Springs

See map on page 83.
General description: Two unexpected rock and cement creations at the end of a short hike in the Los Padres National Forest. Swimwear is required, but could be optional with discretion.
Difficulty: Easy to moderate depending on trailhead
Distance: 0.15 mile round-trip if you can drive to the trailhead, but can be way more
General location: About 28 miles northeast of Santa Barbara
Elevation gain: Negligible (if you can drive to the trailhead)
Trailhead elevation: 1,644 feet
Hot springs elevation: 1,666 feet
Map: USGS Hildreth Peak 7.5-minute (springs are shown)
Restrictions: Day-use only

Best time of year: Spring through fall, though summer might be too hot
Camping: Overnight camping must be in designated Forest Service campgrounds: Mid Santa Ynez, Rock Camp, P-Bar Flats, and Mono Campgrounds.
Contact: Los Padres National Forest, Santa Barbara Ranger District: (805) 448-6487
History: For many years, Big and Little Caliente Hot Springs have been accessible by vehicles. Due to wildfires and their effects on erosion control in recent years, the roads to the springs have been closed more often than open. I spoke with the Forest Service in 2021, and their plan is to perform the necessary road work to keep the springs accessible by vehicles; however, the public should expect that some roads will close often.

Finding the trailhead: From the intersection of CA 192 and Mountain Drive (just north of Santa Barbara), drive northeast on Mountain Drive for 0.2 mile, then take a slight left on Gibraltar Road. Continue for 6.6 miles, turn right onto East Camino Cielo, and drive 6.7 miles. Continue straight as East Camino Cielo becomes Romero Canyon Road for 330 feet, then Romero Canyon Road turns left and becomes Romero Camuesa Road for 1.3 miles. Take a slight right to stay on Romero Camuesa Road for 9 miles, then turn right on FR 5N15B/Little Caliente Road for 0.9 mile to the trailhead. GPS: 34.54044, -119.62017

The Hike

From the trailhead near the information sign, head east through the marshy area and reeds. At my last visit, there was a board to help in crossing the marshy area. Once across, follow the trail northeast then east to the pools over the little hill from the reeds (GPS: 34.54053, -119.61951). Alternatively, instead of crossing the marsh, you can follow a faint path northwest and make a clockwise loop along the steep hillside to end up back on the trail coming from the marsh.

The Hot Springs

Hot water comes out of the ground at temperatures up to 120°F (49°C) and flows directly into a 15-by-20-foot, gravel-bottomed pool with another 6-by-12-foot pool fed by the outflow. The pools are formed by rock and cement walls that dam the small canyon. There's a bench and bamboo, but no shade.

Note: These pools are in a new location from the previous pool, but the old concrete tub is still there, overgrown, with some stagnant water in it. No further details are available.

Top: These are new pools at Little Caliente; it appears that the source was rerouted by some very ambitious and clever folk.

Bottom left: The larger pool can be too warm; the second pool stays a bit cooler. Though hard to see in the photo, some rock steps are built going into the water to access the lower pool.

Bottom right: The roads close often for a multitude of reasons, and it is likely you'll be parking at a gate like this and hiking.

19 Montecito Hot Springs

General description: Eight cascading pools at the end of a short hike in the hills above Santa Barbara, managed by the Los Padres National Forest. Swimwear required.

Difficulty: Fairly easy, though a little steep in places

Distance: 2.7 miles round-trip

General location: In an affluent neighborhood approximately 5 miles from downtown Santa Barbara

Elevation gain: 940 feet

Trailhead elevation: 620 feet

Hot springs elevation: 1,485 feet

Map: USGS Santa Barbara 7.5-minute (springs are shown)

Restrictions: No glass, no nudity, no camping; day-use only; no fires or smoking

Best time of year: Spring through fall

Camping: The Los Padres National Forest has several campgrounds in the hills above Santa Barbara, but none are very close. RV parks and motels are the only options in the area.

Contact: Los Padres National Forest, Santa Barbara Ranger District: (805) 448-6487

History: Reported history goes back to the Spanish and Mexican periods when Californios would visit the springs to do laundry, often camping for days because of the difficulty in making the trip. The property was later purchased by Wilbur Curtiss, who arrived in the area in the late 1850s. His "broken health" was rejuvenated by drinking and bathing in the water. Mr. Curtiss purchased the property with grandiose dreams of a large hotel, saloon, and bathhouses. The lack of investors scaled back the fulfillment of his dream to much less. After a reported fire in 1871, he built a three-story hotel, but that too fell on hard times, and the property was seized and sold. Several owners later, the property was reported to have been a private hot springs club for many decades, until the inevitable wildfires destroyed it all. In 2012 the Land Trust for Santa Barbara raised enough money from generous local donors to purchase Hot Springs Canyon and give it to the Los Padres National Forest for stewardship. Hikers can still view the ruins of the former resorts.

Finding the trailhead: The trailhead address is pretty close to 1217 E. Mountain Dr., Montecito, CA. You can enter "hot springs trail" or the address in your phone or GPS and it will take you to the trailhead. There is very limited parking.

From Santa Barbara, take US 101 South for 2.7 miles to exit 94A (signed for Olive Mill Road) and continue 0.2 mile. Continue straight on Spring Road for 463 feet, then turn left onto Olive Mill Road for 0.7 mile. Continue straight as Olive Mill Road becomes Hot Springs Road for 1.3 miles. Turn left onto East Mountain Drive and continue 0.2 mile to the parking area on the right.

From the south: Take US 101 North to exit 94A, except turn right on Olive Mill Road for 0.5 mile and continue as above. GPS: 34.44923, -119.64565

The Hike

The hike starts in a small parking area on the north side of a residential street. The trailhead is not obvious, but if you look around, you will see a brown Forest Service sign for "Hot Springs Trail." The sign points the way to "Information Kiosk in 50 yards" and "Hot Springs 1.3 miles." Follow the fenced path for 50 yards to the kiosk. Continue up the path alongside residences for about 0.4 mile, where you veer to the

Above left: A highly unexpected sight just a few miles from Santa Barbara, these partially shaded pools are well managed by the Los Padres National Forest.
Above right: Hot water comes out of the bank in two different places. The water collects in a small pool and cascades through eight highly picturesque pools on the way down to the creek.
Below: The silky blue water with just a hint of sulfur contrasts well with the red rock and sand pools. At our last visit, the hot water began at 115°F (46°C) and cooled to 95°F (35°C) by the time it hit the eighth pool. PHOTOS BY BLUE MEEK-FIELD

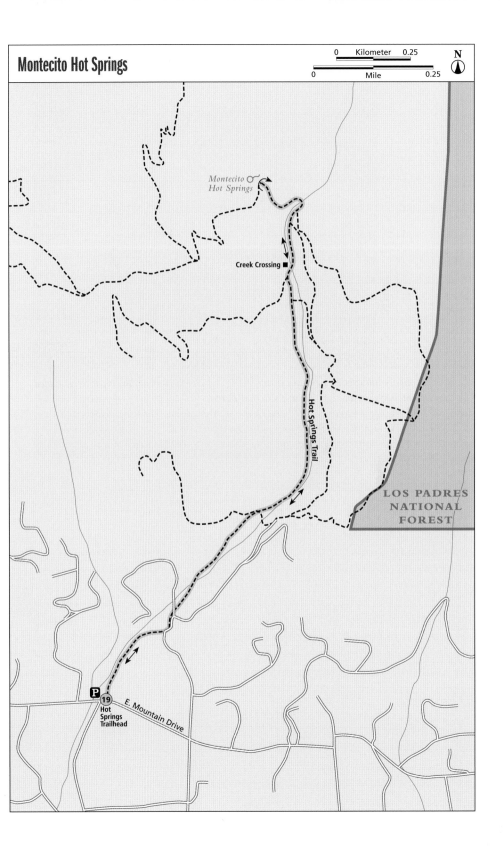

Montecito Hot Springs

Montecito Hot Springs

Creek Crossing ■

Hot Springs Trail

LOS PADRES
NATIONAL
FOREST

0   Kilometer   0.25

0   Mile   0.25

N

P
19
Hot
Springs
Trailhead

E. Mountain Drive

Looking up the trail from the road in this affluent neighborhood

right of a driveway and find a dirt trail heading up the hill. It starts to look more like a hike from here on, though there is just a fence separating the trail from a long private road or driveway. Nearly 0.6 mile from the trailhead is a junction (signed "Hot Springs 0.7 mile") and an alternate route on fire roads. Continue straight past the junction and up the shaded trail for about 0.3 mile to where the trail follows a fire road for another 0.1 mile. Stay right as the trail continues uphill then crosses the creek to the east side, about 1.1 miles from the trailhead (GPS: 34.46114, -119.63945). Continue northeast up the trail for a little over 0.15 mile to the remains of the old hotel and bathhouse. You will find bamboo, cacti, palms, avocado, and banana trees all around the remains of the foundations, and you might start smelling sulfur. Turn left and continue west, then turn northwest for the short distance to the hot springs. GPS: 34.46351, -119.64054

The Hot Springs

A completely unexpected sight just a few miles from Santa Barbara. Hot water comes out of the pipes at 115°F (46°C) and flows down through a series of at least seven well-constructed rock and sand pools in a mostly shady canyon. The water has a slight sulfur smell and a nice blue color from the minerals.

20 Gaviota (Las Cruces) Hot Springs

General description: At least two small pools on a shady hillside in Gaviota State Park. Swimwear required.

Difficulty: Easy

Distance: 1.0 mile round-trip

General location: About 35 miles from Santa Barbara, just off US 101

Elevation gain: 350 feet

Trailhead elevation: 310 feet

Hot springs elevation: 660 feet

Map: USGS Solvang 7.5-minute (springs are shown)

Restrictions: Day-use only; fee for parking; no dogs

Best time of year: Spring through fall

Camping: Gaviota State Park Campground, about 10 miles south

Contact: Gaviota State Park: (805) 968-1033

History: Trespass Trail, Tunnel View Trail, and Underpass Trail are nearby hikes with rich history.

Finding the trailhead: You can enter the Gaviota Peak Trail into Trailhead or something similar in your phone or GPS with much success. Otherwise, from Santa Barbara, follow US 101 North for 33 miles and take exit 132, signed for Lompoc/Vandenberg AFB. Turn right and travel back south on a frontage road for 0.25 mile to the trailhead. GPS: 34.50480, -120.22575

The warmer and clearer of the two soaking pools is far more popular.

Gaviota (Las Cruces) Hot Springs

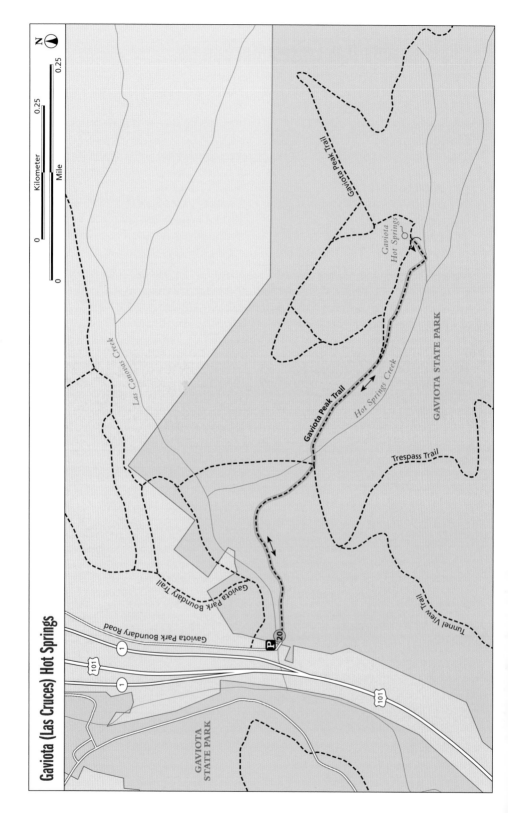

N

Kilometer
0   0.25   0.25

Mile
0

Las Cañvas Creek

GAVIOTA STATE PARK

Gaviota Peak Trail

Gaviota
Hot Springs

Gaviota Peak Trail

Hot Springs Creek

GAVIOTA STATE PARK

Trespass Trail

Tunnel View Trail

Gaviota Park Boundary Trail

Gaviota Park Boundary Road

101

1

1

101

P
20

GAVIOTA
STATE PARK

The Hike

The hike is on dirt fire roads that are inaccessible to vehicles. From the trailhead, walk about 0.25 mile up the dirt road to a signed T junction. Turning right leads you to several historic trails, as listed above, and turning left leads to the hot springs and Gaviota Peak. Turn left on another dirt road and continue about 0.2 mile until you find a faint path heading up the hill alongside a small creek. Turn right and follow the creek up the hill about 180 feet to the hot springs. GPS: 34.50265, -120.21836

The Hot Springs

Gaviota Hot Springs is often known as Las Cruces Hot Springs. I found a large cement-walled pool measuring about 85°F (29°C), and a smaller rock and cement pool that was about 96°F (35.5°C) but can vary in temperature a little with the seasons. This pool can hold four people without being too cramped, though I'm sure it has held many more, as it is quite popular with families on weekends. The source flows directly into the pool, but not always fast enough to maintain the source temperature of 99°F (37°C).

The larger and cooler of the two Gaviota pools tends to be cloudy, with a slimy bottom.

21 Willett Hot Springs

General description: An unexpected pool at the end of a fairly long hike in the Sespe Wilderness in the Los Padres National Forest, Ojai Ranger District. Swimwear is a local decision.
Difficulty: Easy, with some fords
Distance: 20.2 miles round-trip (33 miles round-trip if you visit Sespe Hot Springs too)
General location: About 21 miles northeast of Ojai
Elevation gain: 2,520 feet (4,000 feet if you visit Sepse Hot Springs too)
Trailhead elevation: 3,065 feet
Hot springs elevation: 2,800 feet
Map: USGS Topatopa Mountains 7.5-minute (springs are shown)

Restrictions: Adventure Pass or America the Beautiful Interagency Pass required for parking at trailhead, available at Forest Service offices. Fire permits (free from the Los Padres National Forest website) are required for open flames, including camp stoves.
Best time of year: Spring through fall
Camping: I highly recommend the small camping spot on the trail about 200 feet before reaching the pool (GPS: 34.57549, -119.05126). Otherwise, there is plenty of space down in the valley.
Contact: Los Padres National Forest, Ojai Ranger District: (805) 646-4348

Finding the trailhead: From the junction of CA 33 and CA 150 in Ojai, drive north on CA 33 for 14.6 miles. Turn right on FR 6N31 (aka Sespe River Road or Rose Valley Road) into the Rose Valley Recreation Area. Continue on the main road for 6 miles to the trailhead. (**Note:** The Piedra Blanca trailhead is the same for Willett and Sespe Hot Springs.) GPS: 34.56025, -119.16522

The Hike

This is mostly open terrain with little shade on the route. The trail is narrow and brushy, and wearing pants is highly recommended. The Sespe River Trail generally follows Sespe Creek downstream with multiple side creek crossings and several fords across the larger Sespe Creek. You can usually find rocks to step across for the side creeks; however, the crossings of Sespe Creek are fords. Plan on switching from boots to water shoes several times. You can avoid some fords by bushwhacking through brush along steep sidehills, or hiking up and around to remain on the north side of Sespe Creek. This might be your only option if you are hiking during high-water times.

The trailhead starts on the south side of Sespe Creek, but your destination is on the north side, so you must ford it at least once. From the trailhead, start out with three creek crossings in the first 0.3 mile and another about 0.5 mile after that. Continue on the north side of Sespe Creek as the trail winds and undulates and you gradually lose elevation. At about 4.4 miles, the trail crosses Sespe Creek to the south bank for about 1.2 miles and then crosses back to the north bank. At approximately 9.5 miles, you need to cross back to the south bank for about 0.2 mile, when you ford back across to the north side to a meadow and the remains of an old ranch. You are looking for a trail junction by the old stone fireplace (GPS: 34.57387, -119.04716), which is

Above: A large soaking tank, comfortably deep, and warm, is a perfect way to relax and enjoy the surroundings. Don't ask me how it got there. . . .
Below left: Keep an eye out for this old stone fireplace landmark.
Below right: A campsite about 200 feet from the pool

Willett and Sespe Hot Springs

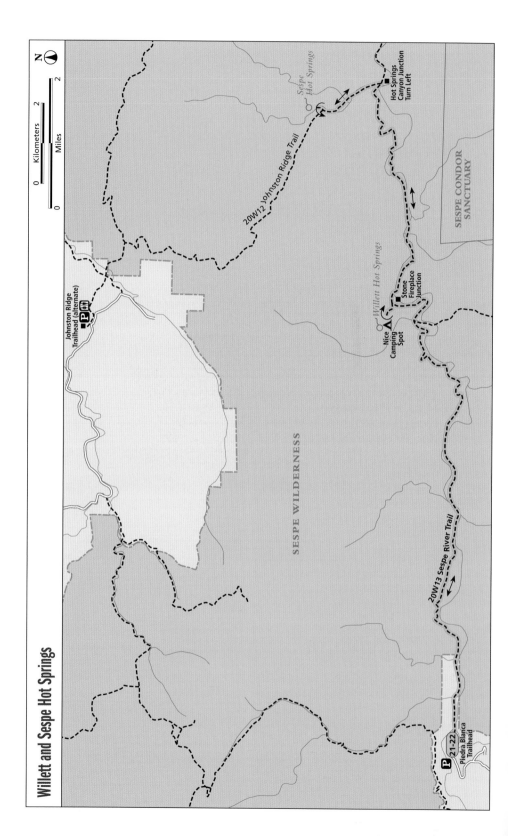

The old bunk-house, which still has bunks for four.

about 9.7 miles from the trailhead. From here, follow the faint trail that heads to the northwest and climbs and then traverses the sidehill heading up the canyon to the hot springs high in the canyon foliage. The pool is 0.4 mile up the trail from the stone fireplace junction, and about 280 vertical feet higher. GPS: 34.57592, -119.05138

The Hot Springs

The pool is a 10-foot-diameter stock tank high up in a canyon overlooking the valley. Hot water comes out of the rocks above at 108°F (42°C), where it is collected and piped to the pool using PVC pipe. Pool temperature can be controlled by moving the pipe. The minerals in the water give it a soft blue color and leave your skin feeling silky.

22 Sespe Hot Springs

See map on page 96.

General description: Multiple soaking opportunities in the hot creek at the end of an easy, but longer hike (Sespe River), or a moderate, shorter hike (Johnston Ridge) in the Los Padres National Forest. Swimwear is a local decision.

Difficulty: Sespe River Trail: easy, with some river fords; Johnston Ridge Trail: moderate

Distance: Sespe River Trail: 32.0 miles round-trip (33.0 miles if you visit Willett Hot Springs too); Johnston Ridge Trail: 19.0 miles round-trip

General location: The Piedra Blanca trailhead is about 21 miles northeast of Ojai; the Johnston Ridge trailhead is about 64 miles northeast of Ojai.

Elevation gain: Sespe River Trail: 4,000 feet if you visit Willett Hot Springs too; Johnston Ridge Trail: 2,400 feet

Trailhead elevation: Piedra Blanca: 3,065 feet; Johnston Ridge: 4,920 feet

Hot springs elevation: 2,690 feet

Map: USGS Devils Heart Peak 7.5-minute (springs are shown), USGS Topatopa Mountains 7.5-minute and Lockwood Valley 7.5-minute (hike)

Restrictions: Adventure Pass or America the Beautiful Interagency Pass required for parking at trailhead, available at Forest Service offices. Fire permits (free from the Los Padres National Forest website) are required for open flames, including camp stoves.

Best time of year: Year-round

Camping: The Forest Service's Middle Lion and Rose Valley Campgrounds are close to the trailhead. There is also plenty of space along the trail. If you are hiking from the Johnston Ridge Trailhead, camping is available at Halfmoon and Thorn Meadows Campgrounds, located along Grade Valley Road.

Contact: Los Padres National Forest, Ojai Ranger District: (805) 646-4348

Finding the trailheads: Piedra Blanca Trailhead: From the junction of CA 33 and CA 150 in Ojai, drive north on CA 33 for 14.6 miles. Turn right on FR 6N31 (aka Sespe River Road or Rose Valley Road) into the Rose Valley Recreation Area. Continue on the main road for 6 miles to the trailhead. (**Note:** The Piedra Blanca Trailhead is the same for Willett and Sespe Hot Springs.) GPS: 34.56025, -119.16522

Johnston Ridge Trailhead: From the junction of CA 33 and CA 150 in Ojai, drive north on CA 33 for 37.3 miles. Turn right onto Lockwood Valley Road and drive 16.4 miles. Turn right onto FR 7N03/Grade Valley Road and drive 10.7 miles to the trailhead. GPS: 34.64320, -119.05550

The Hike

Piedra Blanca Trailhead: This is mostly open terrain with little shade on the route. The trail is narrow and brushy, and wearing pants is highly recommended. The Sespe River Trail generally follows Sespe Creek downstream with multiple side creek crossings and several fords across the larger Sespe Creek. You can usually find rocks to step across for the side creeks; however, the crossings of Sespe Creek are fords. Plan on switching from boots to water shoes several times. You can avoid some fords by bushwhacking through brush along steep sidehills, or hiking up and around to remain on the north side of Sespe Creek. This might be your only option if you are hiking during high-water times.

Clear water, hot waterfalls, and nearby places to take a cool dunk make this a fun soak.

The trailhead starts on the south side of Sespe Creek, with three creek crossings in the first 0.3 mile and another about 0.5 mile after that. Continue on the north side of Sespe Creek as the trail winds and undulates and you gradually lose elevation. At about 4.4 miles, the trail crosses Sespe Creek to the south bank for about 1.2 miles and then crosses back to the north bank. At approximately 9.5 miles, you need to cross back to the south bank for about 0.2 mile, when you ford back across to the north side to a meadow and the remains of an old ranch. You are looking for a trail junction by the old stone fireplace (GPS: 34.57387, -119.04716), which is about 9.7 miles from the trailhead. Continue past the old stone fireplace for another 0.3 mile to the remains of an old ranch. If it hasn't burned down recently, you might see the bunkhouse that still has bunks to sleep four. Continue through the ranch and cross back over Sespe Creek to the south side at about the 10.1-mile mark. The trail will cross back to the north side in less than 0.5 mile, so you could consider following paths through the brush on the north side and picking up the trail when it crosses back. I chose this option because the creek was high enough to make me want to minimize my crossings. At 10.8 miles the trail crosses back to the south side of the creek for about 0.3 mile. Again, it is possible to stay on the north side and bushwhack a little to catch the trail again on the north side, but not as easily this time. Continue on the trail on the north side of Sespe Creek. At 12.0 miles you cross Sespe Creek to the south side for about 0.4 mile, then cross back to the north side. At about 14.1 miles go left (north) (GPS: 34.57693, -118.98920) and hike up Hot Springs Canyon about 1.3 miles to the hot springs. You will see pools in the creek, so take time to explore. There are several nice camp spots along the trail, and the better pools are up by the palm trees. GPS: 34.59154, -118.99610

Hot waterfalls are always a treat for me. There are several along the creek.

Johnston Ridge Trailhead: I have not done this hike, but the Forest Service reports this is Trail 20W12 Johnston Ridge. The signed trail starts from the east side of the parking lot. After a rolling 3.0 miles, the trail drops steeply into Hot Springs Canyon. There is no water and little shade along the first 7.0 miles of the trail. After 8.5 miles from the trailhead, a side trail leads to Hot Springs Creek.

The Hot Springs

There are several rock and sand pools on the creek where 180°F (82°C) hot water flows out of the ground and down into the creek. Rock dams get built in the creek where the hot water comes in, and pools get built seasonally. I once saw a photo of a rock sauna that was built over a hot water source. The entire creek is quite warm, and other hikers have built pools that may need to be rebuilt or dug out. Make sure you explore the whole area as there are many opportunities to soak.

At my last visit, someone had changed the 5 to a 9 in the distance to Sespe, discouraging people who didn't know that Sespe was only 15 miles away (only 15 miles…).

23 Deep Creek Hot Springs

General description: A popular set of pools on Deep Creek along the Pacific Crest Trail (PCT) at the end of 3 different but unique hikes, in the San Bernardino National Forest. Swimwear is a mix.

Difficulty: Varies depending on the trailhead

Distance: 3.6, 5.6, or 12.0 miles round-trip, depending on the trailhead

General location: About 9 miles southeast, as the crow flies, of Hesperia

Elevation gain: Bowen Ranch: 920 feet; Bradford Ridge Path: 1,340 feet; PCT: 1,560 feet

Trailhead elevation: Bowen Ranch: 4,450 feet; Bradford Ridge: 4,365 feet; PCT: 3,125 feet

Hot springs elevation: 3,530 feet

Map: USGS Lake Arrowhead 7.5-minute (springs are shown)

Restrictions: Day-use only; no campfires, no camping. Summer is brutally hot and there is little shade.

Best time of year: Year-round, though fording the creek can be problematic

Camping: Overnight camping is allowed at Bowen Ranch for an additional fee. Deep Creek Hot Springs Campground, a private campground, is located 0.5 mile past Bowen Ranch.

Contact: San Bernardino National Forest, Mountaintop Ranger District: (909) 382-2790

History: For years, Deep Creek Hot Springs was a legendary hangout for people getting away from civilization. People camped there in numbers way beyond what was legal and ethical, and far beyond what the land could accommodate. The Forest Service has implemented some restrictions to manage this very popular hot springs in a manner that is more sustainable. Due to its proximity to large population centers, Deep Creek Hot Springs still seems to attract far more hikers than the ecosystem can sustain.

Finding the trailheads: Bowen Ranch Trailhead: Drive east out of Hesperia on Main Street and turn left on Rock Springs Road. Rock Springs Road becomes Roundup Way after about 3 miles. Continue on Rock Springs Road/Roundup Way for a total of 7.2 miles, then turn right on Bowen Ranch Road and drive another 5.6 miles to the ranch. Though Bowen Ranch Road is graded, this dirt road may be subject to washouts and rutting. There are more complicated ways to get there that involve slightly better roads. You might check what your phone or GPS tells you. GPS: 34.35857, -117.16460

Bradford Ridge Path Trailhead: From San Bernardino, travel north on CA 18 for 13.9 miles, then continue on CA 189/East Grass Valley Road to CA 173 for 10 more miles to the trailhead on the right (east). GPS: 34.31829, -117.19596

Pacific Crest Trailhead: Travel east out of Hesperia on Main Street as it curves south becoming Arrowhead Lake Road. Go past the Rock Springs Road intersection and continue to the intersection with CA 173. Turn left and travel on CA 173 for 0.75 mile to the trailhead and parking area on the left. GPS: 34.33677, -117.24573

The Hikes

Bowen Ranch Access: This 1.8-mile (one-way) hike, the shortest access, is on the Bowen Ranch Road, which accesses the site through private land, for a fee. Pay the fee, park where they tell you, and take the old road as it descends steeply for about 1.8 miles to Deep Creek. There is no shade on this exposed hillside as you descend

Top left: One of my favorite pools. I had to leave Los Angeles early to hike the 6-mile PCT and have this one to myself.

Top right: With all the pools available you'd think there would be room for all. But remember it's just an hour away from one of the nation's largest population centers.

Below: The crystal-clear water in the pool contrasts with Deep Creek, which was not flowing fast at my last visit.

Deep Creek Hot Springs

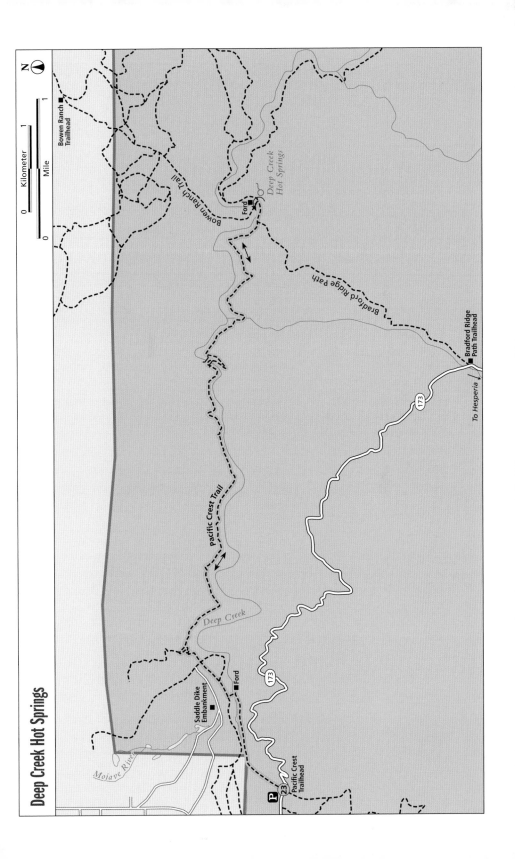

The classic photo from a hot springer's point of view

down to the hot springs, which are on the opposite side of Deep Creek. There is no bridge, and crossing to the hot springs can be a deal-breaker during high-flow times.

Bradford Ridge Path: This 2.6-mile (one-way) hike begins from the trailhead on CA 173. The trail is mostly flat for the first 1.4 miles then starts to descend. The 0.7-mile descent is gentle at first, then descends more rapidly until the trail meets up with the Pacific Crest Trail at about 2.3 miles from the trailhead. Turn right on the PCT and continue about 0.25 mile as it descends gently to the hot springs.

Pacific Crest Trail: This highly scenic 6.0-mile (one-way) hike begins from the trailhead marked for the PCT and descends down below the Saddle Dike Embankment where you must ford Deep Creek. There is no bridge, and fording Deep Creek can be a deal-breaker during high-flow times. Once on the other side of Deep Creek, follow the trail as it climbs the Saddle Dike Embankment and lands you at the northeast end of the embankment where there is a marker for the PCT. Climb some switchbacks and continue generally east to the hot springs. This mostly shady trail stays high above Deep Creek as it winds east. After about 5.7 scenic miles from the trailhead, there is an intersection where the Bradford Ridge Path meets up with the PCT. Continue straight on the PCT for about 0.25 mile to the hot springs. GPS: 34.33941, –117.17689

The Hot Springs

There are at least six pools, depending on the time of year. Hot water flows out of the rocks at 110°F (43°C) and into the pools, in one case as a cascading waterfall. One pool is over 5 feet deep, and the water is usually crystal clear. These pools are nestled among large granite boulders a little way above Deep Creek. They are extremely popular due to their proximity to high population centers, so plan accordingly. Early morning and late evening are good times to get some semblance of solitude if that is your desire.

Nevada

The state of Nevada has more hot springs than any other western state according to the NOAA's *Thermal Springs List for the United States*. Though endowed with so many hot springs, only a small percentage are accessible to the public. You can drive to many of the hot springs, but there is still a handful that involve a hike. Three of those hikes are located downstream of Hoover Dam in the Lake Mead National Recreation Area. The hot springs on both sides of the Colorado River are often accessed by boats; however, this is a hiking guide, so I'll tell you at least one way to hike there.

Looking across the dirt pool and the tanning deck. This is the original pool, while several other cattle troughs have been installed around the other sources. Though hard to see in the photo, there are hoofprints from the wild horses and burros that call this home. PHOTO BY BLUE MEEK-FIELD

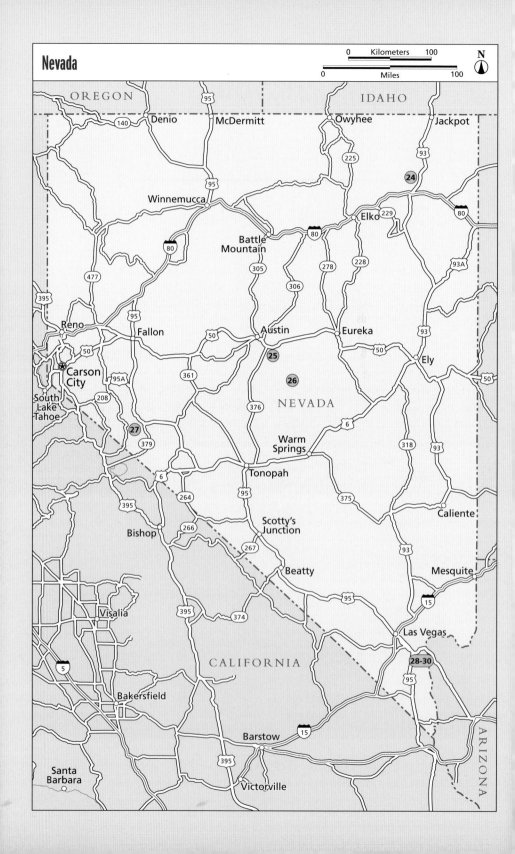

24 Twelve Mile Hot Springs

General description: A huge soaking pool alongside Bishop Creek, at the base of a hill in a remote canyon in northern Nevada. Swimwear is optional with discretion.

Difficulty: Easy

Distance: 4.0 miles round-trip

General location: 12 miles north of Wells

Elevation gain: 260 feet

Trailhead elevation: 5,680 feet

Hot springs elevation: 5,780 feet

Map: USGS Oxley Peak 7.5-minute (springs are shown)

Restrictions: I have found red spider mites at this pool. At the end of this description, I will provide details on how to deal with them.

Best time of year: Spring through fall

Camping: Tabor Creek Campground is about 21 miles away. Primitive camping is available beyond the hot springs on BLM land.

Contact: None

History: If you didn't get enough of a hike after reaching the springs, continue up Bishop Creek for another couple miles and see the impressive dam that created Bishop Creek Reservoir. Not necessarily impressive in the manner of the concrete and steel monstrosities on the Colorado River, but pretty extraordinary to find hidden in the sagebrush hills of northern Nevada. The dam was built around 1911 to irrigate the land and support the planned city of Metropolis; however, the dream city never came to fruition.

Finding the trailhead: From Wells, head northwest out of town on 8th Street. At the edge of town, 8th Street becomes North Metropolis Road. Continue north for 9.2 miles and park just before the road curves sharply to the left (west) and a dirt road heads to the right (east). This is the trailhead, and the hike to the hot springs follows the dirt road to the right. GPS: 41.23699, -114.98305

Looking downstream across the more than 90-foot-long pool at one of Nevada's largest soakable hot springs. The flow is so high it has made the entire creek hot.

The short concrete wall separates the hot water from the cold Bishop Creek. The creek downstream is often hot because of the high flow. PHOTOS BY BLUE MEEK-FIELD

Looking across the hot spring and down Bishop Creek. At this time of year, the hot water flow is over five times greater than the flow of the cold creek flowing down from above it.

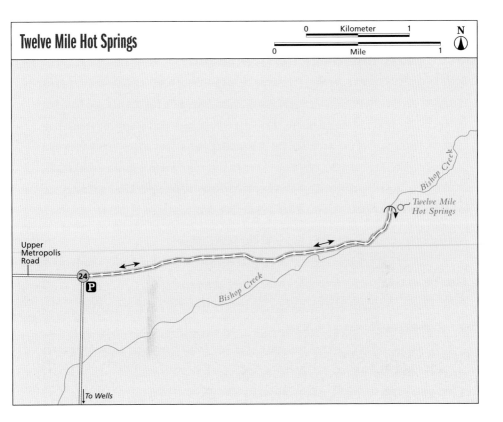

The Hike

From the trailhead, head east on the dirt road. It's often dusty with no shade, but still a nice walk along the road. The last 0.5 mile gets a bit more scenic, and you might have to wade through Bishop Creek. There are definitely four seasons here in northern Nevada, and high-desert flora and fauna abound. GPS: 41.24263, -114.94802

The Hot Springs

The pool measures approximately 12 by 90 feet, and the depth varies from nearly 3 feet at the downstream wall, gradually getting shallower as you progress upstream. A long cement wall was built to contain the hot water and separate it from Bishop Creek. The hot water enters the pool at 105°F (40.5°C) from the upper end and from the hillside along the length of the pool. The property is private and the owner has allowed access as long as it is kept clean. The road is not maintained.

Red Spider Mites (by Sally Jackson)

Don't forget to bring your reading glasses to check for these annoying little critters (also commonly but erroneously known as chiggers), which frequent a few Nevada and Utah hot springs. Barely visible to the naked eye, these tiny orange/red mites scurry with surprising speed on the surface of the water and the surrounding rocks. They attach to the body, and the bites usually result in itchy, mosquito-like welts that can take more than a week to heal. As with many bug bites, different people seem to have varying susceptibilities and reactions to red spider mites. Sometimes the mites appear then disappear again at certain springs.

Minimizing the Chances of Getting Bitten by Red Spider Mites

- Before taking off your clothes, have a good close-up look around the edge of the pool. If you don't see any tiny orange/red critters, you can relax!
- Check out all your soaking options. Sometimes the mites are at one part of a large spring complex and not another.
- If you spy mites, be sure to put your clothes and towel in a plastic bag or hang them in a tree, as the mites can crawl into clothing left on the ground.
- Soak in the center of the pool; the mites tend to frequent the edges.
- Soaking near the outflow sometimes works; the mites seem to know that this is a hazardous location for them.
- Keeping your soak short when there are mites around will greatly reduce your chances of being bitten.
- Dry yourself off thoroughly, immediately after getting out of the pool.
- If you do get bitten, don't scratch; try lotions as you would for other bug bites.
- If you can deal with the occasional mosquito and deerfly bite, you're probably going to survive an encounter with red spider mites.

25 Spencer Hot Springs

General description: No hikes are involved getting to this perennial favorite, consisting of a ground pool and several tubs spread around a sea of sagebrush in the high desert. Located on BLM land, this is a great place to spend a few days and rest from other hiking adventures. Swimwear is optional with discretion.

Difficulty: Easy

Distance: 1.2-mile loop

General location: About 19 miles west of Austin

Elevation gain: Negligible

Hot springs elevation: 5,700 feet

Map: USGS Spencer Hot Springs 15-minute (springs are shown)

Restrictions: The extreme temperatures and lack of shade should be considered when visiting these springs.

Best time of year: Spring through fall

Camping: Primitive camping is available on BLM land, but please do not camp too close to the pools. Bob Scott Campground is approximately 10 miles away.

Contact: Bureau of Land Management, Battle Mountain District: (775) 635-4000

History: Burros often got away from, or were abandoned by, miners a century ago. They have thrived and reproduced, and are now common natives of the area.

Finding the hot springs: Due to the improvements of GPS navigation software available on phones and other devices, you can simply enter Spencer Hot Springs and find directions easily. Otherwise, from Austin, drive east on US 50 approximately 11 miles to the junction with NV 376. Turn right (southwest) for 0.3 mile, then turn left (southeast) on NF 001 for 5.4 miles to a junction. Turn left (northeast) and follow this road about 1.6 miles to the hot springs area. Consider parking in the vicinity of the main pool and looking for the other three sources on foot. The maze of rough dirt roads connecting the tubs are dusty, and on foot you'll be less likely to disturb campers and soakers in this dispersed area.

From the main pool (GPS: 39.32718, -116.85577), tub one is 0.13 mile east (GPS: 39.32701, -116.85840), tub two is 0.24 mile northeast (GPS: 39.33071, -116.85489), and tub three is 0.32 mile southeast (GPS: 39.32506, -116.85041).

The Hot Springs

Upon arrival, the most obvious soaking situation is a 15-by15-foot pool dug into the ground. There's a large platform to one side, and it is often called Platform Hot Springs. It has rock benches and a muddy bottom, and the temperature can be adjusted by blocking the inflow pipe from the adjacent source pool (take care not to step in this!).

Hot water comes out of the ground in several places at temperatures of about 160°F (71°C) and is piped and channeled to the pools. Temperatures in the stock tanks can be controlled by diverting the pipes. Do not leave the hot water running into the stock tanks, as it takes a long time for the water to cool down enough to soak. It is easier to heat a pool rather than wait for it to cool. Be prepared to find wild burros that frequent the area to drink from the springs.

Top: Looking across the dirt pool and the tanning deck. This is the original pool, while several other cattle troughs have been installed around the other sources. Though hard to see in the photo, there are hoofprints from the wild horses and burros that call this home.
Bottom: These metal cattle troughs, aka cowboy tubs, provide a nice year-round soak.
PHOTOS BY BLUE MEEK-FIELD

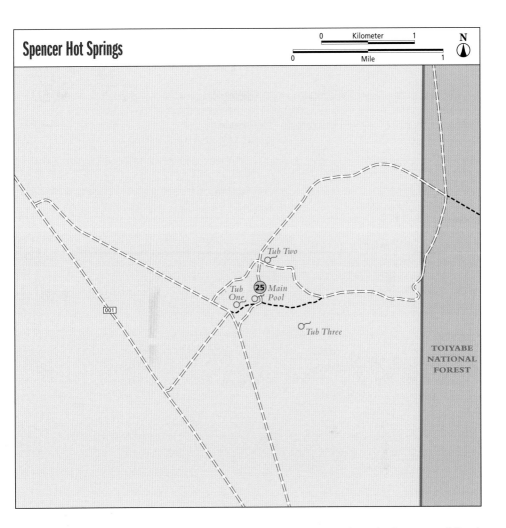

The stock tanks make ideal soaking pools as long as they don't get vandalized. Sadly, delinquents of all ages think stock tanks are targets, and it's not uncommon to find bullet holes.

Note: My friend and legendary hot springs author, Evie Litton, would brilliantly pack apples to use as plugs for pools when they are missing. The added benefit was that birds could eat the apples when she was finished soaking. Carrots are another natural remedy for the bullet hole problem, so I like to pack both when I head out.

Also in the Austin Area

Hickison Petroglyph Recreation Area
Stokes Castle

26 Diana's Punch Bowl Hot Springs

General description: Several pools formed in a hot creek from the outflow of a 50-foot-high, giant travertine dome. Swimwear is optional.

Difficulty: Easy

Distance: 1.0-mile round-trip

General location: 30 miles southeast of Austin in the Monitor Valley

Elevation gain: Negligible

Hot springs elevation: 6,735 feet

Map: USGS Diana's Punch Bowl 15-minute (springs are shown)

Restrictions: None

Best time of year: Year-round

Camping: Primitive camping is available on BLM land.

Contact: Bureau of Land Management, Battle Mountain District: (775) 635-4000

Finding the hot springs: Due to the improvements of GPS navigation software available on phones and other devices, you can simply enter Diana's Punch Bowl and find directions easily. Otherwise, from Austin, head east on US 50 East for 36 miles to the junction of NV 82. Turn right (south) and travel 33.8 miles. Turn left (east) and go 1.2 miles to the dome in the distance. GPS: 39.03063, -116.66793

Diana's Punch Bowl from afar. The steam is rising out of the hole in the top like a volcano. It's about 50 feet tall with a 50-foot-diameter hole in the top. It would be a 30-foot cannonball dive.

Left: A typical rock dam along the outflow. There are several pools-for-two along the outflow. On this cold day, I didn't have to go too far along the hot creek for a soak.
Right top: Some "locals" came along while I was soaking. Though wild, they had manners enough to let me finish.
Right bottom: The view looking down inside this geologic wonder. It's hard to see much because of the steam.

While not really a true hike to get to the hot springs, you might have to hike as far as 0.5 mile to find a pool cool enough to soak in. Diana's Punch Bowl is definitely worth seeing when you're traveling around Nevada.

The Hot Springs

This hot springs is officially named Diana's Punch Bowl, but unofficially called the Devil's Cauldron. The travertine dome is over 500 feet in diameter at the base, and there is a hole in the top about 50 feet in diameter where you can climb up and take a look. When I first climbed up the dome a couple of decades ago, I was so amazed—all I wanted to do was a cannonball jump! I thought better of it and scrambled down inside and measured the temperature at a dangerously hot 150°F (65.5°C)—a close call. The hot water once flowed out of the ground and bubbled up over the surface,

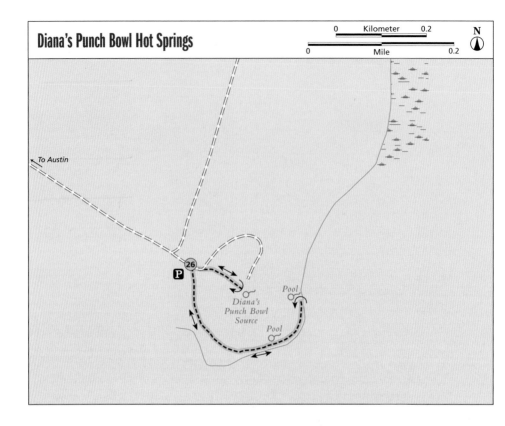

0   Kilometer   0.2

0   Mile   0.2

N

To Austin

26

P

Pool

Diana's
Punch Bowl
Source

Pool

creating the giant travertine dome. The hot water no longer flows over the top, but now streams out of a hole in the southern side of the dome and creates a nice hot creek.

The ambient temperature dramatically affects the cooling of the water. Volunteers have created several pools downstream where the water has cooled to comfortable temperatures. A pool that might be nice on a cold day is at GPS 39.02927, -116.66594. These are still quite close to the outlet from the dome so the water is likely too hot for a soak on a hot day. Many other pools are along the hot creek; you just need to hike along it to find a pool with a comfortable temperature. Make your own pool if you need to. The dome is fenced to keep wayward cattle from living out my cannonball dream.

27 East Walker Hot Springs

General description: A beautifully constructed stone and mortar pool on a hillside overlooking the East Walker River in the Humboldt-Toiyabe National Forest. You'll probably be alone, so swimwear is your decision.

Difficulty: Fairly easy, with a few tough spots

Distance: 2.0, 4.0, or 5.9 miles (each way), depending on the trailhead

General location: About 31 miles west of Hawthorne

Elevation gain: 800 feet (2.0-mile); 1,515 feet (4.0-mile); 1,780 feet (5.9-mile)

Trailhead elevation: 6,310 feet (4.0-mile hike)

Hot springs elevation: 5,380 feet

Map: USGS Aurora 15-minute (springs are not shown)

Restrictions: Temperature extremes can be dangerous; plan accordingly.

Best time of year: Year-round

Camping: Primitive camping is available on BLM land.

Contact: Humboldt-Toiyabe National Forest, Bridgeport Ranger District

Finding the trailhead: Google Maps could send you on a route that is impassable. You might want to stick with this one. From Hawthorne, drive south on NV 359 South for 3.9 miles and turn right (southwest) onto Lucky Boy Pass Road. Continue 18.9 miles to the junction with State Route 3c (signed "East Walker Road"). Turn right and continue 8 miles to a junction, then turn left. The road gets pretty bad with lots of rocks and deep ruts. You may want to consider parking here and walking the remaining 5.9 miles. GPS: 38.47595, -118.91356

If you have a four-wheel-drive vehicle with high clearance, you can turn left from the junction, drive 1.9 miles, and turn right. This is another good parking spot about 4 miles from the hot springs. GPS: 38.46719, -118.94335

It is possible to drive another 2 miles if the roads are dry and you have a four-wheel-drive vehicle with high clearance. If you choose this, after turning right, continue 0.5 mile to a fork where you bear left to remain on the main road. Continue on this road for another 1.5 miles, where you should definitely park. It is a 2.0-mile hike from here. The road is not passable ahead, and you will likely not be able to turn around. GPS: 38.48730, -118.95240

The Hike

The length of the hike varies between about 2.0 to 5.9 miles depending on your vehicle and your level of comfort. From whichever trailhead you choose, walk down the old road, heading for the river at the bottom of the canyon. It's a nice walk and a great chance to enjoy the high-desert flora and fauna. At about a mile away from the hot springs, you will see the remains of an old mine. Not far after the mine, you meet up with the East Walker River. Follow it upstream a short way until you see the pool on your left, up against the hill about 400 feet from the river. GPS: 38.49059, -118.97907

Above and facing page: Built by talented professional volunteers, the clean, clear water really complements the stone and mortar workmanship. An unexpected sight in the Nevada desert. This place is better on cooler days because it is often too hot when people leave the hot water running.
PHOTOS BY BLUE MEEK-FIELD

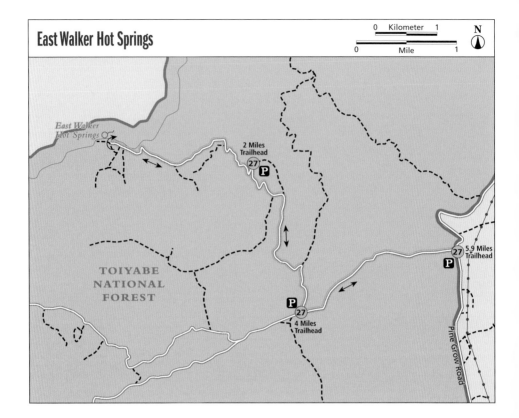

East Walker Hot Springs

The Hot Springs

Also known as Walker Hot Springs, this cleverly crafted, professionally built pool is set into a grassy hillside with views of the river and mountain ranges. The water flows out of the ground at 110°F (43°C) and can be diverted to maintain a comfortable temperature. The pool can fit six close friends and has stone benches with backrests that angle back slightly for comfort. Combine those features with the footbath, and you will agree that the builders did a pretty great job. The pool can be drained for cleaning. Leave the pool empty to help keep it clean. Any cold water must be hauled from the East Walker River. One lone tree provides the shade in the area; other than that, the soak and the hike are out in the elements. At night, there is no ambient light in the canyon, and you can see more stars than you could ever count.

Below Hoover Dam Area

Hot springs enthusiasts visiting the canyons below Hoover Dam must work around the National Park Service closures of Nevada's Goldstrike Canyon, Arizona Canyon, and the associated trails between May 15 and September 30 due to the extremely hot temperatures. Goldstrike and Arizona Hot Springs are still accessible from the Colorado River by boat, but you may not hike down to them from the highways.

The trail to Goldstrike Hot Springs is well marked and so popular that it is rare not to encounter other people on your hike. The route to Moonscape Hot Springs is a different story; it will likely just be you and the buzzards patiently circling above you.

The lower pool at Moonscape Warm Springs, located about 500 feet down the wash from a very large and impressive warm waterfall

28 Goldstrike Hot Springs

General description: Several beautiful pools, grottos, and hot waterfalls at the end of a short but challenging hike down the narrow Goldstrike Canyon, in the Lake Mead National Recreation Area. Swimwear seems to be the custom during the daytime, especially at the upper pool.

Difficulty: Moderate, with some fixed-rope scrambles

Distance: 5.2 miles round-trip if you go all the way to the river

General location: 6 miles northeast of Boulder City, or 32 miles southeast of Las Vegas. The Goldstrike Hot Springs trailhead is about 6 miles from the Arizona Hot Springs trailhead.

Elevation gain: About 1,200 feet

Trailhead elevation: 1,570 feet

Hot springs elevation: 720 feet

Map: USGS Hoover Dam 15-minute (springs are not shown)

Restrictions: The area is closed to hikers between May 15 and Sept 30, but the hot springs are still accessible from the Colorado River by boat. In addition to the extreme summer heat, Goldstrike Canyon, like other slot canyons, can be subject to very dangerous flash floods. Always be aware of the local weather, as well as the weather upstream.

Best time of year: Oct 1 through May 14

Camping: The National Park Service's Boulder Beach Campground is 4 miles north of the Goldstrike trailhead. Vehicle camping is permitted in designated camp areas only. Backpacking primitive camping is available in all areas of the Black Canyon Wilderness unless posted otherwise.

Contact: Lake Mead National Recreation Area, National Park Service: (702) 293-8990

Finding the trailhead: Due to the improvements of GPS navigation software available on phones and other devices, you can simply enter Goldstrike Hot Springs trailhead (or something similar) and find it easily. Otherwise, from I-11/US 93, take exit 2. At the roundabout on the south side of the freeway, head south on Goldstrike Canyon Road for about 0.3 mile to the parking area and trailhead. There are several informational signs that provide detailed trail maps, area information, and great safety instructions. The Lake Mead National Recreation Area staff do a great job communicating information about this popular place. GPS: 36.00982, -114.76878

The Hike

This hike and climb combination leads you down the scenic and often narrow Goldstrike Canyon, where you will be rewarded with beautiful pools, grottos, and hot waterfalls. You can follow the canyon the entire 2.6 miles down to the Colorado River. The total elevation change is about 945 feet between the trailhead and the river. The majority of visitors hike down from the trailhead located just off I-11/US 93. Goldstrike Hot Springs is also accessible by the river, so you might see people coming from both directions. Many people turn around at, or prior to, the first pool due to the steep scrambles. It is a nice hike even if you don't make it to the pools.

The National Park Service describes the trail as strenuous, which sounds discouraging, but it's really not too difficult if you are able to navigate steep descents and ascents using ropes that are already in place. There are several Class 3 scrambles where

Above left: The first pool you find, about 2.1 miles into the hike
Above right: Various pools and warm waterfalls make it worth venturing past the first pool.
Below: Sandbagged, rock-dammed pools with gravel bottoms are typical in these slot canyons.

volunteers have installed fixed ropes. The ropes are not maintained except by other visitors.

The trail descends down the winding Goldstrike Canyon for close to 2.0 miles to the first pool.

The trail from the upper pool down to the lower pools is considerably more difficult, as you are often hopping from boulder to boulder and will likely get your feet wet. You pass several hot waterfalls where the water cascades down rocks, sometimes forming pools. There are a few waterfalls that you can get under, always a nice bonus. Though the trail gets tougher after the first pool, if you are able to continue down the canyon to the lower hot springs and river, it is definitely worth the effort.

If the river level is low enough, you can sometimes access the sauna cave upriver a little way. Use caution because the river level fluctuates rapidly and can leave you stranded. The Bureau of Reclamation's Hoover Dam controls the river level by releasing water.

Looking out from the sauna cave just upriver from Goldstrike. The river levels severely limit your ability to get to this soak (and back).

The Hot Springs

The water comes out of the rocks and ground at about 110°F (43°C) and cools as it flows down the canyon. The flow is enough that the pools maintain a very nice soaking temperature. The first pool you get to is a little past the 2.0-mile mark (GPS: 36.00210, -114.74919) at the bottom of a fixed-rope descent, nestled between some boulders just off the trail. You can get back under the boulders a little and even access a cave via an underwater tunnel. You may want to talk to a local who is familiar with that before attempting it. The next pools are down the canyon nearly another half-mile. The trail gets considerably more difficult, with about four more fixed-rope-assisted descents as you follow the path of the water down the canyon. The lower pools are formed by dams consisting of rocks, sand, and even cement in some cases. The rock dams have been supplemented with sandbags to make them deeper. The pools gradually fill with sand, and helpful soakers often dig them out. These same volunteers rebuild the pools when flash floods wipe them out completely. The second pool (GPS: 36.00019, -114.74452) you get to is about 10 by 15 feet, and the third pool about 40 feet in diameter. The third pool is about 200 yards from the river (GPS: 35.99990, -114.74359), so if the river level allows, it's definitely worthwhile to go down for a cold swim and get a picture of the Mike O'Callaghan–Pat Tillman Memorial Bridge. There is a large camping area down near the river, and it is not uncommon to see boaters camped there.

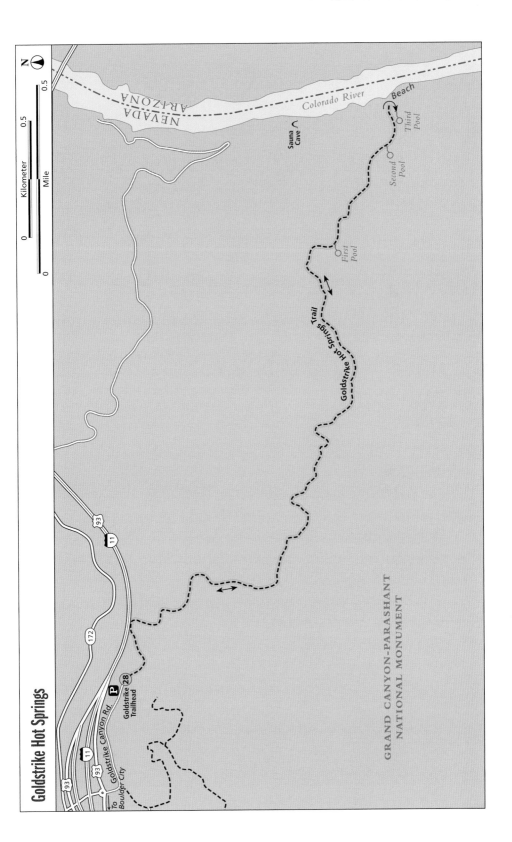

Goldstrike Hot Springs

N

Kilometer
0   0.5   0.5

Mile
0   0.5

To Boulder City

Goldstrike Canyon Rd.

93

172

11

93

11

P Goldstrike Trailhead 28

Goldstrike Hot Springs Trail

First Pool

Second Pool

Third Pool

Beach

Sauna Cave

NEVADA

ARIZONA

Colorado River

GRAND CANYON-PARASHANT
NATIONAL MONUMENT

A rare perspective of the impressive Mike O'Callaghan–Pat Tillman Memorial Bridge, which opened in 2010, spanning the Colorado River joining Nevada and Arizona

About 0.25 mile upriver is the Sauna Cave (approximate GPS: 36.0035, -114.7435), accessible only when the river is low enough. Miners reportedly dug this shaft when the dam was being constructed. They hit hot water and efforts ceased. The cave has a dam across the opening and fills with hot water. The shaft is reported to go back 50 feet, though I stayed closer to the mouth at my last visit. The walls of the shaft are coated with mineral deposits. The temperature at the end of the cave is reported to be 130°F (54.4°C), though the temperature near the mouth was considerably cooler.

Memories

Several years ago, I was in a rented boat with a couple of friends and hot springs writers, Skip Hill and Sally Jackson, exploring the Colorado River hot springs. Our plan was to motor back to Willow Beach Marina and return the boat that evening within the four-hour allotted time. Shortly before dark, Hoover Dam stopped releasing water and the river level dropped six feet in minutes. We were stranded on the sandbar near the mouth of Goldstrike Canyon. It was a last-minute trip in October, and we had only prepared for a few hours. We could not leave the boat for fear of the water coming up and it floating away. Needless to say, it was a long, cold, miserable night. I was the "skipper" on that trip and felt horrible. The next morning a large group of canoeists came paddling down the river and stopped to help. It took ten of us to lift the powerboat back down into the water. It was an expensive "four-hour trip," but even worse was my shame. Whenever the subject would come up in the years following the incident, Skip would get a faraway look in his eyes and say, "What boat?" At the beginning of this story, I referred to Skip and Sally as "friends." It was several years before I dared be so presumptuous as to call them that again.

29 Boy Scout Hot Springs

General description: Stunning hot pools and waterfalls near the Colorado River, in Boy Scout Canyon in the Lake Mead National Recreation Area. Although short, this very tough hike is not for the timid. Swimwear is generally extra weight, but you may see boaters down at the springs.

Difficulty: Difficult, with many Class 3 scrambles and fixed-rope use

Distance: 5.8 miles round-trip

General location: 5 miles east of Boulder City, or 31 miles southeast of Las Vegas

Elevation gain: 1,320 feet

Trailhead elevation: 1,700 feet

Hot springs elevation: 656 feet

Map: USGS Ringbolt Rapids 7.5-minute (springs are shown)

Restrictions: Can be subject to dangerous flash floods. Always be aware of the local weather, as well as the weather upstream. Extreme summer temperatures are problematic. A GPS is essential for this hike, as there is a critical spot you need to find.

Best time of year: Fall through spring

Camping: The National Park Service's Boulder Beach Campground is about 6.2 miles north of the trailhead. Vehicle camping is permitted in designated camp areas only. Backpacking primitive camping is available in all areas of the Black Canyon Wilderness unless posted otherwise.

Contact: Lake Mead National Recreation Area, National Park Service: (702) 293-8990

Finding the trailhead: Due to the improvements of GPS navigation software available on phones and other devices, you can simply enter Boy Scout Canyon Road or trailhead (or something similar) and find it easily. Otherwise, head southeast out of Boulder City on Utah Street and toward the dump. Just prior to the dump, turn right on Canyon Point Road, toward the Boulder City Rifle and Pistol Club. Go past the gun club and under the freeway. Approximately 0.2 mile past the freeway, bear left and continue on Boy Scout Canyon Road. This good gravel road skirts the perimeter of the Boulder City Rifle and Pistol Club for a little over 3 miles until it ends at the trailhead. GPS: 35.97286, -114.76947

The Hike

A GPS is essential for this route as there is a fairly critical waypoint marking the spot where you cross the ridge and descend into the canyon.

In addition to the epic geology, you are likely to see all sorts of flora, fauna, and petroglyphs on this hike. It is a very difficult hike and not to be attempted unless you are experienced. I would not (and did not) make this hike alone. There are steep slopes covered with shale and scree, a corkscrew canyon with fixed ropes, an elevation change of over 1,200 feet, and waterfalls to navigate. Additionally, you must walk through sections of the canyon that are flooded to make the soaking pools, so you will get wet. There may be other ways to bypass the 300-foot waterfall, but I don't know of other reasonably safe routes into the canyon.

From the trailhead, walk down the winding, sandy wash toward the river for 1.5 miles. Turn right (southeast) and scramble up the side of the canyon (there likely

Left: Great friend and hot springs legend Skip Hill, editor of the Hot Springs Gazette, *enjoying a shower in a high-flowing year. I haven't seen the water flowing like that for a while.*
Right: Photographer Blue in her natural habitat. You cross several of these on your way up and down the canyon.

won't be a trail from the wash). You can go up the side of the canyon in several places; just pick what suits you. You will see several sheep trails. I marked GPS waypoint "faint trail on ridge" (GPS: 35.97781, -114.75110) for the faint trail I followed. Follow this trail up along the ridge until you find the "start descent" waypoint (GPS: 35.97934, -114.74826), the only reasonable place I found to belly-down over the edge and begin the descent. There is inherent error with GPS devices for many reasons, and it will not likely be exact. If it is off a little, look around for a spot where you can lower yourself down the cliff about 4 feet to a small shelf. This is a great stop to take pictures as the view is beautiful in all directions.

This is an ideal time to have a short rope and a tall friend (or vice-versa). Before lowering yourself, look down and get an idea of your planned route. As you look down the cliff face, the corkscrew feature is slightly to the right and down a little. Once on the small shelf, sidestep a little until you can get on the rocks that will allow you to scramble down. Remember, your way in is also your way back out, so ensure you don't go down anything you can't get back up. From here, there are likely no real trails, but you might see cairns or other signs of previous use.

Your goal is to lose about 700 feet of elevation to the bottom of the wash. You will have to traverse the sidehill, being careful on the shale and scree, to some rock formations a little way to the northwest. In these rocks is a corkscrew formation where other hikers have installed rock anchors and some fixed ropes. Check the condition of this equipment, and then descend down through the corkscrew. At the bottom of corkscrew you might see faint paths or cairns to lead you down to the canyon floor. Make sure you turn around and get a good look at the corkscrew rock formation, ensuring you can recognize it for your trip out.

Carefully continue down the slope until you reach the bottom of the wash. As you walk down the canyon, look up on the rock canyons above; you will see various patches of vegetation that could potentially hold soaking opportunities. Very soon you will see hot water, grottos, and vegetation. Keep going down the wash, walking through the hot water when necessary. You will walk down through several hot waterfalls along the way until you find a pool.

There are many small pools at the bottom of waterfalls that should not be passed by without a quick dip. Depending on the season, Boy Scout Canyon also has spectacular waterfalls where hot water drops from side canyons. These are a treat not to be missed.

Trekking poles can be helpful, but sometimes are a hindrance as you often need both hands to hold the canyon walls as you traverse the waterfalls and other obstacles.

Left: Sandbagged, rock-dammed pools with gravel bottoms give you an array of soaking choices in this stunning river canyon.
Right: A small but relaxing pool at the base of a waterfall

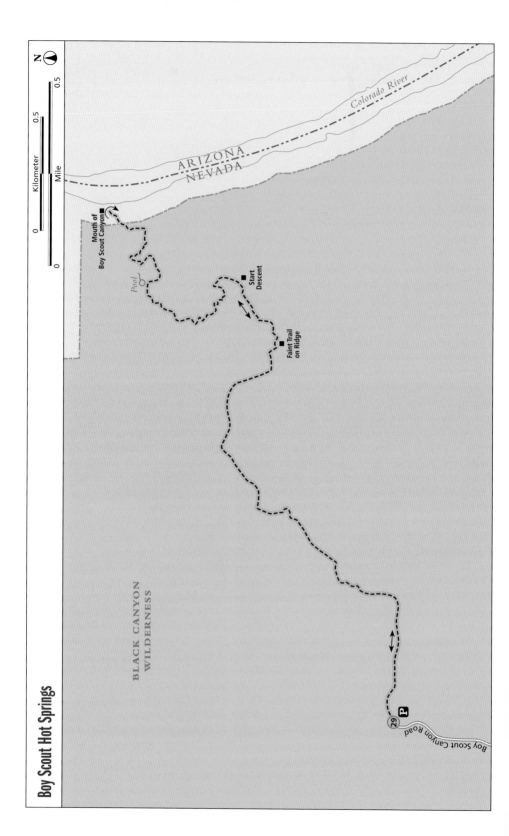

Boy Scout Hot Springs

My tall friend exiting the bottom of the corkscrew rock formation

The sandbag dams that flood the canyons to form the pools leave you no option except to wade through the pools and climb over the dams. Some pools are pretty deep at the lower ends by the dams, and you may get wet up to your waist, even close to waist-high on your tall friend, if they are still with you at this point.

When you reach a sandbag dam that you must cross, you will find that volunteers have placed sandbags as steps so you can safely get over them without hurting yourself or the dam. It's still a short walk to the river, but worth it, especially on a hot day. I took GPS coordinates for one pool on my last trip (GPS: 35.98285, -114.74820), as well as the mouth of Boy Scout Canyon, where it opens to the Colorado River (GPS: 35.98489, -114.74450).

The Hot Springs

The hot pools are in a slot canyon at the end of a fairly short but arduous hike. The water comes out of the rocks and the ground, and sometimes falls from side canyons above at about 110°F (43°C), which cools as it flows down the canyon. The flow is enough that the pools maintain nice soaking temperatures. You will encounter many hot waterfalls in the trail through which you must traverse. Depending on the season, some hot water drops off cliffs into the canyon. Fellow soakers have made sandbag dams that fill the narrow canyon making beautiful pools, generally at ideal soaking temperatures. Pool sizes vary based on the locations and height of the sandbag dams. The water coming out of the rocks is close to 110°F, so the pools must be large enough for the water to cool to a comfortable temperature. If you want a hotter soak, remove a sandbag to allow some of the cooler water to drain. Replace the sandbag and the pool fills up with hotter water.

The sandbag-dam pools get moved up and down the canyon depending on the hot water flow. At my last visit, the best pool was about 0.25 mile from the river. But pool locations change, and GPS signals can be sketchy in slot canyons. I'm able to confirm most coordinates via Google Earth, but it's hard to see anything in these deep slot canyons.

More Information

The pools in Boy Scout Canyon are generally accessed by boats; however, there is at least one route that can be navigated on foot—well, mostly on foot. Much of my descent was on my backside (sometimes intentionally). If you try to follow the wash down Boy Scout Canyon you will find yourself at the top of a 300-foot dry waterfall with no way down except for ropes. I read about people rappelling down the 300 feet; however, climbing back up is problematic for most. If you attempt this hike, you likely won't encounter other hikers on the trip, but you may see boaters at the pools. There are flat areas where people camp near the river, so it is possible that you will not be alone. From the lowest pool, it is a short walk down to the Colorado River for a cold dip. The river flow fluctuates very rapidly based on water releases from Hoover Dam, so be very careful. You can inquire about the Boy Scout Canyon hike at the Lake Mead National Recreation Area Visitor Center, and they will likely tell you that hiking the canyon is beautiful, but you can't make it to the river because of the 300-foot dry waterfall. If you keep inquiring, you might gain access to their "hike book," which is interesting and entertaining. The authors apparently have keen senses of humor.

If you want to take a look at the 300-foot drop, you can follow the directions above, but rather than scramble up the side of the canyon, continue down the wash for another quarter-mile. Descend about 15 feet down a smaller dry waterfall on fixed ropes, then continue down the wash for a couple hundred feet to the edge. Once down below it, I suggest you walk up the wash a short way to view it from the bottom.

30 Moonscape Warm Springs

General description: Located in the Black Canyon Wilderness of the Lake Mead National Recreation Area, Moonscape Warm Springs is one of the largest flowing, natural warm waterfalls in the United States. Swimwear is a local decision.

Difficulty: Moderate, with some scrambling

Distance: Close to 8.4 miles round-trip, including a trip to the river

General location: 6 miles southeast of Boulder City, or 32 miles southeast of Las Vegas

Elevation gain: 2,320 feet

Trailhead elevation: 2,280 feet

Warm springs elevation: 780 feet

Map: USGS Ringbolt Rapids 7.5-minute (springs are shown)

Restrictions: Can be subject to dangerous flash floods. Always be aware of the local weather, as well as the weather upstream. Extreme summer temperatures are problematic. A GPS is handy for this trail-less hike.

Best time of year: Spring through fall

Camping: The National Park Service's Boulder Beach Campground is about 12 miles north of the trailhead. Vehicle camping is permitted in designated camp areas only. Backpacking primitive camping is available in all areas of the Black Canyon Wilderness unless posted otherwise.

Contact: Lake Mead National Recreation Area, National Park Service: (702) 293-8990

Finding the trailhead: Head southeast out of Boulder City on Utah Street and travel southeast toward the dump. Just prior to the dump, turn right on Canyon Point Road, toward the Boulder City Rifle and Pistol Club. Stay on Canyon Point Road past the junction of Boy Scout Canyon Road and continue about 3.2 miles to a pullout and the trailhead on the east side of the road. GPS: 35.93671, -114.75650

The Hike

There is no water on this route unless you walk down to the Colorado River. This is a long, dry hike with no shade. There are no trails, so you will have to rely on your GPS, occasional cairns, or maps. These directions are general, but they will get you there. They do not replace a map and a GPS. I took one route in and another route out. The route shown on the map is the better of the two. It generally follows washes, but at times you'll be walking across the desert floor. If you see a route that looks better than this one, don't hesitate. Whichever way you choose, I recommend you head for the waypoint "canyon junction" (GPS: 35.96580, -114.73941), which is where you turn left and go up to the springs. Any other way to the waterfall will involve a difficult scramble down the steep canyon wall.

From the trailhead, pick your way down the steep slope covered with loose rocks and lots of broken glass. There was no specific trail at my last visit, but I found a few faint, short switchbacks that helped me quickly lose 600 feet of elevation. You will lose another 200 feet of elevation within the first mile from the trailhead.

Once down to the bottom of the hillside, your GPS will tell you to head north-northeast. You start out in the wash heading northeast, and pretty soon the wash

Geothermally heated waterfalls are rare, so this is a real treat. The few who know about it generally come in from the river.

you're following heads east. Leave the wash and continue north across bare desert for about a mile. Some is on smooth, bare rock and is nice walking. It's a mostly gentle downgrade without too many ups and downs. You want to lose elevation, but also stay far enough away from the river to avoid the deep canyons.

Approximately 2.0 miles from the trailhead, there's a wash that heads northeast for about 0.3 mile then heads north (and slightly west) for about a mile. If you encounter obstacles in the wash, just go around them on the west side of the wash. Continue in this wash; eventually it angles northeast toward the canyon junction. The canyon you intersect is the one that boaters use to walk from the river to the warm springs. Once at the junction, the river is to the right (0.3 mile); the warm springs are to the left. Turn left and hike up the canyon to the warm springs.

You'll pass the first pool in about 650 feet; the waterfall pool is another 500 feet beyond that (GPS: 35.96530, -114.74267). Though it's a tough walk, you can follow the warm water up another 750 feet to the source, an overgrown smaller waterfall. It is not nearly as impressive as the lower waterfall.

Top left: A friend, John Blackwell, told me about Moonscape and showed me a photo. He said he went by boat. I studied my map and came up with this route. This is the first time this has shown up in a book. There might be a better way, but I haven't looked. It's only a little over a mile south of Boy Scout Canyon. That was plan B, which I did not attempt because plan A worked. Maybe I'll give it a try on the next revision.

Top right: The warm water flows down the canyon into a rock and sand pool. It is easier to relax in this pool without the crashing waterfall noise. If only it were a little warmer.

Bottom left: Looking northeast and down from the start of the route, this vast, open landscape explains how the warm springs got its name.

Bottom right: The overgrown source pool and small waterfall, upstream of the large waterfall and pool

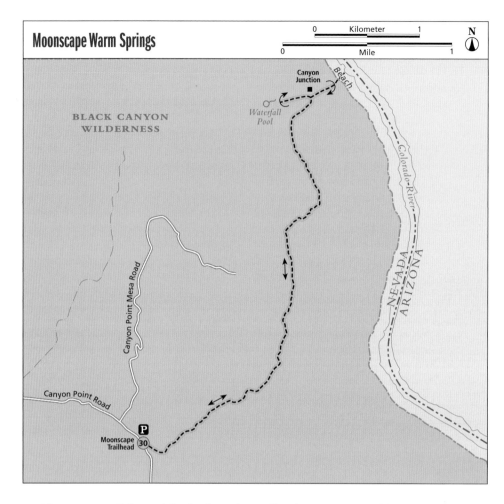

If you want a different hike back to the trailhead, you can scramble up the steep canyon wall just below the waterfall and walk across bare desert. Within a mile you should be able to see the trailhead, and maybe your vehicle. It's a change of scenery from walking washes.

The Warm Springs

Warm water comes pouring out of the ground at about 87°F (30.5°C), falls over an overgrown waterfall, and continues down the wash to another larger waterfall under which you can stand. There's a 12-foot-diameter pool at the base of the waterfall, but the noise makes relaxing difficult. Though the water is only in the high 80s (31–32°C), it feels wonderful after a hot hike. The water flows down the wash 500 feet more to another 10-by-12-foot pool. Both pools might need a little digging out, as they tend to fill up with sand and gravel. Moonscape can also be accessed from the river via a 0.6-mile hike. It is not well known and does not get many visitors.

Arizona

The state of Arizona has a mere sixty hot springs that are documented according to the NOAA's *Thermal Springs List for the United States*. Only about a quarter of those are available to the public, and seven of these are via a hike. The trail to Arizona Hot Springs is well marked and quite popular and it is rare not to encounter people on your hike. The route to Lone Palm Hot Springs is much less popular, and you may not see any life except the ubiquitous lizards.

The soaking pool at Hannah Hot Springs doesn't get a lot of use, so it may need a little cleaning. It's quite a hike, and the last quarter-mile has some tricky spots. The canyon is simply stunning. I think it is the best hot spring hike that Arizona has to offer.

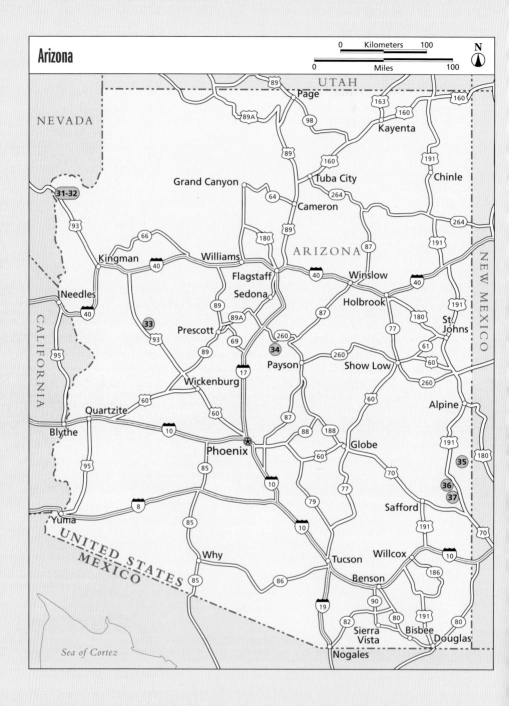

31 Lone Palm Hot Springs

General description: Two pools situated about 30 feet above the Colorado River at the end of a fairly short hike in the Lake Mead National Recreation Area. Swimwear is a local decision.

Difficulty: Easy

Distance: 3.4 miles round-trip

General location: About 8 miles east of Boulder City, or 34 miles southeast of Las Vegas. The Lone Palm Hot Springs trailhead is about 2 miles from the Arizona Hot Springs trailhead and about 3.5 miles from the Goldstrike Hot Springs trailhead.

Elevation gain: 1,060 feet

Trailhead elevation: 1,550 feet

Hot springs elevation: 675 feet

Map: USGS Ringbolt Rapids 7.5-minute (springs are shown)

Restrictions: Extreme summer heat and flash-flood risks.

Best time of year: Fall through spring. Though not subject to the summer closure of Arizona Canyon by the National Park Service, it is very close by and a similar hike. If this hike was more popular, it would be closed as well, as the risks are nearly identical.

Camping: It is legal to camp in the area. You can camp along the trails, or head east on Kingman Wash Access Road.

Contact: Lake Mead National Recreation Area, National Park Service: (702) 293-8990

Finding the trailhead: Due to the improvements of GPS navigation software available on phones and other devices, you can simply enter Kingman Wash trailhead (or something similar) and find it easily. Otherwise, from Boulder City in Nevada, head east on I-11/US 93 toward Hoover Dam. In approximately 6 miles you cross the Mike O'Callaghan–Pat Tillman Memorial Bridge. Continue on US 93 South for approximately 0.9 mile and take exit 2 toward Kingman Wash Access Road. Turn left and park in the parking area. There are information signs at the trailhead. GPS: 36.00241, -114.72429

The Hike

The hike begins at Kingman Wash Trailhead. Follow the sandy wash west as it winds about 1.7 miles to the springs. If you're hiking in the spring, you will see cacti flowering, one of my favorite desert sights. This trail doesn't get many visitors, so you are likely to see bighorn sheep on this hike, and, of course, the lizards roam free.

The Hot Springs

Hot water flows out of the rocks at about 110°F (43°C) and cools as it flows down the small wash toward the river. Volunteers have created dams to form pools. There is a single palm tree down by the river's edge, hence the name. The pools are not easily accessible by boat.

Upper pool (GPS: 35.99519, -114.73851): Rocks and sandbags create a 3-by-5-foot pool big enough for two, if you're close friends.

Lower pool (GPS: 35.99551, -114.73930): A cement wall dams the hot creek in a narrow gap between the canyon walls to form a pool about 30 vertical feet above the Colorado River. You can enjoy the hot water in this 7-by-12-foot pool and look

Top left: Looking out at the Colorado River through the narrow window between the canyons' walls. Boaters don't expect to see people and are often surprised to see soakers, if they do at all.
Top right: The same pool from another angle showing the crystal-clear water
Below: Desert in the springtime is hard to beat.

Lone Palm Hot Springs

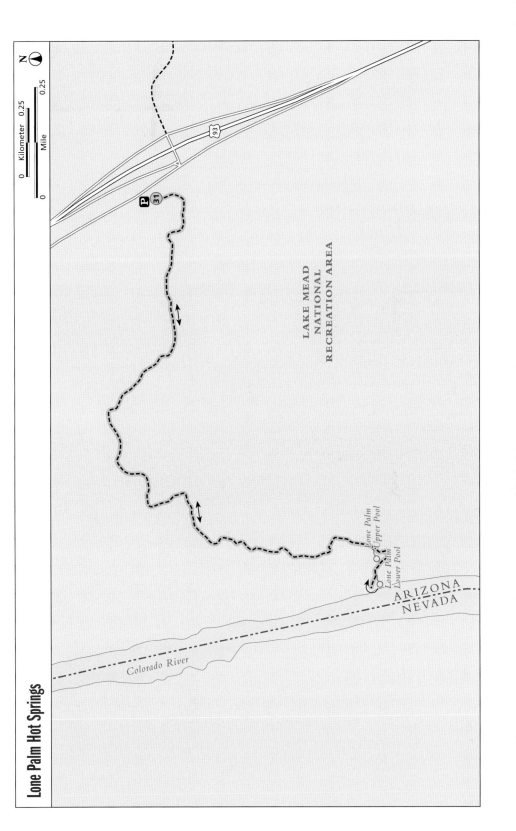

N

| 0 | Kilometer | 0.25 |
| 0 | Mile | 0.25 |

93

P 31

LAKE MEAD
NATIONAL
RECREATION AREA

*Lone Palm
Upper Pool*

*Lone Palm
Lower Pool*

ARIZONA
NEVADA

Colorado River

Rocks and sandbags create this upper pool that's big enough for two close friends.

out over the river through a narrow window between the canyon walls. Not many people know about this pool, so the boaters usually aren't looking. They often seem surprised to see soakers, if they see them at all.

Also in the Area

Lost Man Hot Springs shows up on the USGS Ringbolt Rapids 7.5 minute topo map at about GPS: 35.985, -114.741. It is approximately across the river from Boy Scout Canyon in Nevada, and accessible from this trailhead. I only found a seep when I explored the area; maybe you will find something different if you choose to look for it.

32 Arizona (Ringbolt) Hot Springs

General description: A wonderful series of pools, plus a waterfall, in a spectacular slot canyon on the Colorado River below Hoover Dam, at the end of a scenic canyon hike in the Lake Mead National Recreation Area. Swimwear is mixed; keep it handy.

Difficulty: Easy

Distance: About 5.0 miles round-trip, or a 5.5-mile lollipop loop by hiking out through White Rock Canyon

General location: About 11 miles east of Boulder City, Nevada, or 37 miles southeast of Las Vegas. The Arizona Hot Springs trailhead is about 6 miles from the Goldstrike Hot Springs trailhead.

Elevation gain: 960 feet out and back; 1,170 feet for loop through White Rock Canyon

Trailhead elevation: 1,550 feet

Hot springs elevation: 793 feet

Map: USGS Ringbolt Rapids 7.5-minute (springs are shown)

Restrictions: The National Park Service closes the area to hikers between May 15 and Sept 30 due to the extremely hot temperatures. Arizona Hot Springs is still accessible from the Colorado River by boat, but you may not hike down to it from the highway.

Best time of year: Oct 1 through May 14

Camping: Camping is available on the beach at the canyon mouth, where you will find flat areas and a pit toilet.

Contact: Lake Mead National Recreation Area, National Park Service: (702) 293-8990

History: The hot springs are sometimes called Ringbolt Hot Springs because of their proximity to Ringbolt Rapids on the Colorado River. Prior to the Hoover Dam, when the Colorado River ran wild, there were large rapids near the canyon mouth that were named Ringbolt Rapids. Workers would connect cables to ringbolts in the rocks to winch steamboats through the rapids. Though the steamboats didn't get stuck, the name for the rapids did.

Finding the trailhead: Due to the improvements of GPS navigation software available on phones and other devices, you can simply enter Arizona Hot Springs trailhead (or something similar) and find it easily. Otherwise, from Boulder City in Nevada, head east on I-11/US 93 toward Hoover Dam. In approximately 6 miles you cross the impressive Mike O'Callaghan–Pat Tillman Memorial Bridge, which opened in 2010, spanning the Colorado River joining Nevada and Arizona. Continue on US 93 South for approximately 3.1 miles to mile marker 4. The large parking area is on the east side of the highway. GPS: 35.98011, -114.69742

The Hike

The trail to Arizona Hot Springs is well marked and quite popular, and it is rare not to encounter people on the hike. From the trailhead, this 2.5-mile hike follows a wide trail across sand and gravel as it heads under US 93 and continues gently downhill following the wash. Walk about 0.4 mile in full sun to the trail junction where the trail splits into the Hot Spring Canyon and White Rock Canyon Trails (GPS: 35.97581, -114.70430). Turn left to stay on the Hot Spring Canyon Trail, the fastest way to the hot springs. Continue on the well-defined trail for another 0.7 mile to where the trail enters the canyon and you might get some shade for a little way.

Above left: Soak in this nice small pool tucked into the canyon wall.
Above right: Arizona Hot Springs pools. A dedicated group of volunteers does a fine job of maintaining these springs.
Below left: The short trail to White Rock Canyon begins by the outhouse below the hot springs before you get to the river. This is the path you take across the ridge into White Rock Canyon if you are making the loop.
Below right: The trail drops into the canyon and becomes narrow.

Arizona (Ringbolt) Hot Springs

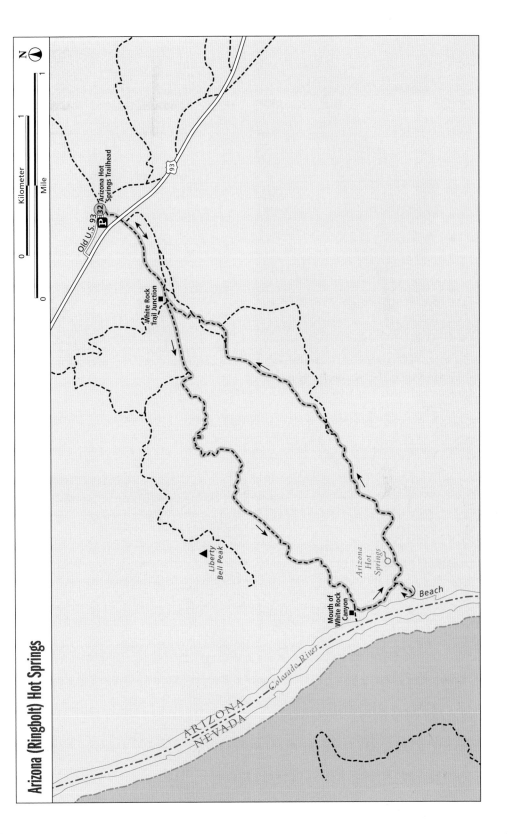

Old U.S. 93

P 32 Arizona Hot Springs Trailhead

93

White Rock Trail Junction

Liberty Bell Peak

Mouth of White Rock Canyon

Arizona Hot Springs

Beach

ARIZONA
NEVADA

Colorado River

N

Kilometer
0   1

Mile
0   1

From the river, you have to climb this ladder to reach your pool.

Hike down the wash as the vegetation becomes sparse and the canyon walls get higher and steeper until you arrive at the first hot pools (GPS: 35.96049, -114.72539). Don't stop yet, there's another pool around the corner. The trail goes through the lower pool and down a 16-foot ladder, then continues down to where the canyon opens up to a beach area on the Colorado River (GPS: 35.95965, -114.72822). Boaters often stop at this beach to walk up the canyon and climb the ladder to visit the hot springs.

An option for the return trip is to take a rocky trail north for about 0.5 mile to White Rock Canyon, and hike that trail back to the junction at 0.4 mile and the trailhead. Both canyons are beautiful, and many hikers make a loop by hiking down Arizona Canyon and returning up White Rock Canyon.

The Hot Springs

Hot water comes out of the rocks at about 105°F (40.5°C) and cools as it flows down the slot canyon where volunteers have built several pools with sandbags. Dedicated volunteers work tirelessly to build and maintain the pools and keep the area clean. A fixed ladder allows access down a 15-foot warm waterfall and to the trail to the river. The pools get washed out during floods and must be rebuilt. In 2021 the ladder was washed out, so there was no access from the river or the White Rock Canyon Trail route. These springs are also accessible by boat; however, the majority of visitors are hikers.

Other Things to See

If you are returning to the trailhead via White Rock Canyon, there is a scenic 3.0-mile out-and-back hike to Liberty Bell Arch that is accessible from the White Rock Canyon Trail, about 0.5 mile west of the Hot Spring Canyon Trail/White Rock Canyon Trail junction.

33 Kaiser Hot Springs

General description: A small pool up against a cliff wall on the side of a wash at the end of a short hike. Swimwear optional, though you may keep it handy. The area is getting more popular.

Difficulty: Easy

Distance: 2.6 miles round-trip

General location: About 66 miles southeast of Kingman

Elevation gain: 280 feet

Trailhead elevation: 2,020 feet

Hot springs elevation: 1,774 feet

Map: 1:250,000 (AMS) Prescott (springs are shown)

Restrictions: The area gets extreme summer heat and flash floods.

Best time of year: Fall through spring

Camping: Burro Creek Campground is about 7 miles south of the trailhead. Primitive camping is available on BLM land along Burro Creek.

Contact: Bureau of Land Management, Kingman Field Office: (928) 718-3700

Finding the trailhead: From the town of Wikieup, travel south for 11 miles on US 93 and turn left (northeast) across the divided highway just before a large divided bridge that curves over a wash. Continue on the dirt road for 0.25 mile to the trailhead. From Wickenburg, drive north on US 93 for 63 miles and turn right just past the large divided bridge that curves over a wash. Continue on the dirt road for 0.25 mile to the trailhead. Many people park under the highway bridge to avoid the direct sun. GPS: 34.57762, -113.49109

A primitive rock-walled and graveled-bottom pool provides a mineral-rich soak.
PHOTOS BY BLUE MEEK-FIELD

Top left: The start of the trail as it drops down from the parking area into the wash for the short hike.
Top right: The trailhead starts here. Many people park under the highway to get out of the sun.

Bottom: This tree is doing its best to provide shade for this lonely pool built up against the side of the wash.

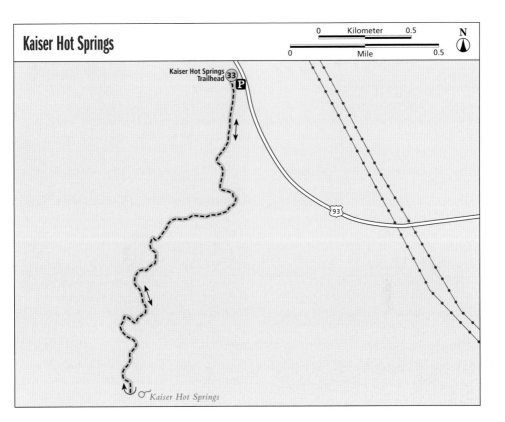

Kaiser Hot Springs

Kaiser Hot Springs Trailhead 33

P

93

Kaiser Hot Springs

The Hike

Wherever you choose, walk down the wash for 1.3 miles until you see the pool on your left (GPS: 34.56309, -113.49680). The canyon walls get higher as you walk south. It's a pretty straightforward hike through the sand and rocks. There are beautiful views and more vegetation than on the hikes farther north. Keep your eyes out for bighorn sheep; you might also see bobcats on this short hike.

You can continue down the wash for another 0.2 mile to Burro Creek. On my last visit, there was some mining activity along this route and vehicles were driving in the wash. I ran into a guy who was driving his family down to the creek to camp. He said that the BLM was working to improve the area down by the creek.

The Hot Springs

A small three-person pool is tucked up against the canyon wall. Water flows out of the rocks at about 99°F (37°C), directly into a shallow pool that often needs to be dug out and flushed. A bucket might be handy if there is not one there.

General description: Two amazing concrete pools at an abandoned resort and bathhouse on the banks of the Verde River in the Coconino National Forest. Though it's a short hike, you must ford the Verde River, which can be impassable during or after rain. Swimwear is a local decision.

Difficulty: Easy unless the water is high

Distance: About 2.5 miles round-trip

General location: About 28 miles east of Camp Verde

Elevation gain: 190 feet

Trailhead elevation: 2,630 feet

Hot springs elevation: 2,640 feet

Map: USGS Verde Hot Springs 7.5-minute (springs are shown)

Restrictions: Fording the Verde River cannot be done during or after rain; access roads are often closed; extreme summer heat

Best time of year: Fall through spring

Camping: Dispersed camping is available at or near the trailhead at the Childs Dispersed Camping Area. The Forest Service's Clear Creek Campground is about 1.5 miles west of the trailhead.

Contact: Coconino National Forest Service office: (928) 527-3600

History: Built in the 1920s, this resort was a popular vacation spot until it burned in 1962, leaving only the foundation and a few walls that have become a canvas for some talented folk.

Finding the trailhead: From Camp Verde, go east on AZ 260 about 7 miles and turn right on FR 708 (Fossil Creek Road). Travel 14 miles to the junction of FR 708 and FR 502. Turn right on FR 502 (Childs Power Road) and drive approximately 6.5 miles to the Childs Power Plant and the Verde River. This last 6.5 miles involves some steep descents, especially near the end. GPS: 34.34902, -111.69853

Left: One of the smaller pools is brightly and beautifully painted.
Right: A waterfall cascades into a beautiful swimming hole on Fossil Creek. Though the crystal-clear water is cold, it is still highly alluring. PHOTOS BY BLUE MEEK-FIELD

The Hike

The Forest Service has recently moved the trailhead, and it is now 100 feet southwest of the Childs Power Plant. From the trailhead, just below the power plant and on the east side of the river, follow the foot trail northwest through the trees for about a mile to a popular place to cross the river (GPS: 34.35730, -111.71065). There are at least two trails heading northwest, and they both end up at the same place.

An alternative route is to pick your way north past the power plant, get back up on the Childs Power Road, and follow it for about a mile. There is no shade on the road, but the views are better. After walking the mile, pick your way down through the brush to the river. You get a good view of the former resort and the pools from this road.

Once at the river, where it crosses under the power lines, ascertain whether it is safe to wade through the swift-flowing water. It's usually muddy, so it's difficult to see

◀ *These pools are remnants from a once-thriving resort built in the 1920s that was destroyed by fire in the 1960s. You can still walk up the concrete stairs that lead to the now-gone buildings.*

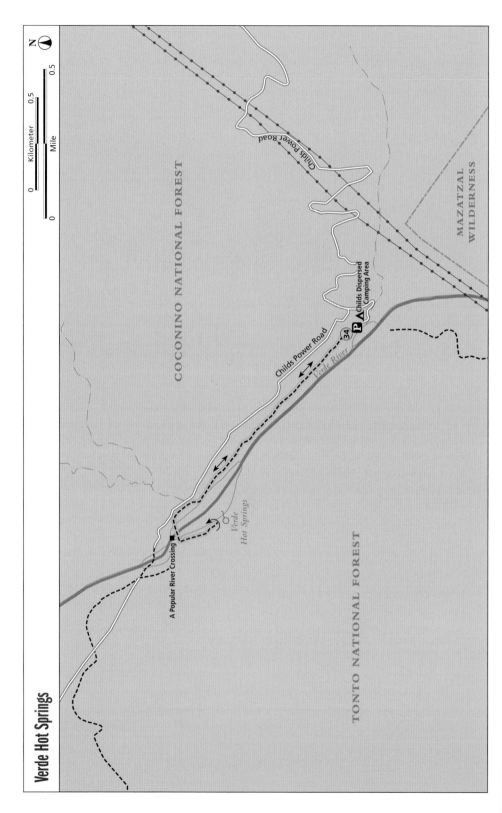

Verde Hot Springs

N

0   Kilometer   0.5

0   Mile   0.5

COCONINO NATIONAL FOREST

Child Power Road

MAZATZAL WILDERNESS

Childs Power Road

Childs Dispersed Camping Area

P

34

Verde River

A Popular River Crossing

Verde Hot Springs

TONTO NATIONAL FOREST

I just could not pass by this swimming hole without taking a swim. There's a semi-flat spot on the rock near the right side of the photo where I was able to lie down and enjoy some sun.

the bottom and any potential hazards. Once on the other side, follow the well-worn trail southeast about 250 yards to the pools. GPS: 34.35538, -111.70964

The Hot Springs

The remnants of the old resort have become a colorful canvas for some beautiful graffiti. The largest pool is built against the cliff with concrete forming two sides. This pool is usually around 100°F (38°C) and can fit several people. It is more than 7 feet deep at one end. There is a roofless bathhouse with a pool inside that can hold two people easily in the 100°F (38°C) water. You can also access a third pool, via a tunnel; however, it is too shallow and cool for a serious soaking.

Also in the Area

Fossil Creek has some of the best swimming holes I've seen. Though not hot, they are definitely worth a look. Permits are required between April 1 and October 1 and must be reserved well in advance through www.recreation.gov.

35 Hannah Hot Springs

General description: A large rock and cement pool built on the side of the hill in a spectacular canyon at the end of a trail-less hike in the Blue Range Primitive Area in the Gila National Forest. Swimwear is superfluous (in the words of hot springs legend Evie Litton).

Difficulty: Moderate, with some tough spots in Hannah Springs Canyon

Distance: 14.4 miles round-trip

General location: About 43 miles north of Clifton, or 86 miles northeast of Safford

Elevation gain: 765 feet

Trailhead elevation: 4,325 feet

Hot springs elevation: 4,780 feet

Map: USGS Dutch Blue Creek 7.5-minute (springs are shown)

Restrictions: Roads may be impassable in winter. The flash-flood danger is real in Hannah Canyon. A GPS is helpful to ensure you make the correct turn up the Little Blue River.

Best time of year: Fall through spring

Camping: The Forest Service's Upper and Lower Juan Miller Campgrounds are en route to the trailhead on Juan Miller Road. There are a couple of small tent spots in Hannah Springs Creek Canyon, one right across the creek from the hot springs. Additional camping is farther up the canyon, or anywhere along the route.

Contact: Gila National Forest: (575) 388-8201

History: The Fritz Ranch (XXX Ranch) was established in the 1880s, but is now owned by the Forest Service after a land swap. Information signs in the area describe the reintroduction of the Mexican wolf. I was not lucky enough to see one; perhaps you will.

Finding the trailhead: This is a beautiful drive through the mountains, but is likely to take you longer than expected. Stock up on gas and supplies in Clifton or Morenci, because you might not have a chance again for a while, especially if you are going to continue north or east to some nearby New Mexico hot springs.

From the mining town of Morenci, follow US 191 north as it winds and winds for about 26.5 miles through the forested mountains. At 0.1 mile south of mile marker 189, turn right (east) on Juan Miller Road. Continue on Juan Miller Road as you pass Upper Juan Miller Campground and, a little farther, Lower Juan Miller Campground.

At 12.1 miles after turning off US 191, turn left (north) on Fred Fritz Road, maybe still signed for the XXX Ranch. A high-clearance vehicle is recommended from here on, as the road crosses washes and is bumpy and rutted. At 3 miles you come to the ranch, and at 3.1 miles, the road ends and the trail begins. Exploring around the old ranch is interesting—you never know what you will come across. GPS: 33.32415, -109.18889

The Hike

There is no getting lost on this hike because you never really leave the riverbeds. The only risk is mistaking a side creek for the Little Blue River, so watch your mileage or your GPS. My internal odometer was thrown off by the multiple river and creek crossings, and all the walking through the muddy riverbed. To me, this trip felt like an additional couple of miles. It should go without saying: Do not enter Hannah Springs Canyon if there is danger of rain in the vicinity or upstream. The flash-flood risk is real.

From the trailhead, follow a short piece of trail as it heads up the Blue River. If you ever see a trail following the river upstream in the direction you want to go, you should take it. On my last visit, there was no trail beyond the first quarter-mile. I walked the riverbeds, crossing back and forth as needed. Hiking poles were very helpful. Pay attention to your mileage or GPS so you don't walk past the mouth of the Little Blue River. By this time, you've crossed the river so many times it all looks the same from ground level. GPS: 33.37515, -109.17638

Continue up the Little Blue River as it winds and winds up the amazing river canyon. Though much of the area might be sparsely vegetated outside the river canyons, there are plenty of shady spots for lunch or a nap in these thick forests. At about 2.3 miles up the Little Blue River, you will see Hannah Springs Creek coming out of a canyon on your right. You might notice the creek is warmer than the river you've been in so many times. GPS: 33.39803, -109.15706

Start up Hannah Springs Creek. In about 200 feet, you might consider leaving your clothes there, because you're going to get wet and won't need them from here on. The only way up the canyon is walking through the water, and in one place it is

Left: An isolated rock and cement pool perched about 8 feet above the canyon floor. Warm water flows out of the pool and mixes with the cold water flowing down, making cooler pools to enjoy. Right: Picturesque views can be found throughout these canyon walls. PHOTOS BY BLUE MEEK-FIELD

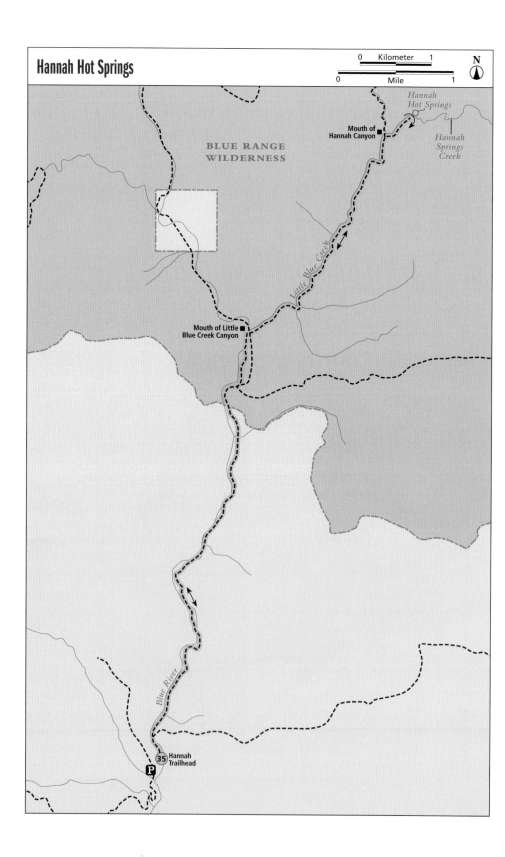

Hannah Hot Springs

BLUE RANGE
WILDERNESS

Mouth of
Hannah Canyon

*Hannah
Hot Springs*

*Hannah
Springs
Creek*

Little Blue Creek

Mouth of Little
Blue Creek Canyon

Blue River

35 Hannah
Trailhead

P

N

0   Kilometer   1

0   Mile   1

Left: Hannah Hot Springs pool (foreground) looking down Hannah Springs Canyon toward the Little Blue River.
Right: Wading through this chest-high, slimy pool was an adventure in itself. It's a good time to leave behind everything you don't need.

chest-deep. Wade through the water, scramble over rocks, go around the obstacles you can't go over. After about 0.3 mile, you find the hot pool on your left, about 8 feet above the canyon floor. GPS: 33.40011, -109.15367

From the springs, you can continue up the canyon about a half-mile to a spectacular view. A little farther, the canyon flattens out and there are places to camp if you still have your clothes with you.

The Hot Springs

An impressive 6-by-18-foot pool is built up on a ledge about 8 feet above the canyon floor. Hot water comes out of the rocks at around 120°F (49°C) and flows into the pool, which is large enough to maintain a comfortable temperature. It may need some cleaning as it doesn't get used much.

36 Eagle Creek Hot Springs

General description: A hot water source and great spot for a small pool at the end of a short hike up Hot Springs Canyon. Swimwear is a local decision.

Difficulty: Easy, with a difficult climb at the end

Distance: About 3.5 miles round-trip

General location: About 13 miles from Clifton, or about 60 miles northeast of Safford

Elevation gain: 390 feet

Trailhead elevation: 3,600 feet

Hot springs elevation: 3,800 feet

Map: USGS Clifton 15-minute (springs are shown)

Restrictions: No shooting, no littering; if you open a gate, close it; leave no trace; and do not camp for more than 7 days. This property belongs to a subsidiary company of the Morenci copper mine, which allows access as long as you abide by their basic rules, with the understanding that access could be revoked at any time.

Best time of year: Fall through spring

Camping: The Forest Service's Granville Campground is about 16 miles north of Morenci.

Contact: None

History: The town of Clifton is packed with history. There is a hot springs hotel and a few hot springs along the San Francisco River, which flows through town. The locals can tell you more about them. I suggest you visit the old Clifton jail and the visitor center adjacent to it. There are many other historic buildings in Clifton that are worth checking out. If you are a ghost-hunter, there have been reported ghost sightings, or "non-sightings," however that goes. Just up the road in Morenci is the Morenci copper mine. This impressive operation is one of the largest copper reserves in the United States and the world. Tours are available on Fridays and Saturdays (reservations required).

Finding the trailhead: From the historic Clifton jail, travel north on US 191 for approximately 7.3 winding miles through the Morenci mine, then turn left (south) on the unsigned Lower Eagle Creek Road. GPS: 33.07449, -109.37063 (I marked the coordinates because it is easy to miss.) Continue 5.1 miles to an electrical substation, then 0.2 mile more to a large water pumping plant. Continue another 150 yards and park at the trailhead. GPS: 33.05753, -109.43958

The Hike

From the trailhead, follow the old dirt road as it winds down Eagle Creek. You must cross the creek at least five times, maybe more if water levels are high enough to flood the road. The road and the creek both share the sometimes narrow canyon bottom, and when water levels are high, the roadbed becomes part of the creek. The creek is generally not difficult to get across, and often there are stones to use when crossing. Otherwise, ford the creek when necessary. There are some deep spots near Hot Springs Canyon. You reach the mouth of Hot Springs Canyon at about 1.3 miles. GPS: 33.04559, -109.43917

At the canyon, cross the creek, leaving the shady creek bottom, and hike up the canyon, staying to the right whenever you can. Head toward the waterfall and some grottos. The waterfall is cool water—at the top warm water mixes with cold water

Look for this mountain as a landmark toward the canyon. PHOTOS BY BLUE MEEK-FIELD

and drops over the edge. On the ridge above the waterfall, you will find the hot sources shown in the photos. One way to climb the ridge is to start near the base of the waterfall and scramble the steep hillside north of the falls. Alternatively, you can backtrack to the mouth of the canyon and look for easier ways to climb to the top. Continue following the source of the waterfall to find the cold source and the two warm rivulets that mix with the cold water and flow down the canyon to create the

Above left and right: A cozy two-person temporary pool could be made by rearranging some rocks and using a tarp. Remember to leave no trace.

Below left and right: Poke around in the grotto on the rocky face to the right of the waterfall. The pool might still be accessible on your visit. Follow the warm water to its source.

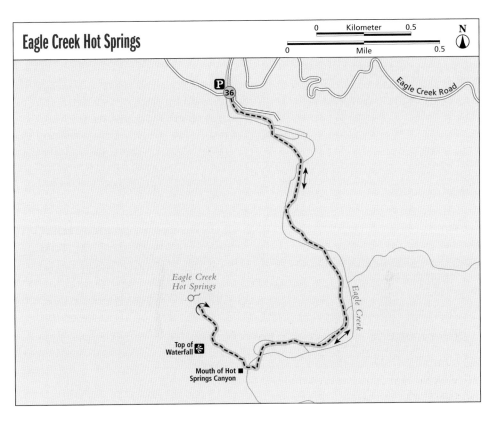

Eagle Creek Hot Springs

waterfall. It is fairly difficult to scramble the last 0.4 mile and about 200 feet of elevation to the hot sources.

There is additional warm water seeping out of the rocky wall to the right of the waterfall and up a little higher. It will take a short scramble, but you may discover a small pool hidden in a cave in the grotto. When you find warm water seeping, follow it to the source and you will likely be pleasantly surprised. GPS: 33.04841, –109.44150

The Hot Springs

If you do not find the pool hidden in the grotto, the other source is above the waterfall. Water seeps out of the ground in two places at 97°F (36°C) and flows down the canyon a short way before joining a cold stream. There are some natural spots where a pool could be made without much trouble. To respect the leave no trace principle on this private land, you can use a tarp to form a temporary pool big enough for two. If you try to make it larger, there may not be enough flow to maintain a comfortable soaking temperature.

37 Gillard Hot Springs

General description: A long, sunny hike to a scalding, high-flowing hot source on the banks of the Gila River in the Gila Box Riparian National Conservation Area. Swimwear is up to those present.

Difficulty: Easy

Distance: 9.2 miles round-trip (less with the right vehicle)

General location: About 9 miles southwest of Clifton

Elevation gain: 1,240 feet

Trailhead elevation: 3,740 feet

Hot springs elevation: 3,295 feet

Map: USGS Guthrie 15-minute (springs are shown)

Restrictions: Extreme heat can be a problem; there is no shade.

Best time of year: Fall through spring

Camping: It is all BLM land; unofficial camping is available anywhere along the trail or near the trailheads.

Contact: Bureau of Land Management, Safford Field Office: (928) 348-4400

History: Gillard Hot Springs were popular before floods dramatically changed the hot springs and its accessibility. At one time, it was easy to drive right up to the pedestrian gate. Floods have dramatically washed out many of the roads, making driving to the gate problematic.

Finding the trailhead: Your phone or GPS will get you to the trailhead, and will also give directions close to the hot springs as if the road was still drivable. Otherwise, from Clifton, drive south on US 191 for 3.6 miles and turn right (west) on the Black Hills Back Country Byway, also known as Old Safford Road. Travel 2 miles and turn right on Gillard Hot Springs Road. There is a small sign near the ground that says, "Gillard HS." The road beyond has been washed out at least once by a flood and was not passable at my last visit. This is the trailhead, and the hike directions start from this point. Though there is no shade, I recommend hiking from here through this beautiful desert area. GPS: 32.98441, -109.29719

If you have a high-clearance, four-wheel-drive vehicle, you can consider driving as far as you feel comfortable to shorten the hike.

The Hike

From the trailhead, follow the rough and rocky Gillard Hot Springs Road as it passes through washed-out areas, often following the washes themselves. When I last hiked this, there was a small BLM sign on the main route, helping guide me through a particularly confusing intersection. Stay on the main road as it winds through small hills with all kinds of wildlife and desert flora, until you come to an intersection at 2.8 miles with San Francisco River Road. Continue straight through the intersection onto what is now called San Francisco River Road on the maps. Pause for a few minutes and enjoy the view before you begin the gradual 1.65-mile descent to the Gila River. Continue mostly southwest on the road as it curves mostly west for a short way, then heads southwest in its curvy descent to the pedestrian gate (GPS: 32.97212, -109.34777). Cross through the gate and walk down the wash for about 200 feet, then head northwest for about 750 feet to a lone sign that warns of scalding water.

Above: Floods have significantly altered the area and made access to Gillard considerably different. The road, as well as any pools, have been washed away, so you must hike to the area and maybe build your own rock and sand pool. There is plenty of hot water available; that's in your favor. The source is scalding hot, so use caution.

Below left and right: Tricky springs as you can see. With the springs source being very hot, these pools need to be mixed with river water to be soakable. Be cautious. PHOTOS BY BLUE MEEK-FIELD

Gillard Hot Springs

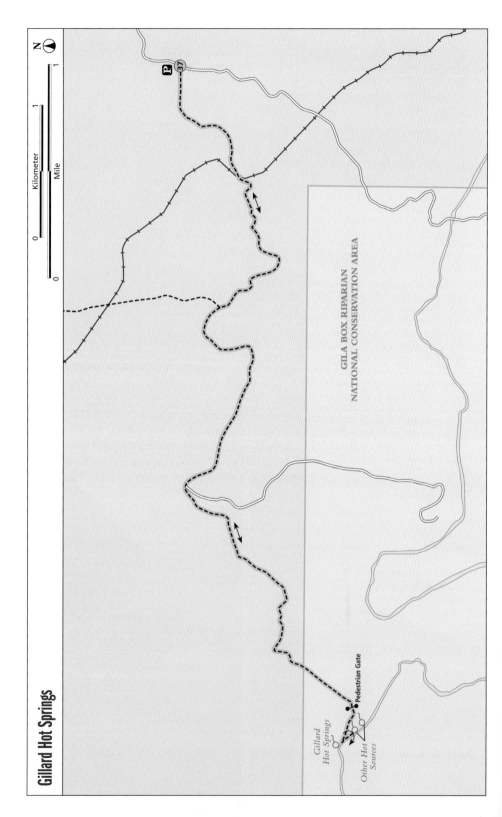

The main hot springs are another 175 feet to the northwest from the sign, down on the Gila River (GPS: 32.97292, -109.35062). There is another hot water source about 260 feet upstream (GPS: 32.97231, -109.35010), and one more about 140 feet farther upstream (GPS: 32.97201, -109.34981).

The Hot Springs

Hot water comes out of the ground at 180°F (82°C) and flows into the Gila River. Rock, sand, and mud pools are washed out and rebuilt seasonally. On my last visit, I found hot water at the expected site, as well as at two other spots upstream within about 400 feet, but there were no remnants of pools. It is very likely that rock and sand pools have been reconstructed by the time you're reading this. Hopefully you find pools on your visit; if not, it is relatively easy to build pools here thanks to the large water flow.

Left and right: The river was low at our last visit, which allowed us to locate the other hot sources.

Utah

The state of Utah has 116 hot springs according to the NOAA's *Thermal Springs List for the United States*, but only about a dozen of those are available to the public. About half of that dozen are in natural locations, and three of those involve a hike of some kind. One is a real hike, while another is more of a paved walk through an urban park on the edge of Utah Lake. The third hot springs involves a short loop in a grassy field surrounded by farm land. Though on private land, the owner has generously made it available to the public so long as it is respected.

The waterfall at Diamond Fork Hot Springs. The water is just trickling over now, but it is a spectacular sight during high-water times. Diamond Fork is Utah's crown jewel of hot water.
PHOTO BY BLUE MEEK-FIELD

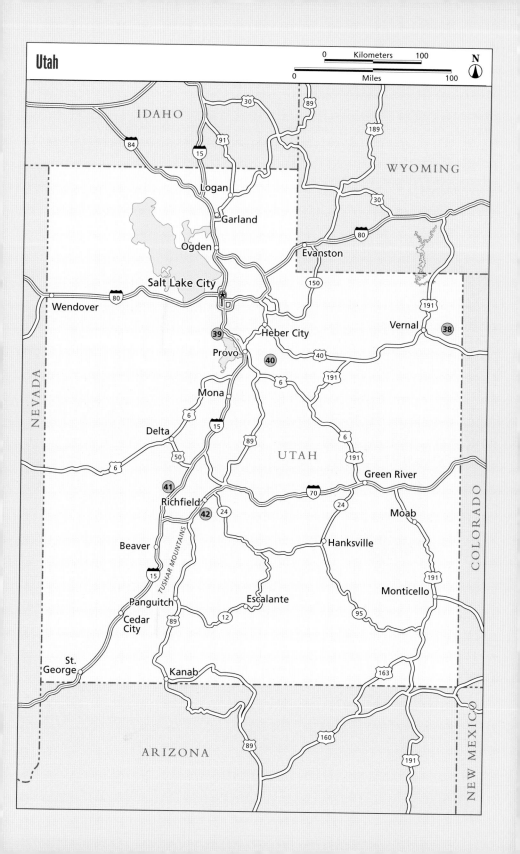

Utah

Kilometers
0 ⎯⎯⎯⎯⎯ 100
0 ⎯⎯⎯⎯⎯ 100
Miles

N

IDAHO

WYOMING

NEVADA

UTAH

COLORADO

ARIZONA

NEW MEXICO

84
30
89
91
189
15
Logan
Garland
Ogden
80
30
Evanston
80
Salt Lake City
150
Wendover
191
39
Heber City
Vernal
38
40
Provo
40
Mona
6
191
6
Delta
15
89
6
191
50
Green River
6
41
70
Richfield
24
24
Moab
42
24
Beaver
Hanksville
15
TUSHAR MOUNTAINS
191
Monticello
Panguitch
Escalante
95
Cedar City
12
89
St. George
Kanab
163
89
160
191

38 Split Mountain Warm Springs

General description: A tepid warm pool on the Green River, in the Split Mountain Canyon, at the end of a very difficult hike. This part of Dinosaur National Monument does not get many hikers, and though brutal, it was one of the best hikes of my season. Swimwear is a local decision.

Difficulty: Difficult

Distance: 4.4 miles from the back side via Horse Trail and Mitten Canyons, or about 4.0 miles (each way) from either up- or downriver on the Green River

General location: About 18 miles east of Vernal

Elevation gain: Horse Trail Canyon: 2,550 feet

Trailhead elevation: Horse Trail: 5,270 feet

Warm springs elevation: 4,880 feet

Map: USGS Split Mountain 7.5-minute (springs are shown)

Restrictions: There is an impassable dry waterfall that needs to be skirted. Permits are required for overnight camping and fording the Green River. There is a fee to enter the monument.

Best time of year: Spring through fall

Camping: Rainbow Park and Split Mountain Campgrounds are at 2 of the trailheads.

Contact: Dinosaur National Monument: (435) 781-7700

Finding the trailhead: Your GPS or phone will get you to Split Mountain or Rainbow Park Campgrounds easily enough, and even to the Horse Trail trailhead if you enter the coordinates. Otherwise, from Vernal, head north on South Vernal Avenue toward West Main Street for 0.5 mile. Turn right on 500 North Street for 3 miles. Continue straight as it turns into Diamond Mountain Road for 5.1 miles. Turn right onto Brush Creek Road for 0.8 mile, then turn right to stay on Brush Creek Road. Continue for 1.1 miles, then turn left on Island Park Road. Drive 8.3 miles and park wherever you want. The canyon is on your right. This is not an official trailhead, just a wide spot in the road from which to start your hike. GPS: 40.50876, -109.23657

The Hike

Horse Trail Canyon: From the trailhead, follow the road heading south for about 0.3 mile until the road heads west; at that point, leave it and aim for the big notch in Split Mountain. You pass through small meadows hidden in the junipers as you cross over the rolling hills to get to the canyon that will take you up to the notch. Continue on this trail-less route until you get closer to the base of the mountain, where you will start walking in the dry creek bed of Horse Trail Canyon. Make sure you stay in the main wash on the way up, as there are tributaries that can lure you off-course. Continue following the seasonal stream bed up small waterfalls, around boulders, and across bare granite as it becomes steeper and steeper before leveling off on the aspen-shaded saddle. The only trails are the abundant game trails as you wind around fallen trees and other obstacles. Wildlife is everywhere as you reach the high point of the saddle at an elevation of 6,130 feet. The grassy saddle starts sloping down as you start descending in Mitten Canyon.

Split Mountain Warm Springs is right down below my position at the bottom of Mitten Canyon. It's a little tricky. If we can't figure out how to hike there, we'll have to wait for Kayaking Hot Springs in the Southwest.

The route now follows the bed of the dry Mitten Creek. It gets steeper quickly, and there are many deadfall obstacles that you must climb over, go up and around, or just get through. Keep following the creek bed, scrambling down waterfalls and across more granite faces as the canyon walls get higher and higher. You descend over 1,000 feet of elevation on your hike down Mitten Canyon. At about 0.2 mile away from the warm springs, you reach the top of a 100-foot waterfall that you need to skirt. When I was there last, it was late in the day and I had to turn around and backtrack through

"At the lower end of the park, the river turns again to the southeast and cuts into the mountain to its center and then makes a detour to the southwest, splitting the mountain ridge for a distance of six miles nearly to its foot, and then turns out of it to the left. All this we can see where we stand on the summit of Mount Hawkins, and so we name the gorge below, Split Mountain Canyon."—Major John Wesley Powell, June 24, 1869 PHOTO BY NPS

one of the best hikes of the year. No warm water for me that day. It was an unforgettable hike through spectacular geological features that are virtually untouched and have rarely been seen by others. Approximate GPS: 40.4652, -109.2217

The Warm Springs

Warm water comes out of the ground at about 86°F (30°C) and flows into a rock and sand pool that can fit four close friends. This is a popular stop for rafters and kayakers, but very few hikers. This warm springs is not worth the hike unless you're doing it for the sake of the hike. There are certainly better springs in this book, but the hike was unforgettable.

Notes about the Hikes

It is not difficult to ford the Green River during low-water times, or to get to the springs from either the upriver or downriver trailheads. But to do this legally, you need a permit from the National Park Service. Permits are required to be in the river, even for a bank-to-bank crossing. They may require that you have a personal flotation device or equivalent before granting you a permit. At my last visit I was surprised to learn that fording the river required a permit. I was discussing this in the visitor center with the staff when a lovely young rangerette promised me that if I put one toe in

Split Mountain Warm Springs

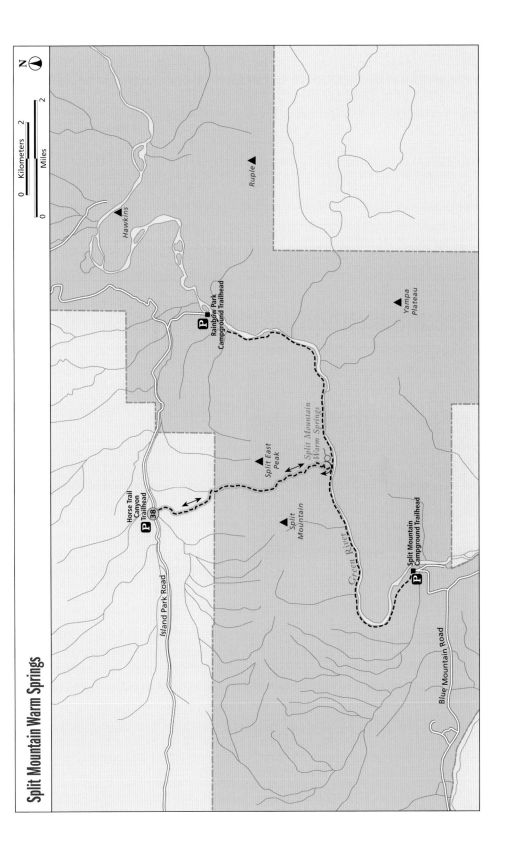

the river without a permit, she would personally cite me. I don't recall the exact conversation prior to that, but I remember that clearly. As you drive by Split Mountain on the BLM-owned Island Park side, it is an impressive sight. Imagine yourself hiking down through the middle of the canyon between the mountains. Soak or not, hiking up Horse Trail Canyon and down Mitten Canyon again is a priority for me.

Options

Split Mountain Campground (GPS: 40.44546, -109.25330) or Rainbow Park Campground (GPS: 40.49534, -109.17425) trailheads: There are no trails. The hikes from these trailheads are difficult because you quickly get to points where you must ford the river or climb up and around the cliffs that were created by the river bends. The river is deep in these spots and fording is often not possible. Hiking up and around these cliffs is challenging because you will likely have difficulty losing the elevation and getting back down to the river's edge. The entire canyon is steep, and you need to take a hard look at a topographical map to choose your route. The best plan from these trailheads is to stay close to the river, fording back and forth as needed. Fording the Green River is difficult during high-water times. These routes

The warm springs are about halfway down this six-mile canyon. Photo by NPS/Jake Holgerson

are possible in low-water times, but still challenging. They require a permit from the National Park Service, who may not allow it because of water level. To obtain a permit, you need to demonstrate that you can do it safely. Their trained staff will scrutinize your plan thoroughly and you should trust their judgment. I have a firsthand report from a friend who started from the Split Mountain Campground and walked upriver. He forded when necessary and made it to the warm springs.

Also in the Area

The Dinosaur National Monument Fossil Bone Quarry is unbelievable. It is built into the side of a large hill that was being excavated by paleontologists. The excavation stopped and an in-place exhibit was built showing the "Wall of Bones," a huge rock face that has been chipped away to reveal hundreds of dinosaur bones still embedded in the sandstone in their original positions.

The outflow winds toward Utah Lake, and volunteers have dug a second ▶
pool that is much cooler for hot days. Photo by Lexi Miller

Inlet Park Hot Springs

General description: A popular 40-foot-diameter rock and mud pool in a park on the northwest corner of Utah Lake. Swimwear is required.

Difficulty: Easy

Distance: 0.7 mile round-trip

General location: About 30 miles south of Salt Lake City

Elevation gain: Negligible

Trailhead elevation: 4,500 feet

Hot springs elevation: 4,500 feet

Map: USGS Saratoga Springs 7.5-minute (springs are shown)

Restrictions: Day-use only; no alcohol; swimwear required.

Best time of year: Open year-round

Camping: No nearby camping except for RV parks and KOAs

Contact: City of Saratoga Springs: (801) 766-6506

History: Inlet Park Hot Springs, also known as Saratoga Hot Springs, has been a resort or place to swim since 1884. I remember visiting Saratoga Hot Springs as a child (considerably after 1884) and going down the waterslide. The medicinal value of geothermal water is a common belief, and Saratoga Hot Springs is no exception. A century ago, the water and mud were sold worldwide.

Finding the trailhead: Entering Inlet Park in your phone or GPS will take you to the general vicinity, then watch for signs to the park. There is a north and south parking area; park at the southern one, which also shows up as the Jordan River Parkway Trailhead on some maps. Otherwise, from Salt Lake City, drive south on I-15 for about 24 miles and take exit 283 to merge onto North Thanksgiving Way, then turn right onto 2300West/Triumph Boulevard. Continue south 0.8 miles as Triumph Boulevard becomes 2300West. Continue 1.8 miles until the road becomes Saratoga Road. Continue on Saratoga Road for 2.6 miles, then turn left into the south parking area for Inlet Park. The trail begins from the south side of the parking area. There are signs with information about the hot springs. GPS: 40.35720, -111.89975

A large mud-bottomed pool in a public geothermal park. The main pool is often too hot on most summer days, but the water cools as it flows into the smaller pool (pictured above).
PHOTO BY LEXI MILLER

Additional Hike

Walk east from the south parking area and find the Jordan River Parkway Trailhead. This paved trail follows the Jordan River north (away from the hot springs) for 45.3 miles through urban areas and Salt Lake City communities until it reaches the Great Salt Lake.

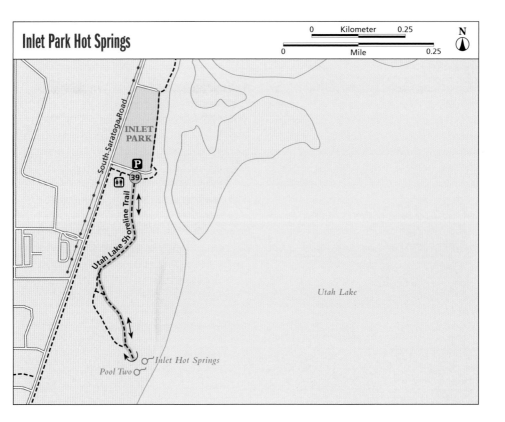

The Hike

Follow the paved path south toward the hot springs for about 0.2 mile until the path splits. Take either path, as it forms a loop, then continue 0.1 mile to the end of the loop. The main pool is another 100 feet south from there. GPS: 40.35301, -111.89969

The Hot Springs: A large mud-bottomed pool is at the end of a 0.33-mile walk on a paved path in a park that lets you feel you're away from town, though you're really not. It's located in the wetlands on the shore just northwest of Utah Lake and is maintained by community efforts. Water comes out of the ground at 110°F (43°C) and wells up from the squishy bottom, enough to keep the temperature comfortable in cooler months. The outflow from the pool meanders toward the lake, and volunteers have dug another pool that is much cooler and the better choice in the summer months (GPS: 40.35269, -111.89960). From here, follow the outflow, pushing through reeds, to find an even cooler third pool, which is not very popular.

40 Diamond Fork Hot Springs

General description: Also known as Fifth Water Hot Springs, there are multiple soaking pools in a beautiful canyon at the end of an easy hike in the Uinta-Wasatch-Cache National Forest. Swimwear is required by county law.

Difficulty: Fairly easy with a few tough spots

Distance: 4.6 or 5.0 miles round-trip, depending on the trailhead

General location: The lower trailhead is about 21 miles east of Spanish Fork and the upper trailhead. Coming from Salt Lake City, the lower trailhead is about 63 miles and the upper trailhead 88 miles away.

Elevation gain: Diamond Fork: 730 feet; Ray's Valley: 725 feet

Trailhead elevation: Diamond Fork: 5,540 feet; Ray's Valley: 6,895 feet

Hot springs elevation: 6,140 feet

Map: USGS Rays Valley 7.5-minute (springs are not shown)

Restrictions: Access roads often closed in winter. Dogs must be leashed.

Best time of year: Spring through fall; mid-week best to avoid crowds

Camping: The Forest Service's Diamond Fork Campground is 4 miles down Diamond Fork Road from the lower trailhead. Primitive camping is available in some places around the trailheads and along the lower trail.

Contact: Uinta-Wasatch-Cache National Forest, Spanish Fork Ranger District: (801) 798-3571

Finding the trailheads: Due to the improvements of GPS navigation software available on phones and other devices, you can enter the trailhead names or GPS coordinates to get there. Otherwise, for the Diamond Fork lower trailhead: From Spanish Fork, travel east on US 6 East for about 10.7 miles and turn left onto Diamond Fork Road (FR 029). Continue 9.9 miles to the parking area and trailhead on the right. GPS: 40.08439, -111.35487

Ray's Valley trailhead: From Spanish Fork, drive east on US 6 for about 22 miles and turn left onto Sheep Creek Road (FR 051) Continue about 14 miles to a junction, which is often signed. The trailhead is on the left. GPS: 40.10573, -111.29112

The Hike

On these hikes, you'll be walking through forests of maple oak, which often turn spectacular colors in the early fall. When the leaves fall, they form a multicolored carpet on the trail that is incredibly photogenic.

From Diamond Fork lower trailhead: From the trailhead, do not cross the footbridge, but follow the trail along the side of Sixth Water Creek. After a mile there is a footbridge over Sixth Water Creek. Cross this footbridge and continue as the trail heads east and uphill along the north side of Fifth Water Creek. You will cross a few side creeks over the next mile and often start smelling sulfur. After about 2.2 miles, the lower springs are on the right, along the creek. While these are lovely pools, the better pools are up the trail in the next few hundred feet. GPS: 40.08299, -111.31862

From Ray's Valley trailhead: This is sometimes called the upper trailhead. Despite being considerably steeper than the lower trail, it's preferred by many because you avoid the crowds, and you can get a parking place (a problem at the trailhead below). From

The milky blue water and multiple pools make Diamond Fork Utah's crown jewel for hot springs. With many pools and the hot creek, it's easy to find a perfect soaking spot. The cascading pools of milky blue water are always popular. PHOTOS BY BLUE MEEK-FIELD

Diamond Fork Hot Springs

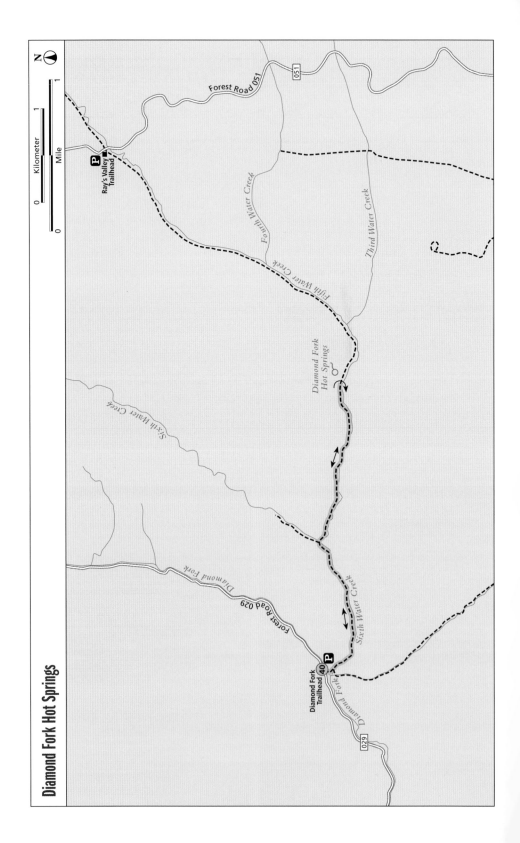

Though not much water is running over it now, the waterfall is spectacular when water is running normally. When the runoff is low, you can get a great picture looking out the little rock peephole behind the falls.

this trailhead, start walking southwest down the moderate, forested trail that follows Fifth Water Creek approximately 2.5 miles to the top of the waterfall. The pools start below the waterfall and continue down the creek. GPS: 40.08299, -111.31862

The Hot Springs

Also known as Fifth Water Hot Springs, I believe these soaking pools are the best natural pools that Utah has to offer. Highly mineralized hot water comes out of the rocks in many places at various temperatures (some over 150°F/65.5°C), where it is diverted into pools that are sized to maintain comfortable soaking temperatures. During dry conditions, the water is likely to be crystal clear. After rain, the pools and even the creek tend to turn a beautiful milky blue color due to the high mineral content. The Emerald Pool is the exception; because it does not mix with creek water, it has an enticing green color. This is likely to be the only pool available for soaking during spring runoff. During the late summer and fall, the entire downstream creek often approaches body temperature, which makes for even more fantastic soaking.

Notes: If the creek water level allows, you can climb up behind the waterfall and stick your head out a hole in the rock, through the water. This is always amusing to the young, and the young-at-heart.

There's a lot of poison oak in the area, especially near the hot springs.

41 Meadow Hot Springs

General description: A short walking loop takes you to two crystal-clear pools surrounded by travertine deposits. As a bonus, there's a third pool that is cool enough to be considered refreshing. Located on private property in a grassy field in central Utah. Swimwear is required.

Difficulty: Easy

Distance: 0.9-mile loop

General location: About 6 miles southwest of Meadow

Elevation gain: Negligible

Trailhead elevation: 4,770 feet

Hot springs elevation: 4,770 feet

Map: USGS Tabernacle Hill 15-minute (springs are shown)

Restrictions: The landowner asks that there be no nudity, no alcohol, and that people clean up after themselves. Walk only on the roads.

Best time of year: Spring through fall. During the summer, heat can be extreme and there is no shade. During the warmer months there have been reports of red spider mites sometimes being a problem, especially in the main pool. You might check for them prior to entering the water. See Hike 24, Twelve Mile Hot Springs in Nevada, for guidance on dealing with red spider mites.

Camping: There is no camping available in the area.

Contact: None

Finding the trailhead: From the center of Meadow, head south on UT 133 for about 0.9 mile and turn right (west) on a dirt road that you can see crosses over I-15. Stay on this dirt road for 4.8 miles to the parking area. It can get very muddy around the parking area and along the dirt roads. Park your vehicle and walk only on the two-track dirt roads to prevent further erosion. GPS: 38.86681, -112.50422

The Hike/Hot Springs

The landowner has built fences and improved trails between the pools, and graciously allows the public access so long as it is not abused. The best way to respect these improvements is to park at the parking area and walk in a clockwise direction to visit all three pools in a 0.9-mile loop.

Main Pool: From the parking area, walk about 850 feet south and a little east along the two-track road to the main pool (GPS: 38.86452, -112.50322). Hot water comes up from the bottom at about 106°F (41°C) and keeps the main pool slightly above body temperature. This 12-by-30-foot pool often has ropes installed across the water to help with access and provide something to hold because there are few places to sit and relax.

Hourglass Pool: From the Main Pool, continue clockwise on the two-track road southwest for about 1,200 feet to the Hourglass Pool (GPS: 38.86211, -112.50527). This pool, shaped like a 45-foot-long, kid-drawn hourglass, is the most beautiful of the three. The pool stays a little below body temperature, but does have travertine ledges that allow you to stand, and even sit in places.

Above left: The crystal-clear water in the two warmer pools makes for an enjoyable soak.
Above right: This main pool is the warmest of the three and most frequently used, likely because many don't know about the others.
Below: The stunning aqua color and mysterious depth make this hourglass-shaped pool a one-of-a-kind soak. Photos by Blue Meek-Field

Known locally as the "Swimming Hole," this is the largest of the three and just warm. You may even find some small fish friends sharing the pool with you.

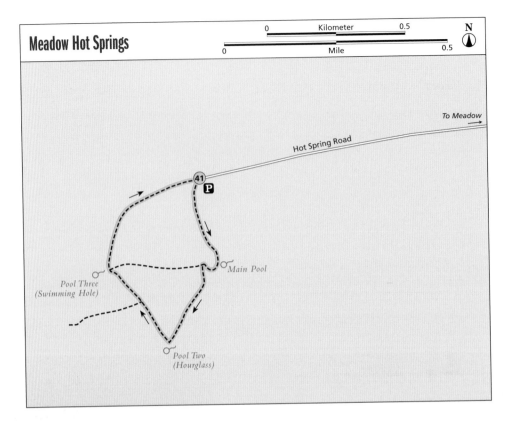

Meadow Hot Springs

0   Kilometer   0.5

0   Mile   0.5

N

To Meadow

Hot Spring Road

41

P

Main Pool

Pool Three
(Swimming Hole)

Pool Two
(Hourglass)

Swimming Hole: From the Hourglass Pool, continue the loop by walking about 1,100 feet northwest on the two-track road to the third pool, the Swimming Hole (GPS: 38.86429, -112.50781). This 40-by-60-foot pool's lukewarm temperature is the coolest of the three, but with the small dock, it has the feel of an old-time swimming hole. You might even find fish swimming with you.

From the Swimming Hole, complete the clockwise loop by walking northeast along the two-track road about 1,600 feet to the parking area.

These unexpected treasures are in a pasture just a few miles from the Interstate 15 in rural Utah. The landowner asks only that they be respected.
All photos by Blue Meek-Field

42 Red Hill Hot Springs

General description: Sometimes called Red Mound Hot Springs, these pools are northeast of Monroe at the base of a deep red travertine mound. This free hot springs is in this book because it is close to Meadow Hot Springs and the commercial Mystic Hot Springs Resort, both of which should be on every hot springs enthusiast's list. Swimwear is required.

Difficulty: Easy

Distance: No hike to get to this one, but plenty of hiking above the pools

General location: About 1 mile east of Monroe

Elevation gain: Negligible

Hot springs elevation: 5,580 feet

Map: USGS Monroe 15-minute (springs are shown)

Restrictions: Day-use only; no glass

Best time of year: Fall through spring; summer might be too hot.

Camping: There is no Forest Service-type camping available in the area; however, there is a lot of BLM ground where primitive camping is available. Alternatively, Mystic Hot Springs Resort has campsites and cabins to rent, as well as converted buses. Parked just outside the resort, they are a funky and fun way to spend a night.

Contact: City of Monroe: (435) 527-4621

Finding the hot springs: From UT 118 in Monroe, head east on East 300 North Street out of town. Continue 1.3 miles to the parking area. GPS: 38.63959, -112.09924

Left: The milky blue water flows into red stone pools, making this springs very photogenic.
Right: The stonework is rustic, yet incredible. PHOTOS BY BLUE MEEK-FIELD

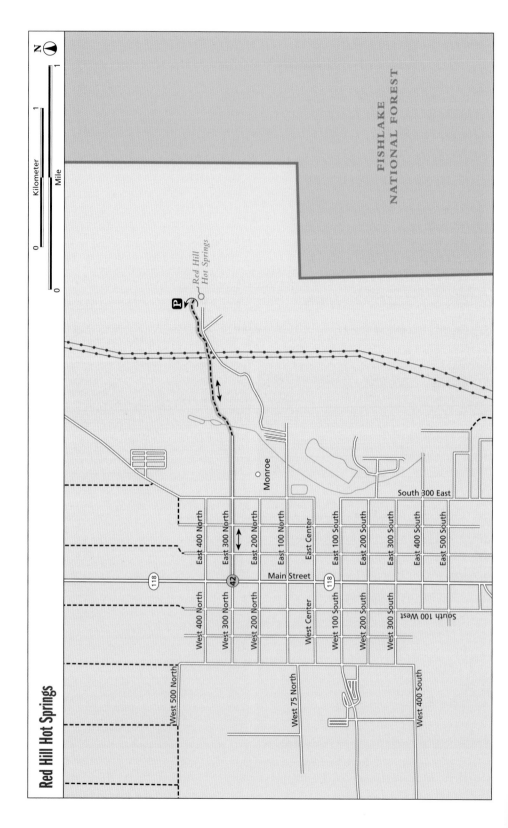

Red Hill Hot Springs

N

Kilometer
0   1

Mile
0   1

FISHLAKE
NATIONAL FOREST

Red Hill
Hot Springs

P

Monroe

South 300 East

118

42

Main Street

118

West 400 North | East 400 North
West 300 North | East 300 North
West 200 North | East 200 North
West Center | East 100 North
West 100 South | East Center
West 200 South | East 100 South
West 300 South | East 200 South
South 100 West | East 300 South
| East 400 South
| East 500 South

West 500 North

West 75 North

West 400 South

The Hot Springs

Hot water comes up out of a tremendous travertine mound at 168°F (75.5°C) and is channeled into pools built near the base. The pools and paths are constructed of local stone, and the travertine deposits have now morphed them into solid formations. Temperature can be controlled by diverting hot water. The flow is reported to be 100 gallons per minute, with enough minerals to make the water a soft blue color. The town is built at the base of the Monroe Mound, a mile-long travertine deposit that is worth exploring. The commercial establishment, Mystic Hot Springs Resort, is a great place to visit and soak in the pools built into the red hillsides.

Left: Hot water comes out of a large dome and flows into soaking pools outside Monroe.
Right: Despite the pools' proximity to the small town of Monroe, it is not uncommon to have one to yourself and watch the sunset.

Colorado

The state of Colorado has forty-seven hot springs documented by the NOAA's *Thermal Springs List for the United States*. Surprisingly, compared to other states, nearly all of these hot springs are used for recreational purposes. Though mostly commercial spas, pools, and retreats, many hot springs are available on public land in their natural state. As the title of this book implies, I am writing about hot springs at the end of hikes, and Colorado has six. I will list these hiking hot springs by their descending latitude, or from north to south.

Also in Colorado

Looking for an above-body-temperature soak? There are several commercial hot springs located in Ouray. Ridgeway's Orvis Hot Springs is a perennial favorite and has the distinction of being clothing optional.

Colorado's Silver Dollar Pond, on the way to the state's crown jewel, Conundrum Hot Springs—North America's highest hot springs

Colorado

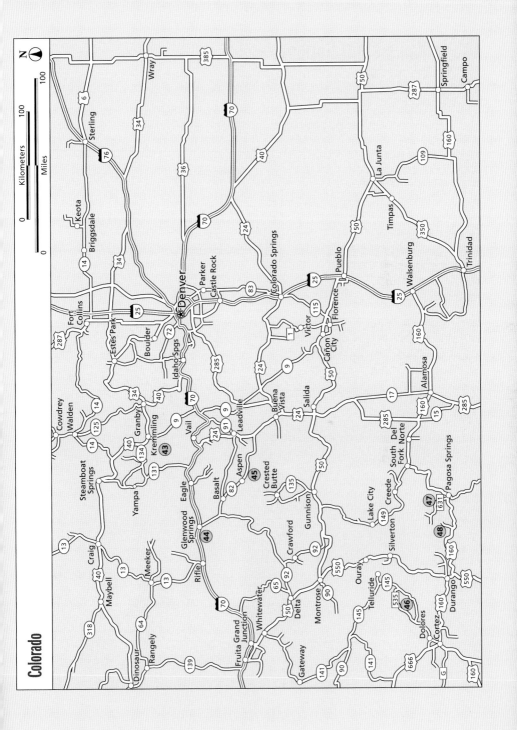

43 Radium Hot Springs

General description: A gorgeous rock and sand pool set against a rock cliff on the banks of the Colorado River, on BLM land. Radium is a popular raft and kayak stop, so swimwear seems to be the norm.

Difficulty: Moderate

Distance: 1.5 miles round-trip

General location: About 18 miles southeast of Kremmling

Elevation gain: 280 feet

Trailhead elevation: 6,940 feet

Hot springs elevation: 6,890 feet

Map: USGS Radium 7.5-minute (springs are not shown)

Restrictions: There is a fee for parking.

Best time of year: Summer and fall. The pool is likely to be underwater during spring runoff, and its temperature is too cold during winter months.

Camping: Mugrage Campground is directly across the road from the trailhead. The BLM-managed Radium River Access Campground is 0.9 mile farther down the road (not reservable and charges a small fee).

Contact: Bureau of Land Management, Kremmling Field Office: (970) 724-3000

Finding the trailhead: From Kremmling, travel south on CO 9 for 2.3 miles and turn right on CR 1 Road (signed Trough Road). Continue on this sometimes paved road for 14.6 miles and turn right on CR 11. Drive 1.4 miles to the parking area adjacent to Mugrage Campground. GPS: 39.95169, -106.54257

The steep trail up the hill to Radium Hot Springs PHOTOS BY BLUE MEEK-FIELD

The Hike

It's approximately 0.75 mile each way, up and across an exposed hilltop, and down to the river. Beginning at the parking lot at the Mugrage Campground, look across CR 11 and find the trail going northwest up the steep hillside. It's tough for about 0.15 mile, then the trail flattens out for about 0.3 mile. You will come to a trail junction (GPS: 39.95705, -106.54402); turn right (northeast) and hike mostly parallel to the

◀ *This rock pool with a gravel bottom set right against the Colorado River offers a great opportunity to watch for wildlife on the surrounding hills or watch and interact with other people floating along the river.*

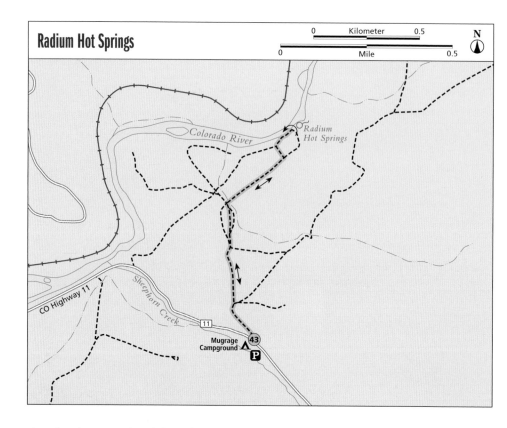

Radium Hot Springs

0   Kilometer   0.5

0   Mile   0.5

N

Colorado River

Radium Hot Springs

CO Highway 11

Sheephorn Creek

11

Mugrage Campground   43   P

river for about another 0.25 mile to another trail junction where you go left (north) down toward the river. It's a bit steep if you go straight down; the way is easier if you follow some of the switchbacks. The trails all go to the same place on the river (GPS: 39.95992, -106.54071). After you start down toward the river, look to your right for a popular cliff that people jump from.

The Hot Springs

Clear, odorless water wells up from the gravel bottom of this pool. On my last visit the rock and sand pool was about 15 feet in diameter, which is a good size to maintain a comfortable soaking temperature of 97°F (36°C). The pool must be rebuilt annually, but when built too big, the temperature of the water drops to the mid- to low 90s (35–33°C). This pool can be too cool, depending on the ambient temperature.

With an easy jaunt to this primitive, murky pool, it gets high traf- ▶
fic. Friendly reminder for this one: Please pack out what you pack in.
Photo by Blue Meek-Field

South Canyon Hot Springs

General description: A large, mud-bottomed pool a little way off a county road, not far from I-70 in western Colorado. Swimwear is at your discretion.

Difficulty: Easy

Distance: 0.15 mile round-trip

General location: About 5 miles west of Glenwood Springs

Elevation gain: 30 feet

Trailhead elevation: 5,840 feet

Hot springs elevation: 5,845 feet

Map: USGS Storm King Mountain 7.5-minute (springs are not shown)

Restrictions: Day-use only

Best time of year: Most popular in the spring and fall, due to temperature extremes in the opposing seasons.

Camping: Primitive camping is allowed in the surrounding area.

Contact: City of Glenwood Springs: (970) 384-6301

Finding the trailhead: From Glenwood Springs, take I-70 west approximately 5 miles to exit 111, signed for South Canyon Road. Turn left under the interstate and follow CR 134 (South Canyon Road) almost 0.6 mile to a large pullout parking area on the right (west) side of the road. GPS: 39.55431, -107.41023

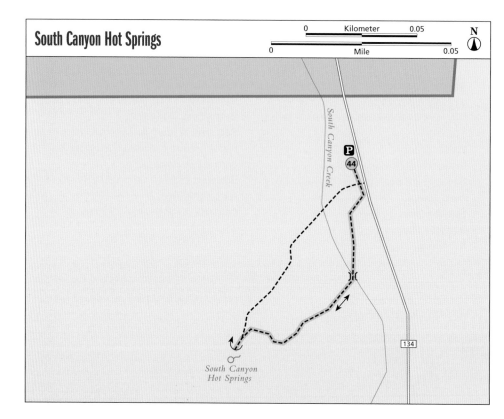

The Hike

There are a few trails to choose from to start this 300-foot hike, all leading to the same place. Pick a trail and drop down through the trees and brush to the small creek where most of the trails come together. Cross the creek and go up the hill to the springs. GPS: 39.55375, -107.41079

The Hot Springs

Hot water at 118°F (48°C) wells up directly into this 10-by-20-foot rock-lined pool, which is maintained by local volunteers. The pool temperature tends to stay well over 100°F (38°C), except in the colder months. This low-flow pool is often murky because of the mud bottom and heavy use. During the warmer months, visiting earlier in the day is recommended due to the pool's lack of shade; the bonus is that the water is likely to be clearer. Some of the state's namesake red rock mountains and hillsides are visible from the pool.

45 Conundrum Hot Springs

General description: Conundrum is likely North America's highest-elevation hot springs. This alpine gem is at the end of a long hike in the Maroon Bells–Snowmass Wilderness of the White River National Forest. Swimwear is a mixed bag, despite the long hike.

Difficulty: Moderate

Distance: Conundrum Creek trailhead: 17.6 miles round-trip; Copper Creek trailhead: 17.0 miles round-trip

General location: The Conundrum Creek trailhead is about 6 miles south of Aspen; the Copper Creek trailhead is about 8 miles northwest of Crested Butte.

Elevation gain: Conundrum Creek: 3,190 feet; Copper Creek: about 5,980 feet

Trailhead elevation: Conundrum Creek: 8,800 feet; Copper Creek: 9,580 feet

Hot springs elevation: 11,250 feet

Map: USGS Maroon Bells 7.5-minute and Gothic 7.5-minute (springs are shown)

Restrictions: Permits are required for overnight camping; campfires are prohibited at all designated campsites at Conundrum Hot Springs

and above 10,800 feet. Dogs must be leashed at all times and left in an area away from the springs.

Best time of year: June through September. Winter is not recommended because the trailhead may be inaccessible and the avalanche danger is real.

Camping: You must have a permit to camp within the Conundrum Hot Springs Permit Zone (permit zone map available on the Forest Service website). There are 20 designated campsites along the trail, which must be reserved in advance at www.recreation.gov. Other primitive camping must be outside the permit zone and no higher than 0.25 mile below the tree line.

Contact: Lincoln National Forest, Gunnison Ranger District: (970) 641-0471

History: In 2019 the trailhead was hit by a "historic-sized" avalanche and the trail was rerouted. Thousands of aspen trees were leveled, and hikers still have to high-step over fallen trees for about 0.3 mile. That doesn't sound like a long way until you try it.

Finding the trailheads: Conundrum Creek: This trailhead will definitely be found on your phone or GPS unit, so you can use that. Otherwise, from Aspen, drive 0.5 mile west on CO 82 to a roundabout and take the Castle Creek Road turnoff. Drive 4.9 miles on Castle Creek Road, then turn right onto Conundrum Creek Road and continue for about a mile to the large parking area. The parking lot can fill up very quickly, so getting there early in the day is best. There are many private residences on Conundrum Creek Road, so ensure you do not block driveways. Due to the popularity of this hike, the Forest Service will likely shuttle visitors to the trailhead in the near future, perhaps even by the time this book is printed. GPS: 39.11921, -106.85610

Copper Creek: This trailhead also can be found on your phone or GPS unit if you enter the GPS coordinates. Otherwise, from Crested Butte, follow FR 317 (Gothic Road) for 8.2 miles to the large parking area on both sides of the road. It's called the Copper Creek/Judd Falls Trailhead. Most of the vehicles parked there belong to people who are walking the 1.1 miles to Judd Falls. GPS: 38.96613, -106.99358

The Hike

Conundrum Creek: This hike is on the Forest Service's Conundrum Creek Trail #1981. The hike is rated as difficult by many, perhaps because of the altitude and length. I believe the rating is closer to moderate, based on my experience. The hike is on a well-defined trail with only a few steep parts. It is mostly just a long, steady, gently uphill climb through a beautiful valley, with a steeper section the last 1.5 miles. The altitude is something to consider on this hike, especially if you have just arrived from a considerably lower elevation.

The trail is around 8.5 miles each way and follows Conundrum Creek south, up a long valley surrounded by towering peaks. The distance is plenty long enough to pass through pine forests, wildflower-filled meadows, and shimmering groves of aspens. The locals refer to aspens as "quakies" because of the leaf movement in the slightest breeze. This is an incredible sight throughout the year, but even better when the leaves are turning color in the fall.

From the trailhead, start out on the well-maintained trail heading south through the valley, along the east side of Conundrum Creek. The first 0.5 mile is mostly flat, then the trail climbs gently through a meadow for about a mile until it flattens out long enough to cross a side creek and then continue in and out of the shade on its steady way up the valley. At about 2.6 miles, the trail crosses to the west side of Conundrum Creek via a footbridge.

The trail continues gently uphill along the west side, high above the creek. There are some shady spots, but it's mostly open terrain as you continue up the valley to the next creek crossing at about 5.8 miles. Cross Conundrum Creek on the footbridge back to the east side of the creek and continue for about a half-mile until you again ford Conundrum Creek to the west side.

Continue gently up for most of a mile before the trail starts to get a little steeper. The final push begins at about the 7.0-mile mark. You have gained 1,700 feet of elevation in the last 7.0 miles and are at about 10,500 feet. The hot springs are about 1.5 miles ahead and 750 vertical feet above you. Keep going as the trail winds in and out of shade on its way up the valley. When you pass the remains of an old cabin, you will start seeing the hot springs on your left.

This amazing hike ends rather anticlimactically, as you can see the hot springs from so far away. It is exciting, though, knowing the uphill climb is almost complete and you are about to soak in natural hot water at the highest elevation in North America. The hot springs are located just below tree line, and it is worth the effort to hike to higher elevations to see the dramatic differences in the landscape. Though the views from the hot springs are spectacular, they get even better as you ascend the valley to Triangle Pass. GPS: 39.01156, -106.89133

Copper Creek: This hike is on the Forest Service's Conundrum Creek Trail #983, which enters the Maroon Bells–Snowmass Wilderness and provides excellent scenery. The hike is very close to the same distance, but with nearly twice the elevation gain. The trail wanders along hillsides where there are loose rocks and downfall. There are many creek crossings, so be prepared for cold, swift, and possibly deep water.

From the trailhead, follow the trail southeast along a sidehill for 1.1 miles until it meets up with Copper Creek near Judd Falls (a popular destination for tourists, and worth the 100-foot detour). From there the trail heads upstream in this heavily wooded canyon for about 3.4 more miles to an intersection. This is the turnoff for Copper Lake and the beginning point of Conundrum Trail #981. Turn right and continue east on Trail #981 toward the scenic Triangle Pass. The trees get progressively smaller until eventually you are hiking above the tree line. In about 2.3 miles you are at the high point of the hike at about 12,900 feet. After crossing Triangle Pass, the trail enters the White River National Forest and gets a name change to Conundrum Creek Trail #1981. Continue on Trail #1981 as it turns north and winds down the valley. Now you can watch the trees get progressively larger as you descend below tree line on the 2.0-mile walk down the valley to the hot springs. GPS: 39.01156, –106.89133

A rewarding soak in stunning surroundings at the highest hot springs in North America

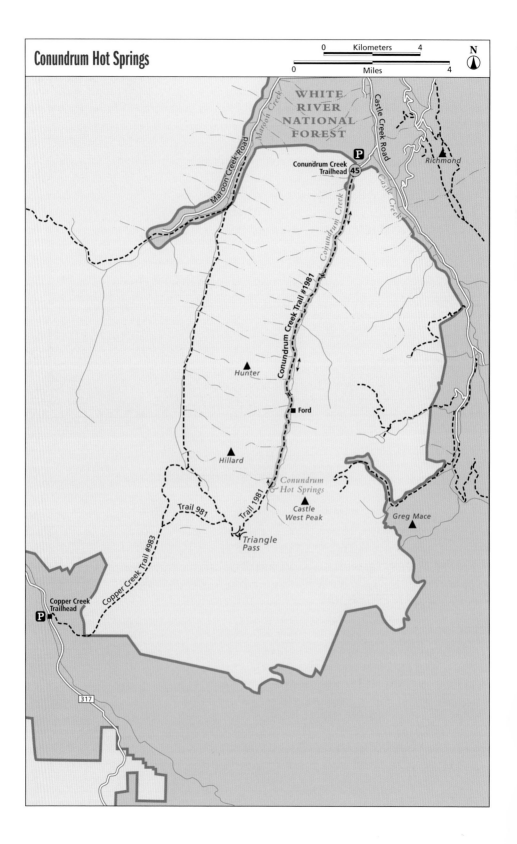

Conundrum Hot Springs

0   Kilometers   4

0   Miles   4

N

WHITE
RIVER
NATIONAL
FOREST

Castle Creek Road

Maroon Creek

Maroon Creek Road

Conundrum Creek
Trailhead   45

P

Richmond

Conundrum Creek

Castle Creek

Conundrum Creek Trail #1981

Hunter

Ford

Hillard

Conundrum
Hot Springs

Castle
West Peak

Greg Mace

Trail 981

Trail 1981

Triangle
Pass

Copper Creek Trail #983

Copper Creek
Trailhead

P

317

Left: There are additional pools that are rarely used.
Right: A small pool in the outflow of the main pool

The Hot Springs

Hot water at 100°F (38°C) bubbles up from the bottom into this 15-by-40-foot oval pool that maintains a temperature in the mid- to high 90s (35–37°C), depending on the ambient temperature. Despite the long hike and high elevation, this hot springs is very popular and gets many visitors, including families. It seems the majority of people wear swimwear, so it is wise to keep it handy during the daytime. Sixty feet down the hill, the outflow forms another pool that is smaller, deeper, and much cooler.

Memories

I have not hiked up the Copper Creek trail, but I have a firsthand account of the hike. Many years ago, I hiked to Triangle Pass via Conundrum Creek. While at the pass, I climbed up the side of a peak until I broke the 13,000-foot elevation mark. Hiking to 13,000 feet was a first for me and was memorable. I imagine that many of you readers have hiked far higher than that, but if not, this is a good opportunity because you're pretty close.

46 Geyser Warm Springs

General description: A large warm pool fed by the only true geyser in the state of Colorado. Not a typical hiking hot springs, but worth seeing, especially since it erupts quite regularly—not as faithfully as another popular geyser in the West, but pretty close. Swimwear not applicable, because you're not going to soak . . . right?

Difficulty: Easy

Distance: 2.6 miles round-trip

General location: About 32 miles northeast of Dolores

Elevation gain: 845 feet

Trailhead elevation: 8,570 feet

Warm springs elevation: 9,100 feet

Map: USGS Rico 7.5-minute (springs are not shown)

Restrictions: The roads are closed in winter due to heavy snow.

Best time of year: Late spring through fall, as this is at high elevation and snow can close access roads.

Camping: West Dolores Campground is about 12 miles away; Mavreeso Campground is about 13.5 miles away.

Contact: San Juan National Forest, Dolores Ranger District: (970) 882-7296

Finding the trailhead: This trailhead can be found on your phone or GPS unit, so you can use that. Otherwise, from Dolores, head east on CO 145 for 12.2 miles to the junction with CR 38/FR 535. Turn left and travel about 19.8 miles to the large parking area and trailhead on your right. GPS: 37.75721, -108.12809

The Hike

This 1.3-mile (one-way) hike is in the San Juan National Forest and on Forest Service Trail 648, Geyser Spring Trail. From the parking area and trailhead, this well-worn trail starts as you cross the footbridge over the West Dolores River. Continue up the trail, through meadows and aspens, as you gain 530 feet of elevation to the pool. GPS: 37.75188, -108.12049

Above and facing page: Colorado's only true geyser, this milky turquoise warm pool erupts for 10 to 15 minutes every 30 to 40 minutes. The geyser softly gurgles during these eruptions, but you can't miss it. PHOTOS BY BLUE MEEK-FIELD

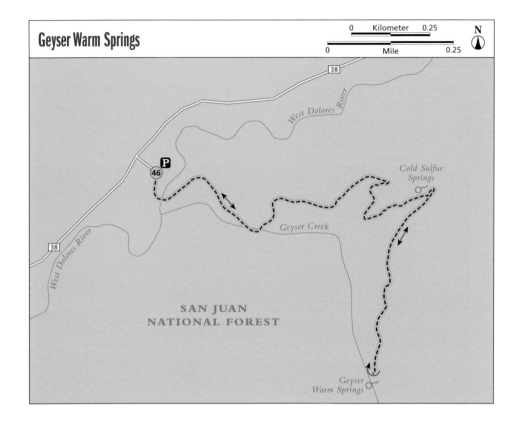

Geyser Warm Springs

The Warm Spring

This 12-by-20-foot pool is fed by the only true geyser in the state of Colorado. The frequency of the eruptions varies; however, 30- to 40-minute intervals are most common. The eruptions look like a boiling pot for 10 to 15 minutes, and emit carbon dioxide and hydrogen sulfide gas, which can create an oxygen-deficient atmosphere. The milky white water looks very inviting, but at 82°F (28°C) it is easy to obey the Forest Service recommendation to stay out of it and view the geyser from the trail above. The gases from the eruptions are heavier than air and fall downhill and away from the trail above the pool. This rock-bottomed pool is surrounded by mineral-coated rocks.

Decisions

The Forest Service website says: "WARNING: Periodic eruptions of carbon dioxide and hydrogen sulfide gas displace oxygen near the water's surface. Swimming or bathing in the geyser is NOT recommended; this exposes one to these gases and could cause a loss of consciousness, and potentially death. If you should feel light-headed or nauseous while viewing the geyser, you should leave the area immediately."

In addition, a sign at the pool reads, "Oxygen Deficient Atmosphere, No Bathing or Swimming."

Did I mention the pool has a rocky bottom?

47 Rainbow Hot Springs

General description: Two sets of riverside pools at the end of a moderate hike in the Weminuche Wilderness of the San Juan National Forest. Swimwear is optional with discretion.

Difficulty: Moderate

Distance: 10.0 miles round-trip

General location: About 18 miles east of Pagosa Springs

Elevation gain: 2,040 feet

Trailhead elevation: 8,100 feet

Hot springs elevation: 9,000 feet

Map: USGS Spar City 15-minute (springs are shown)

Restrictions: No camping near the hot springs except for the 9 designated spaces

Best time of year: Late spring through fall, as this is at high elevation and snow can close access roads.

Camping: The Forest Service's West Fork Campground is about 1.3 miles before the trailhead. The Forest Service does not allow camping around the hot springs except in the 9 designated sites. Dispersed camping is allowed south of the Beaver Creek Trail (Trail 560) intersection or up the trail beyond the next crossing of the West Fork of the San Juan River, as long as you are at least 200 feet from the water.

Contact: San Juan National Forest, Pagosa Ranger District: (970) 264-2268

History: This area is quite fragile as it is still recovering from a devastating fire in 2013 and an ongoing spruce bark beetle epidemic.

Finding the trailhead: The West Fork Trailhead can be found on your phone or GPS unit, so you can use that. Otherwise, from Pagosa Springs, head east on US 160 East for 14.4 miles, then turn left on CR 648 (West Fork Road). Continue for 2.3 miles, then turn right as CR 648 becomes FR 648B. Continue 0.7 mile to the West Fork Trailhead. GPS: 37.45782, -106.91939

The Hike

The popular West Fork Trail (Trail 561) follows the San Juan River upstream to Rainbow Hot Springs and continues on to the Continental Divide Trail. This is an easy day trip, though many prefer to camp. The hike is mostly sunny, but you do pass through many stands of ponderosa pine and aspen. The well-defined trail is easy to follow, but you can expect to encounter many wind-fallen trees.

From the trailhead, follow the dirt road uphill as it makes several curves and eventually ends up heading northwest. Continue past some houses and end up at a gate of a ranch in about 0.4 mile. From here, the West Fork Trail becomes a singletrack dirt trail that goes around the right side of the gate and continues on heavily posted private property until you enter the San Juan National Forest, about 1.1 miles from the trailhead. Continue on the partially shaded trail as it winds through spruce and aspens for a short way and then enters the Weminuche Wilderness shortly before crossing the footbridge over Burro Creek, about 1.5 miles from the trailhead. The trail climbs gently and stays high above the river for a little over a mile, then descends via a few switchbacks and follows the west bank of the river. After about 0.2 mile beyond the

Minerals and algae color the rocks as water runs over them, giving the pool its name.
Top photos by Blue Meek-Field

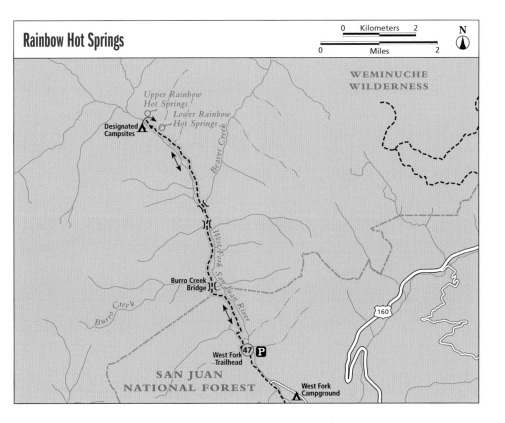

Upper Rainbow
Hot Springs

Lower Rainbow
Hot Springs

Designated
Campsites

Beaver Creek

WEMINUCHE
WILDERNESS

West Fork San Juan River

Burro Creek
Bridge

Creek

Burro

160

West Fork
Trailhead

47

SAN JUAN
NATIONAL FOREST

West Fork
Campground

switchbacks, the trail crosses over the river on a large bridge to the east bank, about 2.9 miles from the trailhead.

Continue along the east side of the river for about 0.15 mile, then cross over Beaver Creek on another sturdy footbridge and meet the Beaver Creek Trail (Trail 560) heading northeast. When I was there last, the Forest Service had rerouted the trail along the north side of Beaver Creek for about 500 feet. Then the trail switched back, gained elevation, and continued its path along the east side of the West Fork of the San Juan River. It appeared that the trail change may not be temporary. Whatever situation you find, you want to hike northwest on the West Fork Trail, along the east side of the river.

Continue on the trail going mostly uphill for about 0.3 mile, then stay on the trail high above the river and gently undulate for about 1.5 miles. This gives you some time to look across the valley and see how the forest is recovering after the devastating West Fork Fire of 2013. Though nearly two decades ago, the area is still quite fragile from the impacts of the fire and the ongoing spruce bark beetle epidemic. There are still dense forests of standing dead trees, killed or weakened by either fire or the bark beetle infestation. It reminds you to minimize your impact and be extra careful, not only here but also wherever else your hiking takes you.

Smaller warm pools can sometimes be found along the riverbank at the upper springs.
PHOTOS BY BLUE MEEK-FIELD

At about 4.9 miles from the trailhead, cross a side creek and pass the designated campsites off the trail. Just past the campsites, watch for a path on your left that takes you down to the river and back downstream to the lower hot pools. GPS: 37.50881, -106.94770

To reach the upper pools, walk back up the path to the West Fork Trail and continue upriver for another 600 feet. You soon see a meadow, and when closer to it, you see the pool. Just below that pool is the seasonal pool(s) on the edge of the river. GPS: 37.51093, -106.94991

The Hot Springs

Rainbow Hot Springs have sometimes been referred to as Wolf Creek Pass Hot Springs.

Lower Rainbow Hot Springs: These pools are the first set as you head upstream on the West Fork Trail. Twelve feet above the fast-flowing San Juan River, 104°F (40°C) water cascades down a bank leaving a wide path of all shades of green before entering a large pool. This pool is slightly above the edge of the river, and the temperature tends to stay around 100°F (38°C). The outflow feeds smaller and cooler seasonal pools in the riverbed.

Upper Rainbow Hot Springs: On my last visit I found a small, shallow, mud-bottomed pool in the meadow. This pool redeems itself because it is a little warmer than the others and not so prone to flooding. The hot water bubbles up from the bottom of this pool then flows down into a rock-bottomed pool slightly above the river. This riverside pool is often flooded during spring runoff.

48 Piedra River Hot Springs

General description: A series of shallow, primitive pools along the east side of the Piedra River, at the end of a hike in the San Juan National Forest. Swimwear seems optional.

Difficulty: Easy

Distance: 2.8 miles round-trip

General location: About 31 miles west of Pagosa Springs, or 45 miles east of Durango

Elevation gain: 770 feet

Trailhead elevation: 7,470 feet

Hot springs elevation: 6,870 feet

Map: USGS Devil Mountain 7.5-minute (springs are not shown)

Restrictions: The trailhead is likely to be inaccessible during winter months, and the pools will be underwater during spring runoff.

Best time of year: Summer and fall

Camping: Primitive camping is available around the trailhead. Lower Piedra Campground is approximately 9 miles away.

Contact: San Juan National Forest, Pagosa Ranger District: (970) 264-2268

Finding the trailhead: From Pagosa Springs, travel west on US 160 for about 21.8 miles, then turn right on FR 622. Continue north on FR 622 for 6.8 miles to the trailhead on the left.

From Durango, take US 550 South/Camino Del Rio for 4.7 miles, then continue east on US 160 for 33 miles and turn left on FR 622. Continue north on FR 622 for 6.8 miles to the trailhead on the left. GPS: 37.30297, -107.33647

The number of pools vary from year to year. It is always worth the hike to see what a new year brings. PHOTOS BY BLUE MEEK-FIELD

The pools need to be rebuilt annually and some years are better than others, but we still had an enjoyable soak.

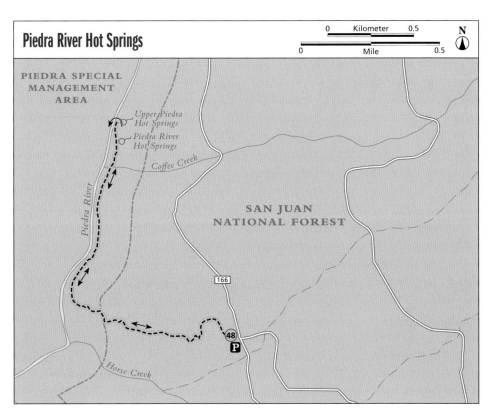

The Hike

From the Sheep Creek Trailhead, follow the well-defined trail through the ponderosa pine forest as it heads north and down multiple switchbacks. You lose 610 feet of elevation in 0.8 mile to reach the Piedra River. Continue on the trail upriver about another 0.6 mile to reach the hot springs. GPS: 37.31287, -107.34429

The Hot Springs

Hot water comes out of the rocks at about 104°F (40°C) and fills shallow rock and sand pools on the east side of the Piedra River. The pools get washed away annually and must be rebuilt. Additional rock and sand pools are located about 500 feet upstream, also on the east side of the river. GPS: 37.31412, -107.34391

Also in Colorado

I was scanning a map not long ago and spied a warm springs on the Yampa River in Dinosaur National Monument. It took me several days of hard trying before I finally got the route figured out and hiked to it. The cliffs are steep and it was not a pleasant hike. I finally arrived to find the water was 76°F (24.5°C). There was not even a pool. GPS: 40.53196, -108.92872

New Mexico

The Land of Enchantment has seventy-seven hot springs documented by the NOAA's *Thermal Springs List for the United States*, and thirteen of those have hikes involved. New Mexico has a law regarding indecent exposure that could apply to soaking-sans-swimwear. New Mexico often relies on other agencies to enforce their laws, which can further complicate the matter. If enforced and you are in the wrong place at the wrong time, it could lead to citations and fines. It is possible that this law may have changed by the time you're reading this; we can check in on the law when it's time to revise this guide. Some locations post signs requiring swimwear, and I will note that requirement.

A couple of decades ago, this pool on the Chama River was previously written about in the Hot Springs Gazette *by Skip Hill. Otherwise it's a new destination for hot springs hikers.*
PHOTO BY BLUE MEEK-FIELD

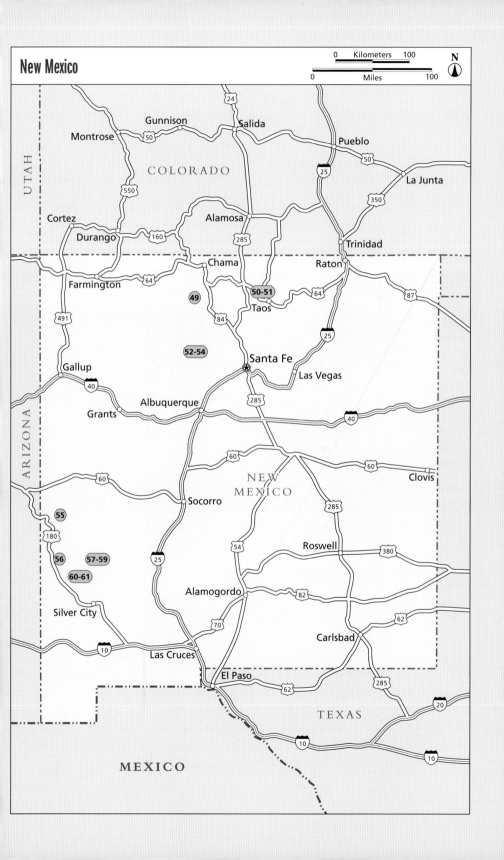

49 Chama River Hot Springs

General description: A cozy 10-by-12-foot pool in a large meadow on remote BLM land near the Chama River. This hot springs is at the end of a 0.8-mile hike and has long been known to rafters and anglers. Swimwear is a good idea in New Mexico, so you should keep it close.

Difficulty: Easy

Distance: 1.6 miles round-trip

General location: The hot springs are 15 miles southwest of Cebolla, or 91 miles northwest of Santa Fe. The meadow is approximately 5 miles downriver from El Vado Dam.

Elevation gain: 480 feet

Trailhead elevation: 7,040 feet

Hot springs elevation: 6,640 feet

Map: USGS El Vado 7.5-minute (springs are not shown)

Restrictions: None

Best time of year: Summer and fall

Camping: No camping at the hot springs, but there are several primitive spots along the trail that follows along the river.

Contact: Bureau of Land Management, Farmington Field Office: (505) 564-7600

History: Approximately 20 years ago, my friend and hot springs writing legend, Skip Hill, wrote a teaser in *The Hot Springs Gazette* about a homestead with a hot spring in the basement. There were few details that I recall, but obviously I was teased. I conferred with another friend and hot springs writer, Sally Jackson (also a legend), who confirmed the homestead was indeed across the Chama River and upstream from these soaking pools. The buildings were all lost to a fire a few years back, but the corrals remain as well as other evidence of a homestead. It can be tough to ford the river; I chose a waist-deep spot that was upstream near the bend in the river. I found the foundation, and found the hot spring in the basement. It was in pretty bad shape, with low flow and only about 85°F (29°C). The mysterious story was better than the reality, which is often the case.

Finding the trailhead: On my last visit, a high-clearance vehicle was helpful, but it's not required if the roads are dry. From Santa Fe, travel about 77 miles north on US 84 toward Cebolla. About 2.4 miles south of Cebolla, turn left on CR 303 and drive for about 6 miles, then turn left again. Continue on CR 303 for 3.4 more miles, then bear left to head west. Continue 3.1 miles to a fork, and go straight on the right fork. In 1.7 miles continue straight through a four-way intersection for 0.9 mile to another intersection near a large windmill (GPS: 36.53746, -106.69530). Turn left at the windmill intersection, continue 0.35 mile, and turn left. Stay on the main road for 0.65 mile until a fork. Bear left at the fork and continue 0.4 mile, then park in a pullout on the left side of the road. GPS: 36.53645, -106.71817

The Hike

From the parking pullout, cross the dirt road to the trailhead. Follow the steep, rocky trail north as it winds down through trees. In approximately 0.5 mile the trail will intersect with a smaller trail coming from the west. Stay on the main trail and continue northeast and down to the meadow. The main pool is about 25 feet from the base of a hill and about 60 feet away from the river. GPS: 36.54235, -106.71937

Above left: A nice pit stop for kayakers and hikers alike Photo by Blue Meek-Field
Right: A one-person soak right on the edge of the Chama River. You can see that it is occupied.
Below: The myth of the house with a hot spring in the basement is finally verified. (It's not that hot.)

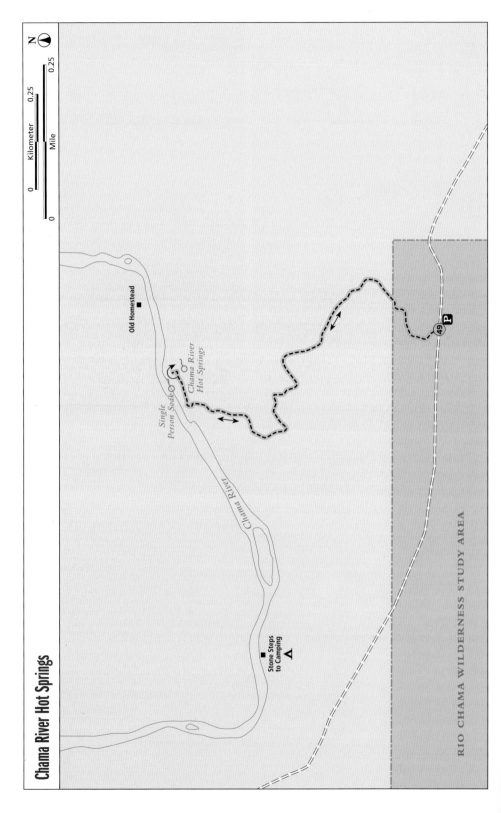

Chama River Hot Springs

Blue enjoying an evening soak in the peaceful meadow pool

There is a trail running along the south side of the meadow that follows the river in both directions. Follow this trail west about 0.47 mile to stone steps leading up to a few campsites (GPS: 36.54035, -106.72691). Several campsites can be found in either direction. If you skirt some private property about 0.5 mile upstream, you can follow this trail all the way to the El Vado Dam in about 5.0 miles. An alternate trailhead for this hike is at GPS: 36.58226, -106.72742.

The Hot Springs

Hot water comes up from the bottom of this 10-by-12-foot pool with enough flow to keep the pool at about 100°F (38°C), depending on the ambient temperature. The water flows out of the pool down to the Chama River. This has been a popular kayak and raft stop for years. In addition to the large pool, there is a one-person pool about 110 feet straight west, just above the river (GPS: 36.54236, -106.71978). There is also hot water bubbling up through the reeds 220 feet southwest of the main pool, at the west end of the meadow.

Note: This is a new addition to hot springs guidebooks.

50 Black Rock Hot Springs

General description: At least two pools on the west side of the Rio Grande River in a spectacular canyon at the end of a short but steep hike. Signs say swimwear is required.

Difficulty: Easy, though steep and rocky

Distance: 0.4 mile round-trip

General location: About 3 miles northwest of Arroyo Hondo

Elevation gain: 195 feet

Trailhead elevation: 6,570 feet

Hot springs elevation: 6,470 feet

Map: USGS Arroyo Hondo 7.5-minute (springs are not shown)

Restrictions: The pools can be underwater in the spring, and roads can close in winter.

Best time of year: Summer and fall

Camping: The Forest Service's Cebolla Mesa Campground is about 12 miles north of Arroyo Hondo, and there is always primitive camping on BLM land.

Contact: Bureau of Land Management, Taos Field Office: (575) 758-8851

Finding the trailhead: From the intersection of NM 522 and Cam Del Medio Road in Arroyo Hondo, travel west on Cam Del Medio Road for about 1.6 miles to the junction with CR B-007. Turn right on CR B-007 and continue for about 1.1 miles to where the road crosses over the Rio Grande via the John Dunn Bridge. After crossing the bridge, stay left and continue on CR B-007 for 0.25 mile to the parking area and trailhead. GPS: 36.53260, -105.71220

Note: There is a hot springs in Nevada with the same name. It's not included in this book because you can drive right to it.

◀ *Left and Above: Rock-walled with a sandy, mud bottom, this is the warmest of the two pools.*
Right: The coolest pool because of the mixing with the river water PHOTOS BY BLUE MEEK-FIELD

Black Rock and Manby Hot Springs

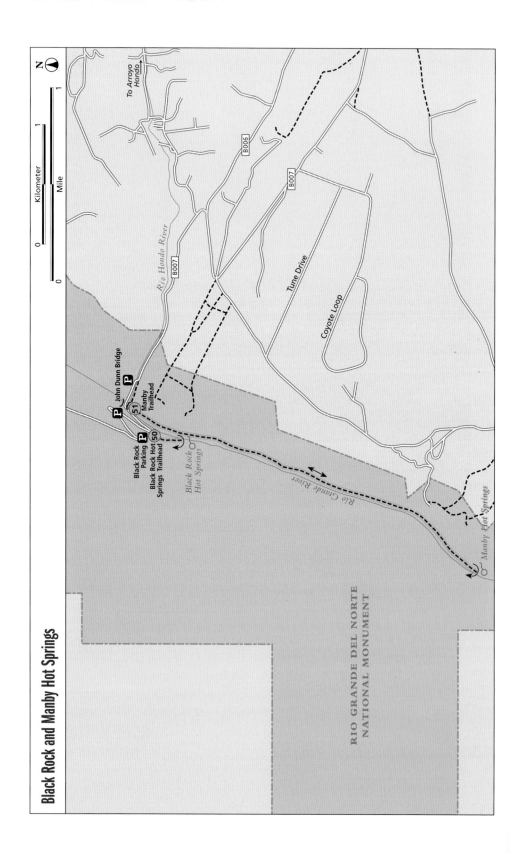

N

0   Kilometer   1

0   Mile   1

To Arroyo Hondo

Rio Hondo River

B006

B007

B007

Tune Drive

Coyote Loop

John Dunn Bridge

P

P

51

Manby Trailhead

Black Rock Parking

P

Black Rock Hot Springs Trailhead

50

Black Rock Hot Springs

Rio Grande River

Manby Hot Springs

RIO GRANDE DEL NORTE NATIONAL MONUMENT

You can snuggle in among the boulders and find a perfect soaking spot.

The Hike

From the trailhead, walk south on the well-worn trail as it winds through the rocks down to the hot springs. There is no shade on the trail or at the pools. GPS: 36.53069, -105.71215

The Hot Springs

Hot water at 106°F (41°C) comes out of the rocks and flows directly into a rock and sand pool big enough to fit eight people. The flow is enough to keep the pool in the high 90s (36–37°C), depending on the ambient temperature. From there the water flows into at least one more pool closer to the river. More pools get built as the season allows. Manby Hot Springs is 1.7 miles downriver from Black Rock Hot Springs on the opposite side of the river.

51 Manby Hot Springs

See map on page 220.

General description: At least three pools on the east side of the Rio Grande River in a spectacular canyon at the end of a short hike. Swimwear is not addressed by signs.

Difficulty: Fairly difficult; trail is not clear and you must look for arrows showing the route.

Distance: 4.0 miles round-trip

General location: About 3 miles northwest of Arroyo Hondo

Elevation gain: About 200 feet

Trailhead elevation: 6,480 feet

Hot springs elevation: 6,450 feet

Map: USGS Arroyo Hondo 7.5-minute (springs are not shown)

Restrictions: Trail and hot springs can be underwater in spring.

Best time of year: Year-round, though the roads can close in winter, adding to the hike.

Camping: The Forest Service's Cebolla Mesa Campground is about 12 miles north of Arroyo Hondo, and there is always primitive camping on BLM land. Camping and overnight use at Manby Hot Springs is prohibited.

Contact: Bureau of Land Management, Taos Field Office: (575) 758-8851

History: Manby Hot Springs is also known as Stagecoach Hot Springs due to the incredible stagecoach trail high above it, which was a miraculous feat to design and build. It is worth seeing. Manby Hot Springs was a stage stop and the site of a bridge where travelers could pay to cross the Rio Grande River. Visitors can see the lower section of the stagecoach trail and pilings for the historic bridge by hiking 200 feet downstream from the hot springs.

Finding the trailhead: *Note:* This is the only legal access to Manby Hot Springs as the previous trailhead was closed because of property issues.

From the intersection of NM 522 and Cam Del Medio Road in Arroyo Hondo, travel west on Cam Del Medio Road for about 1.6 miles to the junction with CR B-007. Turn right on CR B-007 and continue west for about 0.9 mile to the Rio Hondo Bridge (about 0.13 mile before crossing the John Dunn Bridge). Park at one of the available spots near the Rio Hondo Bridge or continue across the John Dunn Bridge to a larger parking area. From the Rio Hondo Bridge, walk 0.2 mile down the dirt road to the Rio Hondo Beach on the east side of the Rio Grande, south of the John Dunn Bridge. The signed trail begins at the south end of Rio Hondo Beach. GPS: 36.53404, -105.70982

The Hike

From the trailhead, follow the sometimes overgrown historic John Dunn Trail south as it winds along the east side of the Rio Grande. After about 0.25 mile you can look across the river and see Black Rock Hot Springs, but keep heading south and enjoy the flora and fauna for an additional 1.75 miles down to the hot springs. Help protect the sensitive riparian plants along the riverbank by staying in the upland and following directional arrows. GPS: 36.50832, -105.72425

Note from BLM: The trail is not recommended for novice hikers; it is classified as difficult with route finding required. Make sure to carry plenty of water, food, and sun protection. The current can be quite strong during spring runoff, and it is advised

Above: Historical bathhouse ruins are the backdrop for this pool.
Below left: Large gravel pool overlooking the Rio Grande
Below right: This pool's water temperature fluctuates with the amount of river water seeping in.
PHOTOS BY BLUE MEEK-FIELD

You can lie in the hot water all day and watch fish swim by.

to not swim in or try to cross the river during this time. A PFD is recommended for either activity. Black Rock Hot Springs is 1.7 miles up the river from Manby Hot Springs on the opposite side of the river. Take care in making appropriate decisions to cross the river, as an unintentional swim could lead to serious injuries or death.

The Hot Springs

Hot water flows out of the rocks at 100°F (38°C) directly into at least three rock and sand pools at the edge of the river that keep a temperature in the mid- to high 90s (35–37°C), depending on the ambient temperature. These pools were constructed at some point during the 1980s. One pool is at the base of a rock and cement wall, which is the remnant of a bathhouse, reportedly built in the early 1900s as part of a resort dream by Arthur Rochford Manby. The Rio Grande River can be quite shallow here, so it might be possible to take a cold swim if the water level allows.

Valles Caldera Area

The next three springs lie within the Valles Caldera, a 13.7-mile-diameter crater created by a sensational volcanic eruption about 1.25 million years ago. The youngest eruption, about 68,000 years ago, formed Battleship Rock and the obsidian flows, responsible for the massive obsidian boulders around McCauley Hot Springs and the area. This accounts for the hot springs, streams, fumaroles, and volcanic domes throughout the caldera. The National Park Service designated the Valles Caldera as a National Natural Landmark in 1975. The Valles Caldera Preservation Act of 2000 created the Valles Caldera National Preserve.

Also in the Area

Battleship Rock: This gigantic chunk of welded volcanic ash rising 200 feet in the air looks as big as a ... well, you know the rest. A natural formation of basalt, it is one of the area's top attractions and is impressive. You cannot climb up on top for safety reasons, but it still draws mountain climbers from all over.

Jemez Falls: A 0.7-mile round-trip detour will let you visit the highest falls in the Jemez Mountains. There is a reported swimming hole above the waterfall, and a way to scramble down to the bottom of it.

Jemez East River Slot Canyon: A slot canyon on the East Fork of the Jemez River, accessible from the Jemez East River Slot Canyon Trailhead. GPS: 35.8276, -106.5898

Battleship Falls: This 40-foot waterfall, Dripping Falls, and a slot canyon are just north of Battleship Rock on Battleship Creek.

52 San Antonio Hot Springs

General description: A popular set of pools on a steep hillside in the Santa Fe National Forest at the end of a short hike. The signs require swimwear and most seem to comply.

Difficulty: Easy

Distance: 1.6 miles round-trip

General location: About 17 miles northwest of Jemez Springs

Elevation gain: 365 feet

Trailhead elevation: 8,290 feet

Hot springs elevation: 8,460 feet

Map: USGS Seven Springs 7.5-minute (springs are shown)

Restrictions: Open sunup until sundown. FR 376 closes in winter, adding 4.4 miles to the hike (I think it would still be worth the hike).

Best time of year: Summer and fall are most popular, though the other seasons are wonderful, if you can get there.

Camping: The Forest Service's San Antonio Campground is about 6 miles away.

Contact: Santa Fe National Forest, Jemez Ranger District: (575) 829-3535

Finding the trailhead: This trailhead comes up in your phone or GPS; otherwise, from Jemez Springs, travel north on NM 4 for 8.7 miles and turn left on NM 126. Travel north on NM 126 for 3.8 miles, then turn right on FR 376 for about 4.4 miles to a gate and the parking area, which is now the new trailhead. GPS: 35.93611, -106.65082

Top left: Hot water spilling out of pipes into this clear, sand-bottomed pool makes this an unforgettable soak.
Top right: Water cascades down the hillside into multiple smaller rock and sand pools.
Right: Steam fills the air as hot water cascades down into lower pools, making a nice foreground for the scenic valley view from this pool.

Facing page: It is rare to find yourself alone in these pools. We arrived immediately after a torrential rainstorm and Blue was able to take some great photos before dark.

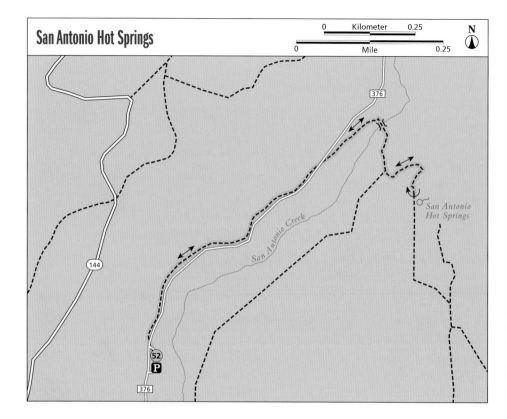

San Antonio Hot Springs

The Hike

This is a new trailhead, but you will walk right past the old trailhead on the short hike. From the trailhead, walk down the partially shaded dirt road (formerly known as FR 376) for about 0.45 mile to where the road forks. The right fork gradually becomes a trail heading for a footbridge 500 feet ahead. Cross San Antonio Creek on that footbridge and continue up the trail another shaded 0.25 mile to the hot springs. The trail splits prior to the springs, and you can access the springs from each side. Water is often running down the trails, so use caution in the mud so as not to hurt yourself or cause excess erosion. GPS: 35.93970, -106.64340

The Hot Springs

Hot water comes out of the rocks at varying temperatures and is collected in a concrete vault then piped out at approximately 115°F (46°C). The pool directly underneath the pipes is large enough to fit a dozen soakers—twice that, if you're all good friends. This pool can be too hot, depending on the ambient temperature, but the water cools as it flows down into many other beautiful rock and sand pools. There is a spectacular view across the canyon and to the mountains beyond.

53 Spence Hot Springs

General description: An extremely popular couple of pools on a hillside in the Santa Fe National Forest, at the end of a short hike. A sign prohibits nudity.
Difficulty: Easy
Distance: 0.8 mile round-trip
General location: About 7 miles northwest of Jemez Springs
Elevation gain: 275 feet
Trailhead elevation: 7,270 feet

Hot springs elevation: 7,330 feet
Map: USGS Jemez Springs 7.5-minute (springs are shown)
Restrictions: Open sunup until sundown. No vehicle parking on the shoulders of NM 4.
Best time of year: Year-round
Camping: The Forest Service's Redondo Campground is about 4 miles north on NM 4.
Contact: Santa Fe National Forest, Jemez Ranger District: (575) 829-3535

Finding the trailhead: This trailhead is easily found using your phone or GPS; otherwise, from Jemez Springs, travel north on NM 4 for 7.2 miles and turn right into the parking lot. The Forest Service reports that the 7-vehicle parking lot is sized appropriately for the size of the hot pools' capacity. Overflow parking is located 0.25 mile north at the Dark Canyon Fishing Access. No vehicle parking is permitted on the shoulders of NM 4. GPS: 35.84912, -106.63157

These pools are usually pretty packed; make sure you get ahead of the crowds on this one to enjoy the stunning views from the pools. PHOTOS BY BLUE MEEK-FIELD

These warm pools are best enjoyed In the warmer months. However, if you look to the left in the upper photo, you can see a rocked-in pool built around the source. PHOTOS BY BLUE MEEK-FIELD

The Hike

From the parking lot, follow the trail down the switchbacks to the San Antonio Creek, cross it on the sturdy bridge, and continue up the hill about 0.25 mile to the hot springs (GPS: 35.84948, -106.62982). It's worth a hike farther up the hill a ways to see if there are any other pools. I have been to Spence when there were hot pools a little higher up the hill. On my last visit, I just saw the remains of the upper pools. GPS: 35.84993, -106.62998

Also in the Area

There is a nice swimming hole (cold) near the Soda Dam, just 0.4 mile north of the Forest Service office on NM 4. At one point, there was hot water here, 117°F (47°C) and smelling of sulfur. The rumors are that the hot spring disappeared when the highway was built. There is a historical marker near the dam with more information. Hot or not, it's a nice place for a swim, if the river is not too high. If you smell sulfur, maybe you ought to poke around a little.

Spence Hot Springs

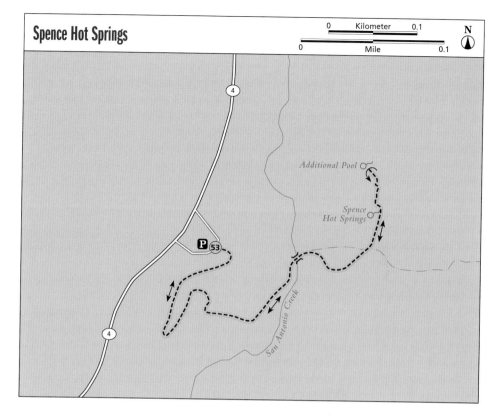

The Hot Springs

Hot water comes out of the rocks at 100°F (38°C) and flows directly into a long, narrow pool that is wrapped around some boulders. The flow is enough to keep the pool in the mid- to high 90s (35–37°C).

Due in part to the easy hike, these hot springs get overused and often abused. Despite the efforts of law enforcement, there is still a lot of trash and broken glass. New Mexico prohibits nudity, and they have asked the Forest Service to enforce that on federal land. At my last visit there were signs saying that nudity is prohibited by New Mexico state law and you will be fined. The Forest Service has their own regulations regarding nudity, but New Mexico's laws are more restrictive. Regardless of the laws or jurisdictions, this is a good place to wear a swimming suit, or equivalent. Please be prepared to pack out extra trash.

54 McCauley Hot Springs

General description: Two sets of warm pools and ponds in a stunning location at the end of fairly short hikes from two separate trailheads. Located in the Santa Fe National Forest. Signs say swimwear is required.
Difficulty: Easy
Distance: 3.5 miles or 3.4 miles round-trip, depending on the trailhead
General location: The lower trailhead is 5.5 miles north of Jemez Springs; the upper trailhead is 15.5 miles north from Jemez Springs.
Elevation gain: Battleship Rock: 840 feet; Jemez Falls: 895 feet
Trailhead elevation: Battleship Rock: 6,810 feet; Jemez Falls: 7,950 feet

Hot springs elevation: 7,500 feet
Map: USGS Jemez Springs 7.5-minute (springs are shown)
Restrictions: Day-use only; fee to park
Best time of year: Summer and fall are most popular.
Camping: Primitive camping is allowed so long as it is not within 400 feet of water or 0.25 mile from a trailhead. Jemez Falls Campground is 0.5 mile from the upper trailhead and 10.5 miles from the lower trailhead.
Contact: Santa Fe National Forest, Jemez Ranger District: (575) 829-3535

Finding the trailhead: Battleship Rock (lower) trailhead: From Jemez Springs, travel north on NM 4 for 5.5 miles and turn right into the Battleship Rock Day-Use Area parking lot. The trailhead is at the south end of the picnic area, between the YMCA Camp Shaver and Battleship Rock. GPS: 35.82816, -106.64406

Jemez Falls Picnic Area (upper) trailhead: From Jemez Springs, travel north on NM 4 for 14.2 miles and turn right on Jemez Falls Road. Continue 0.8 mile to the campground, then another 0.5 mile to the picnic area and trailhead. GPS: 35.81660, -106.60641

The Hike

The East Fork Trail (Trail 137) connects the Battleship Rock Day-Use Area trailhead with the Jemez Falls Picnic Area and Campground trailhead. McCauley Hot Springs is close to the halfway point between them. The ponderosa pine forest, dotted with oaks, creates a stunning contrast against the red sandstone mountains. I was able to walk through an inch of new snow when I last visited, and it was a hike I won't soon forget.

Battleship Rock (lower) trailhead: This 1.75-mile (one-way) hike starts in the day-use area parking lot. Though often rated as moderate, it's a pretty easy hike. The mostly shady hike along the East Fork of the Jemez River begins by crossing a bridge and hiking past the west end of Battleship Rock. At about 0.3 mile there is one switchback, then the trail continues gently uphill to a trail junction at about the 1.2-mile mark. Stay to the right and continue about another half-mile to the hot springs area.

Jemez Falls Picnic Area (upper) trailhead: This 1.7-mile (one-way) hike begins at the Jemez Falls Picnic Area, which is about 0.5 mile south of the Jemez Falls Campground. The trail begins on the west side of the picnic area and heads west. It

These warm pools are best enjoyed In the warmer months. However, if you look to the left in the upper photo, you can see a rocked-in pool built around the source. Photos by Blue Meek-Field

The warmest source pool is in the foreground. People have piled rocks to contain the warmth.
ALL PHOTOS BY BLUE MEEK-FIELD

McCauley Hot Springs

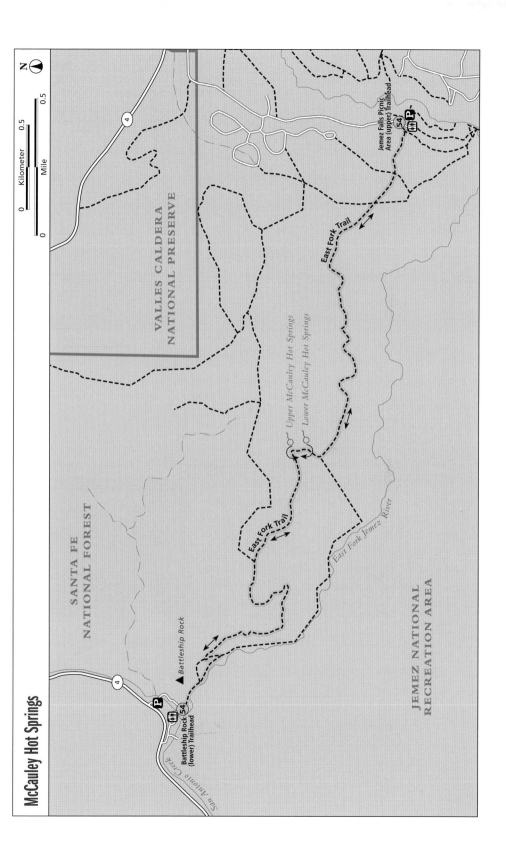

VALLES CALDERA
NATIONAL PRESERVE

SANTA FE
NATIONAL FOREST

JEMEZ NATIONAL
RECREATION AREA

N

Kilometer

0   0.5

0   0.5
Mile

East Fork Trail

East Fork Trail

Upper McCauley Hot Springs

Lower McCauley Hot Springs

East Fork Jemez River

▲ Battleship Rock

Battleship Rock
(lower) Trailhead

Jemez Falls Picnic
Area (upper) Trailhead

San Antonio Creek

54

54

P

P

Take a quick, cool dip in this deep, natural pool.

is mostly downhill going in. Hike through the ponderosa pine and oak forest, then begin a gradual descent for about a mile, before a 0.1-mile climb to the hot springs.

The Hot Springs

The forested hike ends with some of the most picturesque pools in the area. At the upper springs (GPS: 35.82223, -106.62738), hot water comes out of the ground at 99°F (37°C) and flows directly into a 10-by-12-foot rock and sand pool, then into a 40-by-50-foot pool, which rarely is warmer than 90°F (32°C). The water then flows down the hill into a larger pond that would be an ideal soak on a summer afternoon. This cooler pond is full of little fish that nibble on dead skin, similar to the expensive spa treatments. These feral guppies were likely introduced decades ago as an official program for mosquito control.

We had a peaceful walk in the fresh snow at our last visit.

The same kind of cascading pools are located 180 feet to the southeast at the lower springs (GPS: 35.82178, -106.62728), except the pools are deeper and cooler. There is a gorgeous, 3-foot-deep pool that is wrapped around a rock, from which a tree is struggling to grow. Don't miss the obsidian boulders in the area, remnants of recent volcanic activity.

Gila Area

Also in the Area

- **Gila Visitor Center:** Start there.
- The **Gila Cliff Dwellings** are definitely not to be missed.
- **Trail to the Past:** This short hike starts at the Lower Scorpion Campground and gives a lot of history about the prior residents of the area. There are pictographs and even a cliff dwelling at the end. The trailhead starts in the approximate middle of the trail with pictographs at one end and a cliff dwelling at the other.
- Don't miss the **gravesite of William Grudgings**; it's definitely worth the short hike. The Gila area has an ancient past, but also has its more recent place in the history of the wild, wild West.

On your way to Jordan Hot Springs, you will pass by this huge cavern in Little Bear Canyon. This cavern has a long history of use, and if you want, you can be a cliff dweller for a night.

55 Frisco Box Hot Springs

General description: A couple of concrete soaking boxes a little way above the San Francisco River in a remote part of the Gila National Forest. Swimwear is not addressed, and is probably extra weight.
Difficulty: Moderate
Distance: 6.4 miles or 14.0 miles round-trip, depending on the trailhead
General location: The Upper Frisco Hot Springs trailhead is about 20 miles east of Luna, or 27 miles north of Reserve. The Frisco Box trailhead is about 12 miles north of Reserve.
Elevation gain: Upper Frisco Hot Springs: 2,200 feet; Frisco Box: 1,650 feet

Trailhead elevation: Upper Frisco Hot Springs: 8,185 feet; Frisco Box: 6,015 feet
Hot springs elevation: 6,540 feet
Map: USGS Dillon Mountain 7.5-minute (springs are shown)
Restrictions: A GPS is very helpful so you know the destination, as this trail does not get a lot of use. Trail 762 is not recommended for travel during rainy season or spring runoff when high water could pose a risk to personal safety.
Best time of year: May through November
Camping: Primitive camping is available at the trailhead, or anywhere along the trail.
Contact: Gila National Forest, Reserve Ranger District: (575) 533-6232

Finding the trailheads: Upper Frisco Hot Springs Trail #124: From Luna, travel southeast on US 180 for 6.5 miles to the junction of US 180 and FR 35. Travel east on FR 35 (signed "San Francisco Warm Springs Trailhead 13 Miles") for 13.5 miles to a gate and the trailhead. GPS: 33.80131, -108.81554

Frisco Box Trail #762: From Reserve, travel north on NM 12 for 5.2 miles, then turn left on FR 49 (signed "Toriette Lakes"). Continue for 0.45 mile and turn left on FR 41. Continue 6.1 miles to the trailhead. GPS: 33.78557, -108.76977

The Hike

If you're looking for scenery, you can't go wrong with either trail. The upper trail has a significant elevation loss, which you must regain on the way out. There are nearly two miles of walking ridges with unbelievable views. The lower route takes you along the San Francisco River through narrow box canyons that are often described as the best scenery in New Mexico. It would take some planning, but if you could arrange for a vehicle waiting at the lower trailhead, I can't think of a better loop than to start on the upper trail (Trail 124) and walk the 10.0 (or so) miles to the lower trailhead (Trail 762).

Upper Frisco Hot Springs Trail #124: This moderate 3.2-mile (one-way) hike begins at a gate about 13.5 miles east of US 180. Cross through the gate and follow the foot trail as it leaves FR 35 and parallels the west side of a fence. Pinyon pines and junipers provide shade through most of this hike, with the last mile and a half more heavily wooded. You climb gently uphill for about 0.4 mile to reach the high point of the hike at about 8,285 feet. Stop here and enjoy some of the most spectacular 360-degree views in New Mexico. Continue northeast, gently descending along

Concrete soaking boxes are at the bottom of the hill if hiking the upper trail, or just through "Frisco Box" canyon (their namesake) if you took the long way. Spectacular views from either direction. Take an apple with you in case the plug is gone.

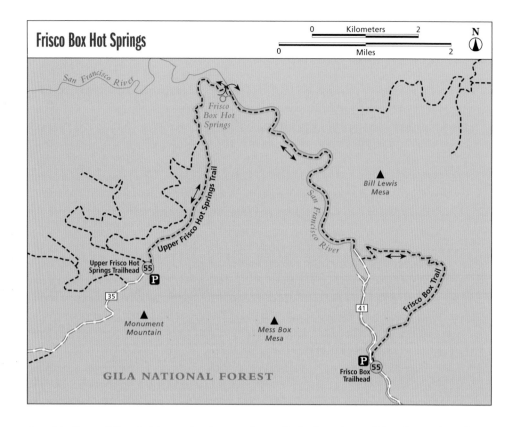

the ridgeline of South Mountain, for another mile before the trail heads north and downhill along another ridgeline for 0.6 mile. Game trails are everywhere along this route, so pay close attention to stay on the correct trail. The trail starts to descend more rapidly as you go down the switchbacks, heading mostly north, until you reach a flatter meadow in another 0.6 mile. The descent becomes more gradual for the final 0.6 mile, as the trail heads northwest and makes a loop back around to the southeast, before turning northeast and down to the hot springs hidden in the trees. I hiked this in early fall and heard elk bugling all around me. To me, this was as good as it gets. GPS: 33.83092, -108.80023

Notes: No facilities are present at the trailhead or along the trail. There are no river fords on this hike. Game trails are everywhere, making it more difficult to stay on track, but on my visit there were many helpful cairns along the way.

If you follow the faint trail down to the river, you will see the Frisco Box Trail, which heads downstream along the San Francisco River, through the narrow canyons of the Frisco Box, and to a trailhead on FR 41, 7.0 miles away. This trail is the alternate hike to the hot springs.

Frisco Box Trail #762: From the trailhead off FR 41, Trail 762 skirts around the east side of private land then ascends a ridge providing excellent views of rock bluffs and unique formations before the trail descends back to the San Francisco River.

At this point the route basically follows a gorge-type river bottom without any developed trail. The farther you go up the river, the rockier the route becomes, until you get to the area known as the Frisco Box. This canyon area is very narrow with high bluffs along its edge and the San Francisco River running through the gorge. Once you get through the narrows, or "Box" area, the canyon gradually widens and you continue upstream for approximately 1.5 miles to the hot springs. GPS: 33.83092, -108.80023

Note: This trail description was provided by the Forest Service; I have not hiked the lower trail.

The trail fords the San Francisco River many times, even following the riverbed at times. The trail also runs

Hopefully you see more of these than I did at my last visit on the upper route.

along the boundary of private land. Please keep to the trail and adhere to signs to respect private landholder rights. No facilities are present at the trailhead or along the trail.

The Hot Springs

Don't ask me how they got there, but there are two concrete soaking boxes on a small, elevated area about 250 feet from the San Francisco River and about 25 feet higher in elevation. One box is about 4 by 5 feet, and the other about 4 by 7 feet. Hot water at about 98°F (36.5°C) is piped into them. There may not be plugs available, but an apple works great! The tubs don't get used too often, so they might need some cleaning.

56 San Francisco Hot Springs

General description: Large warm ponds and small riverside pools alongside the San Francisco River in a scenic canyon in the Gila National Forest. Swimwear is not addressed.

Difficulty: Fairly easy with a few tough spots

Distance: 2.6 miles round-trip

General location: About 6 miles south of Glenwood, or about 55 miles northwest of Silver City

Elevation gain: 580 feet

Trailhead elevation: 5,000 feet

Hot springs elevation: 4,560 feet

Map: USGS Wilson Mountain 7.5-minute (springs are shown)

Restrictions: During spring runoff and storms, the river could be unpassable.

Best time of year: May through November

Camping: The Forest Service's Big Horn Campground is about 5 miles away, near the town of Glenwood.

Contact: Gila National Forest, Glenwood Ranger District: (575) 539-2481

Finding the trailhead: Your phone or GPS may not work for finding this one, as there is another San Francisco Hot Springs a few miles away at the now-closed RV park formerly known as Sundial Hot Springs. From Silver City, travel west on US 180 for about 52 miles and turn left on CR 25, signed for San Francisco Hot Springs Trailhead. Continue 0.6 mile to the parking area and trailhead. GPS: 33.22841, -108.86709

Above: Algae and frog-filled warm pools at the base of fascinating conglomerate cliffs.
Facing page: Primitive rock and mud pool that gets washed out seasonally. A shovel might be
handy if you're the first one there. PHOTOS BY BLUE MEEK-FIELD

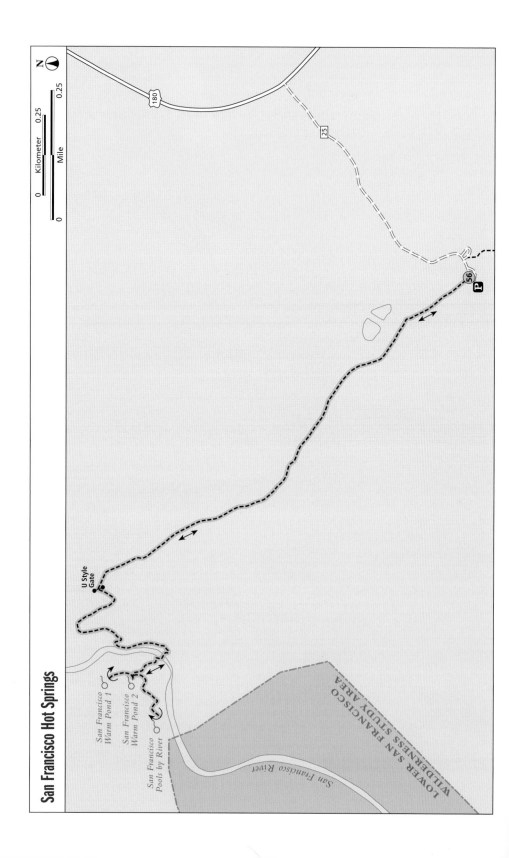

San Francisco Hot Springs

San Francisco Warm Pond 1
San Francisco Warm Pond 2
San Francisco Pools by River

San Francisco River

U Style Gate

LOWER SAN FRANCISCO
WILDERNESS STUDY AREA

180

25

56

P

N

Kilometer
0   0.25

0   0.25
Mile

The Hike

This 1.3-mile hike is on the Forest Service's San Francisco Trail #250. From the trailhead, follow the well-worn trail about 1.0 mile through scrub brush to a maze gate that allows people through but prevents wayward livestock from soaking. After passing the maze gate, switchbacks help you descend the mostly shaded 0.25 mile down to the San Francisco River. Ford the river where you feel comfortable, and head toward the southeast corner of the conglomerate cliff. The cliff face and the river each make a 90-degree turn to the west. Using the corner of the cliff as a reference point, the warm ponds are at the base of the east-facing cliff, about 120 feet north from the cliff corner. There is another warm pond about 200 feet north of that one, also at the base of the cliff. GPS: 33.23821, -108.88071

To get to the river pools, backtrack to the south and turn right (west) around the cliff corner. Follow a trail heading toward (southwest) and then along (west) the river. The river pools are downstream about 350 feet from the corner of the cliff, located on the north bank of the river, which is now flowing west parallel to and about 100 feet from the south-facing cliff (GPS: 33.23717, -108.88165). When walking west along the river's edge, you will pass other hot sources that have potential for pools, but no additional pools were built on my last visit.

The Hot Springs

Hot water comes up from the ground at varying temperatures with enough flow to keep the large warm ponds at temperatures in the high 80s (30–32°C). The warm ponds were not really appealing on my visit, but it is a great place to count frogs. Follow paths when you see them. Pick your way through the brush to find access points to the ponds, which are nearly 100 feet long. The more you look, the more you will find.

The rock and sand riverside pools are washed away seasonally. Hot water comes up from the ground at 120°F (49°C) with enough flow to maintain soaking temperatures over 100°F (38°C). Temperature can be controlled by diverting cold creek water. On my last visit, I found a 6-by-8-foot oval and a 4-foot-diameter round pool. The river pools are about 90 feet upstream from the point where the river turns northwest then makes a 180-degree U turn before flowing southwest out of sight.

57 Jordan Hot Springs

General description: One of the state's best geothermal soaks at the end of a long, but moderate hike in the Gila National Forest's Gila Wilderness. Signs say swimwear is required.

Difficulty: Moderate

Distance: 15.0 miles round-trip

General location: About 43 miles northwest of Silver City

Elevation gain: Little Bear Trail #729: 1,560 feet; Middle Fork Trail #157: about 300 feet

Trailhead elevation: 5,670 feet

Hot springs elevation: 6,010 feet

Map: USGS Woodland Park 7.5-minute (springs are not shown)

Restrictions: River levels are likely to be a problem during spring runoff and rainy times, as you cross the river several times walking up this canyon.

Best time of year: Year-round, though river levels might be a problem during the spring.

Camping: The Forest Service's Lower Scorpion Campground is 0.4 mile beyond the trailhead on NM 15, and Upper Scorpion is 0.2 mile beyond that. You pass several nice campsites along the way. The area close to the hot springs can get congested during summer months. Do not camp too close to the springs or the river. Finding a spot 200 feet from water to bury toilet waste is very difficult; please consider using wag bags to pack it all out.

Contact: Gila National Forest, Wilderness Ranger District: (575) 536-2250

History: Jordan Hot Springs is also known as House Log Cabin Hot Springs.

Finding the trailhead: One easy way to get here is by entering the Gila Visitor Center in your phone or GPS. Otherwise, from Silver City, travel north on NM 15 for about 42 miles. When you're about to enter the Gila Visitor Center parking lot, instead continue on NM 15 for 0.7 mile to the TJ Corral trailhead on the right (northeast). GPS: 33.22709, -108.25145

The Hike

Little Bear Trail #729: This hike is a not-so-short shortcut to Jordan Hot Springs, and provides spectacular views and a memorable walk through the Little Bear (slot) Canyon, which also avoids more than a dozen river fords. The TJ Corral trailhead is about 1.25 miles (by road) away from the Middle Fork Hot Springs trailhead. It would make a nice loop to leave from TJ Corral, visit Jordan Hot Springs, and then enjoy Middle Fork Hot Springs on your way out.

The hike begins at TJ Corral and follows Little Bear Trail #729 northwest until a trail intersection with the West Fork Trail #151. Turn right at that intersection and continue north on Trail 729 up the hill. The climb starts with a few switchbacks, then continues its winding path up the hill for about 2.5 miles. Once on top, and about 670 feet of elevation higher, spend some time enjoying the views across the valley.

Continue on Trail 729 down some switchbacks, through the trees, across a meadow, and through more trees, then start down the winding Little Bear Canyon. Continue down as the canyon becomes narrower until it's just a slot. After about 2.0 more miles, the canyon widens and you descend through the mouth of Little Bear Canyon where

After a long hike with stunning scenery, you will find this two-pooled gem. Some decent camping spots are available nearby, so take a day or two to thoroughly enjoy the area. You can make it a loop and go out on the Middle Fork Trail. PHOTOS BY BLUE MEEK-FIELD

Trail 729 intersects with the Middle Fork Trail #157. Turn left on Trail 157 (GPS: 33.27230, -108.25938) and walk the Middle Fork of the Gila River downstream on its winding route to Jordan Hot Springs.

A right turn on Trail 157 would lead you up the river to the Middle Fork Hot Springs (see that hike) and the Gila Visitor Center about 0.7 mile farther.

After nearly 3.0 more miles, and many river crossings, you will find yourself on the east side of the river and see a rock and sand pool on the right side of the trail. Though it looks very inviting, don't stop yet; this is just the outflow from the soaking pools. Continue up the east side of the river for about 250 feet to a steep path on the right. Follow this path about 100 feet to the hot springs. GPS: 33.29257, -108.26946

Alternate Hike

Middle Fork Trail #157: This route is a little longer than the Little Bear Trail. Though it is pretty flat, there are numerous more river crossings. To reach the trailhead, continue 0.2 mile beyond the Gila Visitor Center and turn left into the signed trailhead parking area (see the Middle Fork Hot Springs hike). Continue on the Middle Fork Trail #157 past the Middle Fork Hot Springs for another 4.5 miles to the intersection with the Little Bear Trail #729. Continue on the Middle Fork Trail about 3.0 more miles (and several more river crossings) to Jordan Hot Springs.

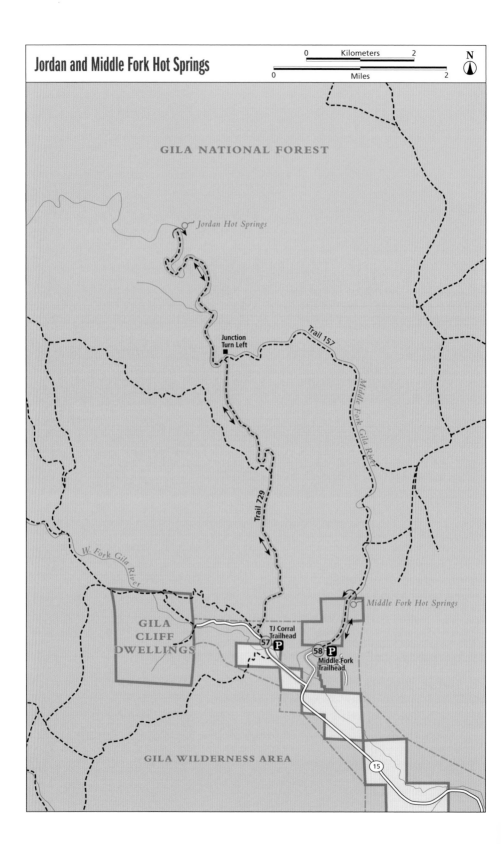

0   Kilometers   2

0   Miles   2

N

GILA NATIONAL FOREST

Jordan Hot Springs

Trail 157

Junction
Turn Left

Middle Fork Gila River

Trail 729

W. Fork Gila River

Middle Fork Hot Springs

GILA
CLIFF
DWELLINGS

TJ Corral
Trailhead

57

58

Middle Fork
Trailhead

GILA WILDERNESS AREA

15

The Hot Springs

Hot water comes out of the rocks at 99°F (37°C) and falls about 3 feet into a very large, beautiful rock and sand pool. The pool is high above the Middle Fork of the Gila River and not subject to flooding, though the trail is likely to be flooded during high-water times. From that pool, the water cascades into a smaller rock and sand pool. The pool temperatures tend to stay in the mid-90s (35°C).

Note: There is also a Jordan Hot Springs in California.

A huge cavern in Little Bear Canyon, big enough to live in. This and other unbelievable scenery make the Little Bear Canyon route a must-do. You can make it a loop and go out on the Middle Fork Trail.

58 Middle Fork Hot Springs

See map on page 248.

General description: Popular pools on the Middle Fork of the Gila River at the end of a short hike near the Gila Visitor Center. Signs say swimwear is required.

Difficulty: Easy, with some river crossings

Distance: 1.5 miles round-trip

General location: About 43 miles northwest of Silver City

Elevation gain: 120 feet

Trailhead elevation: 5,720 feet

Hot springs elevation: 5,680 feet

Map: USGS Gila Hot Springs 7.5-minute (springs are shown)

Restrictions: River levels are likely to be a problem during spring runoff and rainy times, as you cross the river several times walking up this canyon.

Best time of year: Year-round, though river levels might be a problem during the spring.

Camping: The Forest Service's Lower Scorpion Campground is about 2 miles from the trailhead; Upper Scorpion Campground is 0.2 mile beyond that.

Contact: Gila National Forest, Wilderness Ranger District: (575) 536-2250

History: Middle Fork Hot Springs is also known as Lightfeather Hot Springs.

Finding the trailhead: One easy way to get here is by entering the Gila Visitor Center in your phone or GPS. Otherwise, from Silver City, travel north on NM 15 for about 42 miles. Enter the Gila Visitor Center parking lot; continue 0.2 mile beyond the visitor center and turn left into the signed trailhead parking area. GPS: 33.22581, -108.24110

The Hike

The Forest Service's Middle Fork Trail #157 follows the Middle Fork of the Gila River downstream for about 0.7 mile to the hot springs. Start by walking downstream on the trail; in about 0.25 mile you cross the river to the west side. Continue on the west side for another 0.25 mile, then cross back to the east side of the river. Continue downstream on the east side of the river for about 0.2 mile, passing a grotto against the hillside and additional hot seeps, to the main hot springs. GPS: 33.23352, -108.23532

To reach the additional warm water on the west side of the river, do not cross back to the east side of the river at the half-mile point; instead, continue down the west side and follow a warm stream that parallels the Gila River for a short way. The water is not as hot as the east-side pools, but this warm water might be a better alternative on a hot day. It's less well known and may get you away from the crowds.

Notes: The Middle Fork Trail #157 continues downstream past Middle Fork Hot Springs for an additional 7.5 miles to Jordan Hot Springs (see Jordan Hot Springs hike), which is slightly shorter, but has some elevation gain. That trail (Little Bear Trail #729) goes over the mountain, winds down the spectacular Little Bear Canyon, and meets up with Trail 157 about 4.5 miles downstream from Middle Fork Hot Springs.

Popular volunteer-built rock and sand pools on a hot stream that flows to the river where more rock and sand pools are built. Along the Middle Fork of the Gila River and close to the Gila Visitor Center, these springs see a lot of visitors. PHOTOS BY BLUE MEEK-FIELD

The rock and sand pools at Middle Fork Hot Springs, just a short walk from the Gila Cliff Dwellings Visitor Center. This water is high in minerals but does not have the sulfur smell. This water has been used for bathing for thousands of years, all the way back to the Mogollon.

The Hot Springs

Hot water pulses out of the rocks at temperatures between 130°F (54.4°C) and 149°F (65°C) and flows through a hot channel into multiple rock and sand pools. The pool sizes vary by season, as they often wash away during runoff. The hot water cools as it flows into successive pools. Pools can easily be cooled by moving rocks to let river water in.

59 Melanie Hot Springs

General description: A lovely pool hidden in the grass above the Gila River at the end of a fairly short hike. Swimwear is not addressed; you may want to keep it close.

Difficulty: Fairly easy, with several river crossings

Distance: 3.6 miles round-trip

General location: About 40 miles north of Silver City

Elevation gain: Negligible

Trailhead elevation: 5,540 feet

Hot springs elevation: 5,500 feet

Map: USGS Gila Hot Springs 7.5-minute (springs are shown)

Restrictions: River levels can be a problem during high-water times.

Best time of year: Year-round, though river levels might be a problem during the spring.

Camping: Grapevine Campground is just beyond the trailhead; the Forest Service's Forks Campground is 0.4 mile north on NM 15.

Contact: Gila National Forest, Wilderness Ranger District: (575) 536-2250

Finding the trailhead: Grapevine Campground can be entered into your phone or GPS. Otherwise, from Silver City, travel north on NM 15 for about 39 miles and turn right on East Fork Road. Pass the entrance to Grapevine Campground at 200 feet and continue straight 300 more feet to the parking area by the river bridge. GPS: 33.17976, -108.20592

Rock-lined pool hidden in the grass near a cliff. Hot water falls into this little two-person soak, sized to maintain a comfortable soaking temperature.

The pool is located at the base of this cliff.

Signs of a previous pool

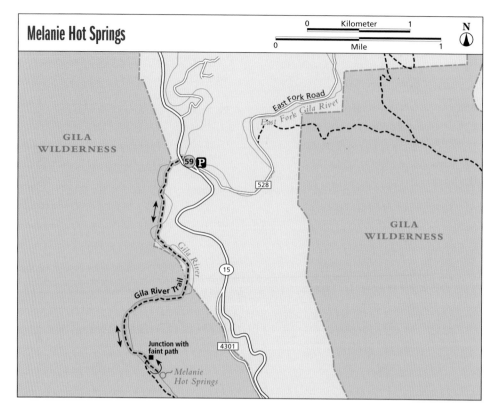

The Hike

From the trailhead, you must immediately ford the Gila River and get on the Gila River Trail #724, heading southwest. Proceed under the bridge where NM 15 goes over the Gila River, and begin following the trail downstream. Not counting the river ford you just made, stay on the trail and start counting your river fords as you hike downstream for the next 1.8 miles. There is a faint path between the seventh and eighth river fords, which is a critical junction. It is right before the eighth ford, so make sure you are on the east side of the Gila River after seven fords. The GPS coordinates for this path are 33.16303, -108.20976. Follow the faint path heading to your left through the grass for 450 feet to the hot springs at the base of the large cliff. GPS: 33.16227, -108.20860

The Hot Springs

This 5-by-10-foot pool is hidden in the grass at the base of a rock cliff along the Gila River. Hot water at 111°F (44°C) trickles out of the rocks and into this 2-foot-deep, squishy-bottomed pool. It's in tall grass, so it is not visible until you're right next to it. Volunteers have dug it out and lined it with rocks, and the grass has grown around the rocks. Though the source is hot, it does not flow fast enough to keep the temperature much over 95°F (35°C). At my last visit, there also was a smaller, considerably cooler pool adjacent to the larger pool.

60 Turkey Creek Hot Springs

General description: Several pools at the end of a moderate hike in the Gila Wilderness of the Gila National Forest. Swimwear is not addressed, and is probably extra weight.

Difficulty: Moderate, with a scramble or two

Distance: 9.8 miles round-trip

General location: About 40 miles northwest of Silver City

Elevation gain: 620 feet

Trailhead elevation: 4,770 feet

Hot springs elevation: 5,132 feet

Map: USGS Canyon Hill 7.5-minute (springs are not shown)

Restrictions: No motorized vehicles permitted in wilderness area. Turkey Creek Road can be dangerous in wet weather.

Best time of year: Summer to late fall; avoid spring runoff

Camping: Primitive camping is available along the trail and near the trailhead in Brock Canyon.

Contact: Gila National Forest, Silver City Ranger District: (575) 388-8201

Finding the trailhead: You can get directions on your phone or GPS for the Turkey Creek Hot Springs trailhead. Otherwise, from Silver City, travel west on US 180 about 23 miles and turn right on NM 211 for 4 miles to the town of Gila. Stay right to continue on NM 153 and drive 5.2 miles. Stay right as NM 153 becomes FR 155 (Turkey Creek Road) and continue about 7.9 miles to the trailhead. Use caution driving the rough and rocky Turkey Creek Road. GPS: 33.06701, -108.49892

The Hike

I read on the information signs that the Forest Service is working on repairing trails and improving trailheads. It's likely that the trailhead described here will be different in the future. The hike sounds a lot tougher than it is, and is rated as difficult by some, though most call it moderate.

From the trailhead, follow the singletrack trail through the overgrowth for about 500 feet, where the trail becomes an old two-track road. The old roadbed crosses the Gila River three times in the first 1.3 miles. There is a trail that bypasses the first two river crossings, but you should follow the designated trail. The crossing at 1.3 miles from the trailhead cannot be avoided.

About 0.3 mile after the last Gila River crossing, you come to an old shack, corrals, and the remains of an old house. Beyond the homestead, the trail takes on a more typical appearance for another 2.0 miles to a junction at GPS: 33.10332, -108.48320. From this junction, leave Trail 155 and stay to the right (east) on a good trail heading up Turkey Creek. Turkey Creek Hot Springs are nearly a mile and a half up Turkey Creek and about 100 feet higher in elevation. If you find yourself walking up switchbacks, turn around and go back down to Turkey Creek, then stay in the bottom of Turkey Creek Canyon. The trail crosses Turkey Creek back and forth, which sometimes involves some scrambling. Keep going up Turkey Creek until you see the algae and hot pools. You start seeing pools long before you arrive at the source; try any that you like. GPS: 33.11458, -108.48397

You're almost there. The entire creek was warm at my last visit and there were pools clear down the creek. Find one with a temperature that suits you and enjoy. The area is still recovering from a major fire.

You'll pass through the remains of an old ranch and see the associated infrastructure, now dilapidated, of course.

New Mexico is improving many trails, and the Turkey Creek Trail is on the list, according to the signs I read.

Lesson Learned

There is one critical junction where you need to take the correct trail. Otherwise, you end up on the wrong side of the ridge with no way to get to the correct side, except for backtracking. If I sound like I know all about it, there is a reason. I'll try to prevent you from making my mistake.

It is not uncommon for me to jump out at a trailhead and hit the trail with only my GPS telling me the straight-line distance to the destination, and Turkey Creek was no exception. I am not proud of this practice, and though it usually works, Turkey Creek was an exception. This time I should have done a little homework and learned about the critical junction. Instead, I took the wrong trail and hiked up the next canyon to the west. I eventually got to a point where my GPS was pointing east and telling me that Turkey Creek Hot Springs was about a quarter-mile away. Sadly, there was the huge ridge between me and a soak. I had to backtrack down to the critical junction and go up the correct canyon. Back at the trailhead, I found detailed directions from my friend and hot springs author Karin Burroughs, which I had failed to read prior to my hike.

Looking up Turkey Creek. You either go around the creek or right through it on your way up.

Turkey Creek Hot Springs

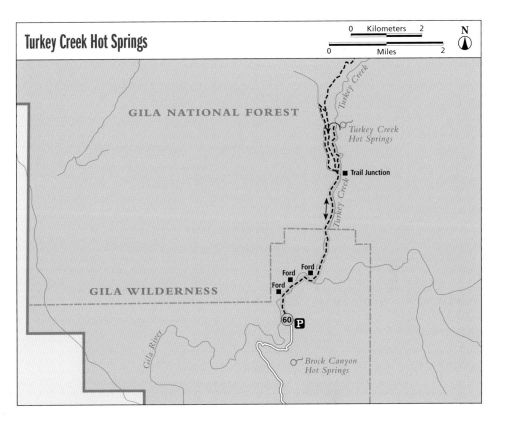

The Hot Springs

Considered one of New Mexico's best hiking hot springs, Turkey Creek should be on your list. Hot water comes out of the rocks at 165°F (74°C) and flows into multiple pools along and in Turkey Creek. You walk along hot water for a long time and pass many pools that are a comfortable temperature. The water gets hotter as you go up, so you might find a pool you like sooner than you think. Clever volunteers have built pools all the way down the creek. A major fire over a decade ago significantly changed the area, causing increased erosion and silty pools. The area is still recovering, but I had an enjoyable soak, and it is definitely worth the hike.

61 Brock Canyon Hot Springs

General description: Though not a long hike, there is a bit of walking around to see all the pools at this location. It is a great place to spend a night as you prepare for, or recover from, the Turkey Creek Hot Springs hike. Swimwear is not addressed.

Difficulty: Easy

Distance: 0.5-mile round-trip

General location: About 39 miles northwest of Silver City

Elevation gain: Negligible

Trailhead elevation: 4,780 feet

Hot springs elevation: 4,830 feet

Map: USGS Canyon Hill 7.5-minute (springs are not shown)

Restrictions: Turkey Creek Road can be dangerous in wet weather and spring runoff.

Best time of year: Summer to late fall

Camping: Primitive camping is available all around the area.

Contact: Gila National Forest, Silver City Ranger District: (575) 388-8201

Finding the trailhead: You can get directions on your phone or GPS for the Brock Canyon Hot Springs trailhead. Otherwise, from Silver City, travel west on US 180 about 23 miles and turn right on NM 211 for 4 miles to the town of Gila. Stay right to continue on NM 153 and drive 5.2 miles. Stay right as NM 153 becomes FR 155 (Turkey Creek Road) and continue about 7.3 miles to the Brock Canyon parking area (GPS: 33.05935, -108.49891) and trailhead (GPS: 33.05898, -108.49879). Use caution driving the rough and rocky Turkey Creek Road.

Note: The Turkey Creek Hot Springs trailhead is 0.6 mile farther on FR 155.

A roughly built, tarp-lined rock pool with full temperature control. It may take awhile to cool if someone left the hot water running. PHOTOS BY BLUE MEEK-FIELD

A rock-lined pool that seems to be losing the battle against encroaching grass

You may need to scoop out gunk and debris, but with a little work, you can have a nice peaceful soak.

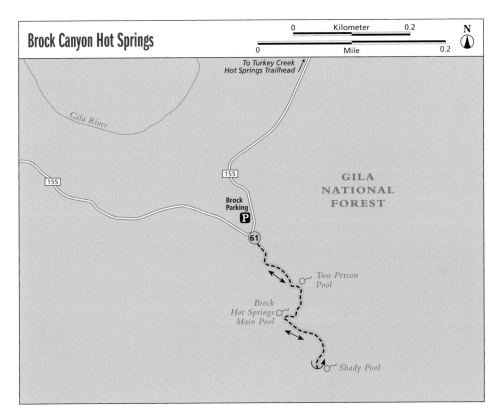

Brock Canyon Hot Springs

Gila River

155

155

Brock Parking

To Turkey Creek Hot Springs Trailhead

GILA NATIONAL FOREST

61

Two Person Pool

Brock Hot Springs Main Pool

Shady Pool

The Hike

From the trailhead, follow the main wash south about 350 feet to a popular camping area. The Two-Person Pool is located in the grass on the edge of the clearing (GPS: 33.05828, -108.49796). From there, follow the wash south and slightly west another 150 feet to the main pool (GPS: 33.05784, -108.49821). To reach the Shady Pool, continue up the wash southeast and look for the trees. It is 350 feet in a straight-line distance southeast of the main pool (GPS: 33.05705, -108.49754).

The Hot Springs

Two-Person Pool: Not surprisingly, this small pool is only big enough for two. The hot water that flows into this rock-lined, squishy-bottomed pool is fighting a battle with encroaching grass. This pool was the coolest of them all at 98°F (36.5°C) on the warm day I visited.

    Brock Hot Springs Main Pool: Rocks, cement, wood, tarps, and all kinds of other stuff come together to create this 10-by-12-foot, aboveground pool. It has 116°F (46.5°C) hot water piped into it, which can be diverted to control temperature.

    Shady Pool: This larger, rock-lined, squishy-bottomed pool is in the shade of some trees that make it pleasant on a sunny day. It's about 6 by 8 feet and maintains a temperature of about 104°F (40°C).

Texas

Although geothermal activity is mostly limited to the western states, the NOAA did document ten Texas hot springs in their *Thermal Springs List for the United States*. It is no coincidence that they are all in West Texas, and there is only one of the ten that is available to soak in. You may have read about a second hot springs in the general vicinity of this one; however, it is considered off-limits by the local authorities and truly is not worth looking for. Consequently, the Lone Star State makes it into this guide with one lone spring.

A peaceful Texas morning at Langford Hot Springs PHOTO BY NPS/CA HOYT

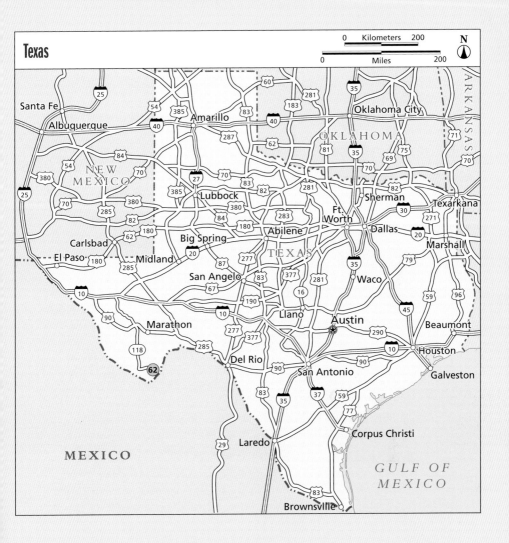

Texas

62 Langford Hot Springs

General description: The concrete foundation of a historic bathhouse on the bank of the Rio Grande River in Big Bend National Park. Swimwear is required.

Difficulty: Easy

Distance: 0.6 mile round-trip

General location: About 85 miles south of Marathon

Elevation gain: Negligible

Trailhead elevation: 1,855 feet

Hot springs elevation: 1,840 feet

Map: USGS Boquillas 7.5-minute (springs are shown)

Restrictions: No glass, no alcohol; day-use only; and the National Park Service prohibits swimming the river to Mexico and buying items from vendors.

Best time of year: Year-round, except during high-water times when the hot pools are flooded and underwater

Camping: The National Park Service's Chisos Basin, Rio Grande Village, and Cottonwood Campgrounds are all available within Big Bend National Park.

Contact: Big Bend National Park: (432) 477-2251

History: Langford Hot Springs is a former resort in what is now Big Bend National Park in Texas. J. O. Langford was a native of Mississippi who as a child contracted malaria. In 1909, Langford heard a gentleman speaking about medicinal waters flowing into a hot springs pool on the Rio Grande. He purchased the site unseen and moved there. In 1912, bandits became a threat along the river and the US Army encouraged everyone to leave the area. Langford returned in 1927 to find much had changed. His home and bathhouse were ruined, or completely gone, so he rebuilt. In addition, he built a post office and motel rooms. Through the 1930s and early 1940s, the hot springs resort was successful. But a national park was being planned and Langford knew his dreams would not last long. In 1942, Langford sold the property to the State of Texas for $10, to be used for park purposes only. In 1944, Langford's dream became a part of Big Bend National Park.

Finding the trailhead: The trailhead is in the Hot Springs parking area in Big Bend National Park. From Marathon, drive south on US 385 for about 84 miles to Big Bend National Park. Continue on Main Park Road, turn right on Hot Springs Road, and drive 1.5 miles to the Hot Springs parking area. GPS: 29.17751, -102.99932

The Hike

From the Hot Springs parking area, follow the historic Hot Springs Trail past the old post office and motel, and along the bank of the Rio Grande River for 0.3 mile to the hot springs. There's a little bit of shade for the first half of this short dirt trail, but it is pretty exposed after that. GPS: 29.17953, -102.99551

If you did not get enough of a hike, you can continue on the trail to the Hot Springs Canyon Rim to enjoy the desert flora and fauna and get spectacular views of the West Texas and Mexican deserts. There are hundreds of miles of backcountry trails for backpacking in the Chisos Mountains; a backcountry permit is required and available online through www.recreation.gov.

A look upriver on a typical Texas day—clear springs, blue sky, muddy river.
PHOTOS BY NPS/JENNETTE JURADO

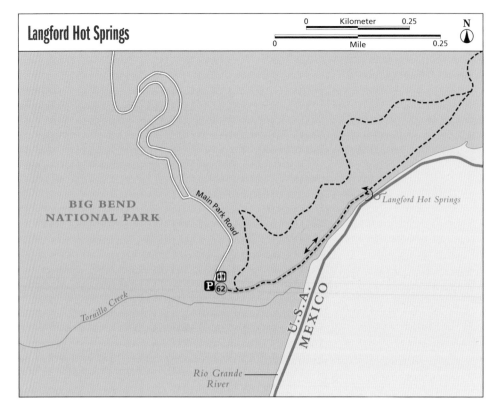

0   Kilometer   0.25

0   Mile   0.25

N

Main Park Road

BIG BEND
NATIONAL PARK

Langford Hot Springs

P 62

Tornillo Creek

U.S.A.
MEXICO

Rio Grande
River

The Hot Springs

Also known as Boquillas Hot Springs, the hot springs are the remains of an old bathhouse. The foundation is about 18 by 18 feet and divided into sections that still remain today. Hot water at 105°F (40.5°C) flows directly into the pools at a flow high enough to maintain comfortable temperatures throughout.

Geoff has the tubs to himself, a rare occasion. PHOTO BY PATSY MATTHEWS

CALIFORNIA APPENDIX: HIGH SIERRA TRAIL, SEQUOIA AND KINGS CANYON NATIONAL PARKS

Published by the National Park Service

The High Sierra Trail leads from Crescent Meadow up the canyon of the Middle Fork of the Kaweah River, crossing the Great Western Divide by the 10,700-foot (3,261 m) pass known as Kaweah Gap. It descends into Big Arroyo, then climbs up to the Chagoopa Plateau and drops down again into the Kern River Canyon. After running up the bottom of the Kern Canyon, it turns east, climbing parallel to Wallace Creek up to the junction with the John Muir Trail, 49 miles (79 km) from the starting point. You can then follow the John Muir Trail about 13 more miles (21 km) to the summit of Mount Whitney. A wilderness permit is required to hike the High Sierra Trail.

Note that a High Sierra Trail permit is needed to access the High Sierra Trail between Seven Mile Hill and Kaweah Gap. A permit for the Alta Trail is not valid for travel on this segment of High Sierra Trail

Altitude sickness is an illness that can occur when at high altitude (typically above 8,000 feet or 2,400 m). Symptoms of mild to moderate altitude sickness include dizziness, fatigue, headache, shortness of breath, and rapid heart rate. The best treatment for altitude sickness is to descend to a lower altitude.

The campsites suggested in the following itinerary are for hikers with a minimum amount of time to make the trek to Mount Whitney. For hikers with more time, a summary of distances between the alternate campsites mentioned is given at the end.

Day 1—to Bearpaw Meadow (11.4 mi./18.2 km): The trail leaves from Crescent Meadow on the southeast edge of the Giant Forest. For the first half-mile, the trail travels through shady, well-watered terrain covered with dense forests of red and white fir, sugar pine, and occasional giant sequoia. The trail then emerges onto a warm, south-facing slope at Eagle View. From here, you can see back to Moro Rock to the west, down to the Middle Fork of the Kaweah River, and ahead to the glaciated peaks of the Great Western Divide. The nearly level trail then passes through part of the area burned by the Buckeye Fire in 1980. Spring-fed streams cross the trail late into the season. *Creek crossings may be hazardous early in the summer.* Be sure to check conditions when you pick up your permit.

Beyond the junction with the Seven Mile Hill Trail, the trail crosses the steep slopes and bluffs of the south side of Alta Meadow and Alta Peak. During 1930, a trail crew working with an air compressor and rock drills spent nearly the entire summer blasting a 1-mile (1.6 km) stretch of trail through this area.

Hikers taking a more leisurely trek to Mount Whitney may wish to camp along one of the two forks of Nine Mile Creek (8.8 mi./14.1 km). After passing Nine Mile Creek, the trail descends to Buck Canyon, a spectacular canyon well known for floods, avalanches, and rockslides. After crossing Buck Creek, the trail climbs some

500 feet in slightly over a mile (152 m in 1.6 km), arriving at the Bearpaw Meadow area 11.4 miles (18.2 km) from the trailhead. In addition to campsites, this is the location of the **Bearpaw Meadow Camp**, a simple tent hotel run by the park concessionaire (reservations required).

Day 2—to Big Arroyo Junction (11 mi./17.6 km): East of Bearpaw, you begin your ascent into the Great Western Divide. After passing some nice campsites at Lone Pine Creek (13.1 mi./21 km from the trailhead), the trail follows a long series of switchbacks, overshadowed by the Angel Wings, a sheer granite wall to the north of the trail. The route crosses Hamilton Creek just above the lower Hamilton Falls and climbs another series of switchbacks to Big Hamilton Lake (16.6 mi./26.6 km). The popular campsites here offer outstanding views and fair to good fishing for brook, rainbow, and golden trout.

Beyond Big Hamilton Lake, there is nowhere to go but up! The climb begins with a series of sweeping switchbacks across the bluffs to the north of the lake, before turning east toward the sheer-walled avalanche chute known as Hamilton Gorge. In 1932, Park Service engineers erected a steel suspension bridge across the gorge, but in the winter of 1937 a massive avalanche tore the bridge from its moorings and swept its twisted wreckage down to the shores of Big Hamilton Lake. You can still see the bridge's concrete foundations and a few scrap metal remains, but the trail now uses a ledge and tunnel that were blasted by the Civilian Conservation Corps the next summer.

East of Hamilton Gorge, the trail enters the alpine life zone of the Sierra, a region where the short growing season, avalanches, and lack of soil make life impossible for plants other than herbs and low shrubs. Precipice Lake, which is nestled beneath the north wall of Eagle Scout Peak, often stays frozen into midsummer. Beyond the lake, the route passes a series of shallow glacial ponds, to finally arrive at Kaweah Gap on the Great Western Divide (20 mi./32 km). From this pass at 10,700 feet (3,261 m) it is only a few hundred vertical feet down to the open valley of the Big Arroyo. The trail continues a steady to moderate descent to the campsites at Big Arroyo Junction (22.5 mi./36 km).

Day 3—to Moraine Lake (8 miles/12.8 km) or Upper Funston Meadow (12 mi./19.2 km): After two strenuous days of hiking, the journey from Big Arroyo to Moraine Lake is relatively easy. If you have a tighter schedule, you may wish to bypass Moraine Lake, an extra 0.8 mile (1.3 km), and proceed directly to Upper Funston Meadow, at the bottom of the Kern Trench.

After leaving Big Arroyo Junction, the trail makes a moderate ascent up the north wall of the Big Arroyo, providing views of the east side of the Great Western Divide. Once it reaches the Chagoopa Plateau, the trail levels off and soon reaches a junction on a tributary of Chagoopa Creek. The right-hand trail branches off from the main High Sierra Trail to Moraine Lake (30 mi./48 km from Crescent Meadow). The left-hand trail follows a more direct route across the Chagoopa Plateau, rejoining the Moraine Lake Trail at Sky Parlor Meadow (30.8 mi./49.3 km). From here it descends to the bottom of the Kern Trench. The drop is moderate at first, but concludes with a series of steep, rocky switchbacks. This stretch of the trail can be long and dry, so be sure to fill your water bottles at Sky Parlor Meadow. To reach Upper Funston Meadow (34.5 mi./55.2 km), turn right (south) upon reaching the bottom of the canyon.

Day 4—to Junction Meadow (13.7 mi./21.9 km from Moraine Lake; 9.7 mi./15.5 km from Upper Funston): If you are coming from Moraine Lake, continue about 1 mile (1.6 km) beyond the lake to rejoin the High Sierra Trail at Sky Parlor Meadow. Descend into the Kern Trench, but turn left (north) upon reaching the bottom. If you are coming from Upper Funston, retrace your steps to the junction with the trail from the Chagoopa Plateau and continue north along the bottom of the canyon.

The Kern River Trail drops into a marshy area beyond the junction, then leads through a forest of Jeffrey pine and incense-cedar. Keep an eye through the trees to the west to catch a glimpse of Chagoopa Falls tumbling down from the rim of the canyon. At 36.8 miles (58.9 km) from the trailhead (excluding the side trip to Moraine Lake), you arrive at Kern Hot Springs, complete with a crude cement bathtub in which to soak your aching muscles. The water from the spring is 115°F (46°C). The tub is only a few feet from the cold, rushing Kern River, and runoff from the tub mixes with river water to create a warm pool, allowing a choice of temperatures for bathing. (Please, no soap in the river or tub.) If your schedule allows, you may wish to camp here, but you must stay in the designated campsites, which are often heavily used.

Beyond Kern Hot Springs, the trail continues along the bottom of the glaciated valley of the Kern River. This canyon runs almost due north and south for about 25 miles (40 km) along the Kern Canyon fault. The trail ascends steadily to Junction Meadow (42 mi./67.2 km). Hiking along the bottom of the canyon can be hot and dry during the middle of the day. If you have camped at Kern Hot Springs, however, remember that cold air from the surrounding peaks flows down the canyon at night, and the sun will not clear the 2,000- to 5,000-foot (610 to 1,524 m) canyon walls until relatively late in the morning.

Day 5—to Crabtree Meadow (8.9 mi./14.2 km): Leave the park-like Jeffrey pines of Junction Meadow and cross a steep, rocky slope covered with manzanita and currant. Soon the trail begins to climb out of Kern Canyon, offering increasingly impressive views of the canyon to the south, and west to the Kaweah Peaks, which were to the east of you three days ago when you came over Kaweah Gap. At 48.9 miles (78.2 km) from the trailhead, you reach the junction with the John Muir Trail, which runs from Yosemite Valley to the summit of Mount Whitney. There are campsites here, as well as at Crabtree Meadow (53.1 mi./85 km). Guitar Lake (56.6 mi./90.6 km) is the last campsite with water before the summit of Mount Whitney.

Day 6—to the summit of Mount Whitney: If you have arranged for transportation from Whitney Portal and this is the last day of your trip, it will be a long day (19.1 miles/30.6 km). You may also camp at Trail Camp (65.7 miles/105.1 km from the trailhead) or Outpost Camp (68.7 mi./109.9 km) on the east side. If you are hiking back to Giant Forest, plan to return to Crabtree Meadow (16.8 mi./26.8 km round-trip to the summit).

The final climb begins with a moderate traverse along the "back" side of Mount Whitney, then the trail begins a switchbacking climb to Trail Crest, the divide between the west and east sides of the Sierra. Fill your water bottles before starting on this climb; there is no reliable water supply between Guitar Lake and Trail Camp on the east side. A hundred yards (91 m) below Trail Crest is the 2.4 mile (3.8 km) spur trail to the summit of Mount Whitney. If you wish to leave your backpack at this junction while you make the climb to the summit, be sure your food is secure from the hungry marmots that frequent this area. The trail to the summit follows an open, rocky route along the west side of the Sierra crest.

The windswept, barren summit of Mount Whitney is home to hardy flocks of rosy finches. When not looking for handouts from hikers (please remember that feeding animals in a national park is illegal), these tame little brown and pink birds eat, among other things, insects that have been blown upslope from lower elevations and become trapped in melting ice or frozen on the surface of snowfields.

The Mount Whitney Hut was built at the summit in 1909 as a station for meteorological observations. The metal roof of this hut attracts lightning, which can be conducted through the building to individuals inside. *Do not seek shelter here during a storm.* It is unsafe to be anywhere on top of the mountain or any exposed high place during a thunderstorm. Check the weather conditions before beginning the hike to the summit.

After returning to Trail Crest, hikers heading out to Whitney Portal descend one hundred switchbacks to Trail Camp, a popular camping area for hikers coming from the east side. Although often crowded, this site offers an impressive early morning view of the rising sun's light striking Mount Whitney. If you camp here, however, be aware that the sun drops behind the crest of the Sierra fairly early in the evening, and at 12,000 feet (3,658 m) the air cools down quickly. If you keep going, the rocky trail follows Lone Pine Creek down to Mirror Lake, a glacial cirque that is closed to camping, then continues along the creek to Outpost Camp, the last camping before Whitney Portal.

Day 7 (if returning to Giant Forest)—to Kern Hot Springs (14.5 mi./23.2 km) or Upper Funston Meadow (18.5 mi./29.6 km): Retrace your previous route.

Day 8—to Big Arroyo (12 mi./19.2 km from Kern Hot Springs; 8 miles/12.8 km from Upper Funston): Retrace your previous route.

Day 9—Explore Nine Lakes Basin and return via Kaweah Gap to Hamilton Lakes (4.8 mi./7.7 km plus side trip): An unmarked trail leaves the High Sierra Trail at the point where it turns west and begins the climb up the east side of Kaweah Gap. Follow this unmarked trail north if you wish to take a side trip to the Nine Lakes Basin. If you plan to hike in this or any off-trail area, always carry a topo map and compass, and be sure you know how to use them.

Day 10—to Crescent Meadow via the High Sierra Trail (15.5 mi./25 km): Retrace your previous route.

Summary of Distances along the High Sierra Trail

Site	Distance from Previous Point	Distance from Crescent Meadow	Distance from Whitney Portal
Crescent Meadow			72.2 mi./115.5 km
Nine Mile Creek	8.8 mi./14.1 km	8.8 mi./14.1 km	63.4 mi./101.4 km ***
Bearpaw Meadow	2.6 mi./4.2 km	11.4 mi./18.2 km	63.4 mi./101.4 km ***
Lone Pine Creek	1.7 mi./2.7 km	13.1 mi./21.0 km	59.1 mi./94.6 km ***
Big Hamilton Lake	3.5 mi./5.6 km	16.6 mi./26.6 km	55.6 mi/89.0 km ***
Big Arroyo Junction	5.9 mi./9.4 km	22.5 mi./36.0 km	49.7 mi./79.5 km ***
(Moraine Lake) *	8.0 mi./12.8 km	30.5 mi./48.8 km	41.7 mi./66.7 km ***)
Upper Funston Meadow	12.0 mi./19.2 km **	34.5 mi./55.2 km	37.7 mi./60.3 km ***
Kern Hot Spring	2.3 mi./3.7 km	36.8 mi./58.9 km	35.4 mi./56.6 km ***
Junction Meadow	7.4 mi./11.8 km	44.2 mi./70.7 km	28.0 mi./44.8 km ***
Wallace Creek Junction	4.7 mi./7.5 km	48.9 mi./78.2 km	23.3 mi./37.3 km ***
Crabtree Ranger Station	4.2 mi./6.7 km	53.1 mi./85.0 km	19.1 mi./30.6 km ***
Guitar Lake	3.5 mi./5.6 km	56.6 mi./90.6 km	15.6 mi./25.0 km ***
Mount Whitney Summit	4.9 mi./7.8 km	61.5 mi./98.4 km	10.7 mi./17.1 km
Trail Camp	4.2 mi./6.7 km	65.7 mi./105.1 km ***	8.3 mi./13.3 km
Outpost Camp	3.0 mi./4.8 km	68.7 mi./109.9 km ***	6.5 mi./10.4 km
Whitney Portal	3.5 mi./5.6 km	72.2 mi./115.5 km ***	3.5 mi./5.6 km

* If you take the side trip to Moraine Lake, add 0.8 mile (1.3 km) to all subsequent distances.

** From Big Arroyo Junction, excluding the trip to Moraine Lake

*** The climb to the summit includes a 2.4-mile (3.9 km) (each way) spur trail. These distances include the 4.8-mile (7.7 km) side trip to the summit.

**** Hikers may not access the High Sierra Trail eastbound between 7 mile creek and Kaweah Gap with an Alta trailhead permit.

HIKE INDEX